SWANNY

SWANNY

CONFESSIONS OF A
LOWER-LEAGUE LEGEND

PETER SWAN

JOHN BLAKE

Published by John Blake Publishing Ltd,
3 Bramber Court, 2 Bramber Road,
London W14 9PB, England

www.blake.co.uk

First published in hardback in 2008

ISBN: 978 1 84454 660 2

British Library Cataloguing-in-Publication Data:

A catalogue record for this book is available from the British Library.

Design by www.envydesign.co.uk

Printed in the UK by CPI William Clowes Beccles NR34 7TL

1 3 5 7 9 10 8 6 4 2

Papers used by John Blake Publishing are natural, recyclable products made from
wood grown in sustainable forests. The manufacturing processes conform to the
environmental regulations of the country of origin.

Every attempt has been made to contact the relevant copyright-holders,
but some were unobtainable. We would be grateful if the appropriate people
could contact us.

To Mam and Dad for all their support
over the last 42 years.

ACKNOWLEDGEMENTS

A lot of people have given me their time and assistance and I'd like to say thank you to them all. To James Mitchell, Imaging Manager at the *Hull Daily Mail*, Martin Spinks at the *Stoke Evening Sentinel*, Tony Dewhurst of the *Lancashire Evening Post* and Ray Simpson, the Burnley FC historian. I'd like to say a big thanks to Alan Roberts, Bradford City Stadium Manager, for finding The Pope. And to Shane Embleton, manager of New Wheel FC of the Wakefield Sunday League, my last club. Thanks also to the staff at the Briar Court Hotel, Huddersfield, for always making us so welcome. And to Andrew Collomosse for pulling everything together; it's been a lot of fun. This is also my chance to say thank you to all the fans that have backed me over the years, people I've never really been able to thank before.

Stan Ternent, manager of Blackpool, Hull City, Bury, Burnley, Gillingham and Huddersfield Town: 'Swanny's an absolutely top-class lad. He was a great bloke around the club and in the dressing room was up there with the best. And an extremely good player; just as effective at centre-forward or centre-back. He was very unfortunate with injuries. Nobody who really knows Swanny will say a bad word about him ... apart from his dodgy golf handicap!'

Phil 'The Power' Taylor, 13-times world darts champion and lifelong Port Vale fan: 'Swanny's always been a good lad and great company, but for me he never reached his true potential as a player. He might easily have gone on to play in the top flight for one of the really big clubs. He could have been that good.'

Gary Speed, over 500 Premier League appearances for Leeds, Everton, Newcastle and Bolton: 'I was Swanny's boot boy for a while at Leeds – so he has a lot to thank me for! When I went there I was fifteen, a little lad from Wales, and what struck me first about Swanny was the sheer size of the man. Frightening! But, from day one, he went out of his way to make me feel at home.'

Shane Embleton, manager of New Wheel FC, Wakefield & District Sunday League: 'Just eighteen months after marking Dwight Yorke in a pre-season friendly, Swanny was turning out for us. And I found myself in midfield alongside a man I used to cheer from the Elland Road Kop. But, from day one, he was just one of the lads ... and he's a legend on our trips away!'

John Beresford, ex-Barnsley, Portsmouth, Newcastle, Southampton and Birmingham: 'People look at Swanny and see a big, brash guy who'll always have a laugh, but, deep down, he's a big softie. If I'm in trouble and need a mate, I know who to turn to. Swanny would always drop everything and help.'

David Burns, sports editor, BBC Radio Humberside: 'Everybody should have a mate like Swanny. He's a one-man band of entertainment. Mind you, I did think that if he ever got round to a book it would either be a pop-up or a colouring book. Enjoy!'

CONTENTS

FOREWORD

As a Torquay United fan, I was always more familiar with players in the lower leagues than some of my colleagues. Port Vale's Peter Swan was a name I knew, but it was only that – a name ... until the 2000-01 season, that is. And then Peter started to loom large in our legend on *Soccer AM*.

We always ask our studio guest a final question. That year it was, 'Who is your best mate in football?' And twice, in the first few weeks of the season, the answer was Peter Swan. The show immediately latched on to this, realising that although Swanny may not have been a household name with everyone, there must certainly have been something special about this enigma for him to be so popular!

We decided to run with the gag and guests were set up to reply, 'Peter Swan', when we asked the question. They were all happy to play along ... and always to good effect. His name always brought a raucous cheer from the crew and studio audience and we never got bored with it.

It was especially funny when foreign players were on the show. I remember Samassi Abou from West Ham – who had to come on with an interpreter because his English was so bad – stammering out 'Pettre Swenn', much to the amusement of everyone else on the show and the viewers at home.

But even though Swanny was a 'regular' on *Soccer AM*, it wasn't until the end of the season that I met him. I'd just finished playing in the Soccer Sixes tournament at Stamford Bridge and I was at the bar having a drink when there was a tap on my shoulder. I turned round to find this huge man grinning down at me, shouting, 'Guess who?' I started laughing; it could only be Peter Swan.

Swanny hung out with us for the rest of the afternoon and long ... long ... long into the night. As I drove home, I passed Peter propping up two *Soccer AM* crew members, one under each arm, and dragging them across the road to the next watering hole. Yes, in one afternoon Peter Swan really had become everybody's best mate.

It is impossible not to like the man. He's so funny, so friendly, and so easy to get on with. Eight years on we are still great friends. The World Matchplay Darts tournament in Blackpool is usually our annual get together. Peter will come along with a few pals and by the end of the night he'll have as big a crowd round him as Phil 'The Power' Taylor!

If Peter is your friend, he's your friend for life. I have lost count of the invites to nights out I've had from him, for no other reason than he's been down in London. He's even taken me to see his pal Robbie Williams in concert. It was a fantastic night, though I do remember being more entertained by John Beresford's ridiculous dancing than whatever Robbie was doing on stage.

What you see is what you get with Swanny. He lives life to the full and he wants you to live it as well. And you rarely find people who are so generous with their time. Nothing's too much trouble for Peter.

It is an absolute honour and a pleasure to have been asked to write a foreword for this book. And believe me this man is so worth a book. I'd far rather read Peter Swan's life story than Ronaldo's – either of them!

A lot of sportspeople write books because they are popular, in the spotlight and because their 'media-relations officer' has told them to do so, not because they have a story to tell. Peter does ... and I'm certain you're going to enjoy it.

Helen Chamberlain, presenter of Sky One's *Soccer AM*

INTRODUCTION: THE WARM-UP

When I was a kid, starting out at Leeds United, there were headlines flying around that Leeds had discovered the new John Charles.

Me.

Like King John, I was big, quick and strong. Like King John, I was equally at home at centre-half or centre-forward. But there the similarity ended. He was a legend, an all-time great who played 38 times for Wales and who became a cult hero in Italy after he joined Juventus in 1957. I was a decent pro who made over 500 appearances in a 16-year career with seven clubs: Leeds, Hull, Port Vale, Plymouth, Burnley, Bury and York. I never played in the top flight. And while John, the Gentle Giant, was never sent off or booked, I saw red ten times, once in a Wembley final. So if Charles was the king, I was the joker. A man who never said no to a drink or a night out with the boys.

Soon after I packed up in 2000, John Rudge, one of my 14 managers told me, 'Swanny, if you'd got your head together instead of going out drinking and enjoying yourself, you could have gone all the way. You could have played for England.'

Maybe so. But I'd have missed out on the best time of my life, the days when a pro footballer could burn the candle at both ends and get away with it. And there would have been no going out and getting pissed with Port Vale's celebrity fan, now a worldwide superstar. His name? Robbie Williams.

I first bumped into Rob, as his mam and his mates used to call him, just before the start of the 1992–93 season. He'd have been eighteen. Port Vale were playing a friendly against Newcastle Town, a local non-league team. We used to make the short trip to Newcastle-under-Lyme every year and quite a few Vale fans went along. Newcastle made decent money from it.

When I went into the bar after the game, I noticed a young lad sitting in a corner, flanked by what looked like a couple of minders. He was wearing a Planet Hollywood jacket and a ridiculous hat. I was halfway down the first pint when one of the minders tapped me on the shoulder and said, 'Robbie would like to meet you,' nodding towards the lad in the corner.

'Fine.' I'd no idea who 'Robbie' was, but I wandered over, shook hands, said pleased to meet you and all that. We chatted about football for a few minutes. He wished me all the best for the season and added, 'See you around.' His minders ushered him out of the bar. When he left, I asked one of our punters, 'Who's that?' 'Robbie Williams. He's from Take That, a band from round here. People say they're going to be the next big thing. Robbie's a massive Vale fan.' I'd heard of Take That, but I'd no idea who was in the band.

Rob used to come to home games whenever he wasn't away on tour. He never made a big deal of it. I'd see him in the bar afterwards, usually with his mam, Jan.

And like the first time at Newcastle, he tucked himself away in a corner and minded his own business. Bex, my wife, sometimes came to games with my mam and dad and I'd spot them having a natter with Jan. I'd say hello to Rob, have a chat about the game over a pint and after a while we'd all piss off home.

This went on for a couple of months or so and then after one game, his mam said, 'Is it all right if Rob comes out for a drink with you tonight?'

'Aye, course it is. But not if he's bloody dressed like that.' He was wearing big baggy trousers with a gusset down to his knees and silly boots. I said, 'He's no chance of a few quiet drinks with us if he's wearing that bloody lot. He'll stand out like a sore thumb. If he gets some normal gear on like ours, no problem at all.'

So Jan ran him home, he got changed and re-appeared a while later wearing a casual shirt and jeans – normal gear for a night out at the Three Crowns in Stone. Bex and I went there most Saturdays with a few mates and Rob started to come with us on a fairly regular basis. The arrangement was that we'd take him home at the end of the night or maybe he'd stay at our place. His mam was happy with that.

We never had any problems with other punters in the pub or, for that matter, when we went to the cricket club in the village. At first, I'd have a quiet word with the landlord or the barman as soon as we arrived. 'Look, we've brought Rob. We don't want any hassle, no pictures, no autographs. He just wants a quiet drink with his mates. And if he gets any grief, he won't come again.'

After we'd been out a few times, Rob grinned: 'That's why I like coming out with you, Swanny. No hassle!' And I like to think he realised that we weren't starstruck or expecting any favours. We thought he was a good lad and thoroughly enjoyed his company.

But don't get the wrong idea. I didn't need Robbie Williams as an excuse for a night out. For 16 years, I was a fully paid-up member of the drink culture that was part of the scene throughout my playing career. Wednesday was usually a day off, so Tuesday night was party night and, at every club I played for, with the exception of Plymouth, I was one of the main men. I still am. If I go back to a players' reunion, my old pals will soon be recalling nights out with Swanny and we'll be back to the jokes and the banter of the good old days. The days when turning up for training with a hangover was all part of life's rich tapestry. I'd just go out and work harder than anyone else.

If a manager decided I'd stepped out of line, I'd pay my fines and get on with it. And I always believed that as long as I produced the goods out on the pitch, what I did with the rest of my life was my business.

There are ex-players out there who went home straight after training, put their feet up in front of the telly, never touched a drop and won medal after medal. Good luck to them but, for me, they've never had a life. And I suspect that if I'd been a good, clean-living lad and followed all the rules, I would have ended up banging my head against the wall. I would have resented the game that I loved. Why? Because it wasn't letting me live my life to the full. I'm sure I would have packed it in far earlier.

When I was at Vale, I played at Wembley twice. In the 1993 Autoglass Trophy final against Stockport and, nine days later, in the Division Two play-off final against West Brom. Before the Autoglass game, I partied until dawn, staggered out on to the pitch after two hours' sleep and picked up the Man of the Match award. We won 2-1. Before the play-off final, I followed the rules and went to bed early. I was sent off after an hour. We lost 3-0. And I blame myself to this day.

I suppose that, deep down, I knew there was an extra 10 per cent in there that would have come out in my performances if I'd looked after myself better but what the hell! And, on balance, I don't think too many of my team-mates felt short-changed. That was the bottom line. Even though I gave it some stick off the field, I set myself very high standards in training and matches. Either as a striker or a defender, I set out to win every individual battle. What's more, I was prepared to use every trick in the book to make sure I came out on top.

I learned most of those tricks in my early days at Leeds. Billy Bremner was the manager who gave me my first chance at league level in 1985, when Leeds were in the old Second Division. And every Friday, one or two of Billy's old mates from Don Revie's great side of the sixties and seventies would come down and join in the five-a-sides.

Men like Norman Hunter, Paul Reaney, Joe Jordan and Jack Charlton – and what they didn't know about the tricks of the trade wasn't worth knowing. I learned all about standing on an opponent's toes, scraping your studs down his heel, anything that took his mind off his game and made my job easier.

Over the years, I learned a few off-the-ball activities as well ... but we won't go into those here. I'll be passing them on to my elder son George, who joined the Leeds United Academy in 2004 when he was ten! And, of course, in those days, there was only a referee and two linesmen to worry about – no television or video cameras watching every move.

I used to bully opponents and, when I played centre-half, I could sense straightaway that some players were scared of me before a ball had even been kicked. They'd want to make a big show of shaking hands before the kick-off. I'd ignore them.

Others would want to exchange a bit of banter when the action was at the other end of the field. I'd ignore them, too. But I knew I was in their heads and that they were thinking more about me than their own performance. And I'd clatter them good and proper at the first opportunity, just to let them know I wasn't going to go away.

As well as being sent off ten times, I picked up a whole pack of yellow cards ... but I don't recall losing too many personal battles. I like to think I usually managed to keep my striker quiet or, if I was playing up front, give my marker a hard time. To me, it was a matter of huge personal pride.

So was my determination to get out there and wear the shirt. Medical science has moved on a million miles over the last twenty years and players, managers and physios know the consequences of taking a chance on a player's fitness. But for most of my career, injured players were prepared to come back ahead of schedule or to play through the pain barrier with the help of an injection here and there. I was no different ... and the result was a chronic condition in my right knee that eventually forced me to quit in 2000. I've been told it's inoperable and that I could be confined to a wheelchair in later life, but I've no regrets. And, in the end, I've done all right for Bex and our two sons, George (who was born in 1994) and Harry (who was born in 1997). Our lifestyle has been good and the kids haven't gone short. Maybe I was never in the big league as far as money was concerned but, for most of my career, I received a decent wage for a decent day's work.

I was on £25 a week when I signed for Leeds as an apprentice. And because I lived at home, my mam was given some brass towards my keep. I also had a bus pass so I could get to work on time. Imagine that today! My first professional wage in 1984 was £85 a week and over the next five seasons at Leeds, my salary rose to £350. That was reasonable money. And when I moved to Hull in 1989, they paid me £400 a week plus a £10,000 signing-on fee. That paid for a new motor.

At first, money wasn't everything. I played football for the love of the game, but I soon realised that money is the be-all and end-all. Why? Because that's what professional football is all about for players. Making money, not winning trophies. And any journeyman pro who tries to tell you anything else is talking a load of bollocks.

OK, if a Premier League superstar is earning £50,000-plus a week it's easy for him to go on television and say that winning the

Champions League or the championship is all that matters, but the average player plying his trade outside the top flight isn't bothered about silverware. He's more interested in having a nice house, giving his missus and kids a good standard of living and enjoying a decent quality of life.

I won the Autoglass Trophy and promotion with Port Vale, but I haven't a clue where the medals are today. I know where the bonus money went. My aim was to make as much as I could – and that's why I played for so many different clubs. Loyalty is a lovely concept, but a footballer is a long time retired and, when he packs it in, he needs a bit in the bank for a rainy day.

I didn't have a lot when I was forced to quit in 2000 when I was playing for York City. For a while, times were difficult. And I learned the hard way that people in football can have short memories.

But football still plays a leading role in my working life. In 2003, I had a few trial runs as BBC Radio Humberside's 'expert witness' at Hull City's games. They gave me the job on a regular basis from the start of the 2004–05 season and I must have been doing something right because, soon afterwards, I was asked to write a column in the *Hull Daily Mail*, the local evening paper. I now write two pieces a week. I've also done a bit for Look North, the local television station.

Also in 2003, I took a career swerve into the construction industry – by building a house in the back garden of our home at Altofts, near Wakefield. I hired my own workforce and we had the job done in eight months. We lived there while I was working on the next project: a ramshackle old place out in the country. We stripped it down, laid new foundations, did a complete renovation job and were soon on the way to our own six-bedroom mansion. It's called The White House.

I keep an eye on George's progress at the Leeds academy. He's a central defender and looks a useful prospect. He's got a sensible head on his shoulders, too. He's listened to some of my stories and says he'll never go down the same road as his dad. That's exactly the advice I've given him.

If he makes the grade, he'll no doubt have an agent, a financial adviser and all the trappings that go with being a pro in this day and age. And he'll have the opportunity to make more money than I ever dreamed of. Whether he'll have as many laughs as I did remains to be seen.

And will he shake hands with the Pope one day? I doubt it. Not like his dad!

1

HARRY'S GAME

My great granddad, Harry Wilson, was one of the 'Terrible Six'. That might not mean a lot to anyone who isn't steeped in Rugby League folklore but, believe me, it's a hell of a sporting pedigree. A bit like having a long-lost relative who played football for Arsenal in the 1930s or cricket for Yorkshire in their golden age. The Terrible Six may sound like a bunch of Wild West gunslingers but they were, in fact, one of the finest packs of forwards the game of Rugby League has ever seen.

In 1908, Hunslet won an unprecedented all four cups – the championship, the Challenge Cup, the Yorkshire League and the Yorkshire Cup. They were the first team to achieve the feat and only two others have followed in their footsteps. Their triumphs were built around the Terrible Six and Harry Wilson, my dad's granddad, was a member of that all-conquering pack. Harry also played for Great Britain. We used to have one of his caps on show at home when I was a nipper growing up in Hunslet, an industrial suburb on the south side of Leeds.

What's more, I picked a pretty good sporting year to arrive on the scene. I was born on 28 September 1966, two months after

SWANNY

England won the World Cup. My dad, another Harry, had a newsagent's shop in Hunslet Park. It wasn't a million miles away from Parkside, Hunslet's legendary home where Wilson and his fellow desperadoes used to batter the opposition into submission. It bit the dust in 1972.

We lived above the shop: Dad, my mam Jean, my big sisters Janice and Diane, and me. A few years later, Dad took another newsagent's on the Parnabys, a couple of miles or so away. It wasn't an estate, just rows and rows of *Coronation Street*-style terraced houses, built years before for workers in the local factories. There was a Parnaby Street, a Parnaby View, a Parnaby Terrace, a Parnaby Row and a Parnaby Mount.

Once again we lived above the shop at No.10, Parnaby Terrace and I stayed there until I signed pro at Leeds United in 1984. That was when Mam and Dad decided to sell up and move on. They must have reckoned that until I'd finally made it as a pro, they'd keep the business on for me, just in case ...

My room was on the first floor, while Mam, Dad, Janice and Diane all slept on the floor above. It was a pretty tough area and I remember being shit scared that if anyone broke into the shop, I'd be first in the firing line if they came charging upstairs. Nobody ever did, although we had the window put through once or twice. But there were plenty of times when I'd wake up with a start and dash upstairs and leap into Mam and Dad's bed. I felt safe there.

We didn't have central heating, so the house was freezing in winter. Condensation froze on the inside of the windows, but I don't remember any of us catching too many colds. We had a little dog called Lassie. She'd followed Dad on his round one day and ended up tailing him all the way home. He asked around the neighbourhood, but nobody claimed her. We took her on board instead. She was a lovely dog. In winter, my sisters and I used to race to see who could be first in bed because, as soon as one of us hit the sack, Lassie would climb in at the bottom of the bed and wriggle all the way up for a cuddle. She was better than a hot water bottle.

Because of the hours involved for my dad, Mam had the most to do with bringing up Janice, Diane and me. There may not have been a lot of spare money around, but we had a happy childhood. Mam and Dad really did have hearts of gold. Janice is eight years older than me and she's done well for herself. She went into nursing and is now part of the management team at St James' Hospital in Leeds. So she's the intelligent one, although I've always told her that she hasn't got a lot of common sense to go with it. She's got a couple of lads, Adam and Jordan.

Diane is four years older than me and she copped for any bad luck that was coming the way of all three of us. She was born blind. Eventually, after several operations while she was still a baby, she was able to see out of one eye. When she was sixteen, though, she had to have cosmetic surgery because one of her pupils was black and the other white and, finally, when she was forty-two, she had to have a glass eye.

Soon after her seventeenth birthday, she developed psoriasis and was in a bad way for quite a while. That was just the start. By the time she was twenty-nine, she was suffering from rheumatoid arthritis. The next year she had to have a non-malignant tumour removed from her left knee and, by the time she was forty, the arthritis was so advanced she had to have yet another operation to save her right hand.

On top of all that, her husband Tom, ex-husband now, had a vasectomy that somehow reversed itself and she ended up having twins, Jessica and Peter. She already had an elder daughter, Rebecca. She's got a couple of grandchildren now so things are looking up for her at long last.

The Parnabys was a good environment for a young kid to grow

up in and I soon made a couple of mates, Ian Johnson and Ian Walker. I've stayed pals with Jonno ever since. He was my best man when Bex and I got married in 1989. 'Whacker', as we called Ian Walker, was one of the few black kids in the area. We also ganged up with a lad called Justin, whose granddad ran the local pub, the Parnaby Tavern. We spent hours in the pub, when it was shut, playing pool and darts. There was a massive concert room upstairs where we used to set up a Scalextric set or play our mini league at Subbuteo. So I grew up in the pub environment ... and I've been there ever since.

The three of us did everything together. In school holidays we'd set off on bike rides across the city to places like Kirkstall Abbey, an old ruin a couple of miles outside the city centre. They were real adventures and we never gave a toss about personal safety. There was far more freedom for kids in those days and no mobile phones if we got into bother. These days parents want to know exactly where their kids are and what they're up to every minute of the day. I don't blame them. I've been just the same with my lads, George and Harry. When they're out, I'm looking out of the window every five minutes to see if they're coming back.

Whacker had huge 'afro' hair. It was his pride and joy. The gang used to go down to what we called the pigsties, an old farm behind the Peggy Tub, the local social club. We'd get up to all sorts down there and, one day, when we were messing around with a box of matches, I accidentally set fire to Whacker's hair. I started patting him on the head to put out the flames straightaway, but he thought I was thumping him and started slapping me back.

Eventually he ran off home to tell his dad what had happened. I set off after him in hot pursuit, desperate to explain my side of the story. But he was quicker than me and by the time I arrived, his dad was already on his way out of the house. He was brandishing a machete. I screeched to a halt, spun round and set off back as fast as I could – with Whacker's dad giving chase. It was like something out of a *Tom and Jerry* cartoon.

I never really got into big trouble at home, but that didn't mean it was a house without discipline. Far from it. There were times when Mam ruled us with a rod of iron. We weren't allowed to swear and I'll never forget the first and only time I got into trouble for it. I would have been around eight at the time. I was playing tennis with Janice and at one point I shouted, 'Fucking hell!' when I missed an easy ball. As soon as I said it, I thought, 'Oh shit' because I knew exactly what she was going to do. She rushed straight in and told Mam.

She made me sit on her knee and tell her what I'd said. Then she got out a lump of carbolic soap, that horrible bloody green stuff, out of the kitchen drawer and rammed it into my mouth. Bubbles started coming out of my nose. It was terrible. I suppose the idea was to clean my mouth out. It must have worked. I've never sworn in front of my parents to this day. If I even think about it, I get a taste of soap. Nowadays it seems a cruel thing to do but that's the way people were back then and nobody seemed to worry. I certainly didn't, and when my eldest son George swore in front of me a few years back, I did exactly the same thing.

I also picked up a red card from Mam for smoking. At that age, you try everything, don't you? One day, I nicked one of her fags and joined Jonno at the pigsties, where we lit up straightaway. Unfortunately, Mam wanted me to go and get some fish and chips and came looking for me. We were caught red-handed. She took me home and made me smoke four cigarettes, one after another, until I went green and puked up. That put me off smoking cigarettes forever, although these days I treat myself to a cigar every now and then.

A few years down the line, I asked her why she'd been so strict. She said that in her day parents tried to stamp their authority on their kids whereas today, we're far more easy-going. Older people like Mam seem to think kids get away with murder and she may be right. I must admit there have been times when I've started to read the riot act to George or Harry and ended up cracking out laughing because they've come back at me with a joke. They're both cheeky little buggers.

We never had a family holiday abroad. I don't think Mam and Dad had the money or could spare the time. We sometimes went to Blackpool at Christmas. We'd take all the presents and open them there. And we had a caravan at Flamborough, near Bridlington, on the east Yorkshire coast. We went in the summer, but holidays came second to making sure us kids had everything we needed and I never had a problem filling in my time during the school holidays. Far from it.

My first school was Hunslet Carr Primary School. That's where I really got into sport. Rugby league was the big deal, but we played soccer, too. When I was eight or nine, I started playing for a local boys' team. It was run by a bloke called Ronnie Wood and my mum got in touch with him to say I was keen. She was soon involved as well and used to organise coffee mornings and all sorts of events to raise money. Eventually there was enough cash to buy a strip. We wanted white like Leeds United; we got sky blue, Manchester City.

Most weeks we struggled to get a team together although two of us eventually made it as pros. The other was Don Goodman, who went on to play in over 550 games with Bradford City, West Brom, Sunderland, Wolves and Barnsley. Don was one of our paper boys and Dad always said he was the quickest of the lot. He was given the first bag and went flying out of the shop on his round. He'd sometimes be back before Dad had finished packing the fourth bag. He was always quick but, at that age, he wasn't the best player in the world. In fact, even if we only had ten players, we'd make him sub!

HARRY'S GAME

Even at primary school I was the joker in the pack. We got up to all sorts. Once one of the kids threw another lad's coat up in the air, it hit a telegraph pole and got stuck on a wire about 20 feet up. The staff tried everything to get it down, but no joy. Mrs Whitehurst, the head teacher, was just getting ready to ring the owner's parents when I came wandering into the playground, bouncing a football. I said, 'I'll get that down for you', and drop-kicked my ball towards the telegraph pole. Bull's eye! I hit the jacket first time. To be honest, it's a tale I'd long forgotten but, a while back, I was invited to a question-and-answer session by a group of Leeds fans and one of them stood up and told that story. It was Mrs Whitehurst.

I was good at all sports at Hunslet Carr and by the time I was ten and ready to move to Belle Isle Middle School I'd gained a bit of a reputation. It seemed the staff and the other kids at my new school knew all about me by the time I arrived. Belle Isle was a tough set-up and, on my first day, a bunch of kids who were three years older decided to put the new sporting superstar in his place. They gave me a battering in the playground.

I took a hell of a pasting. They tore my jumper, ripped my shirt, cut my lip, split my nose and, in the end, I just ran out of the playground and set off home. There was no way I was going back there the next day without my mam. But she and Dad said no, I had to stand on my own two feet. They rang the school to tell the staff what had gone on, but said that basically it was down to me – and the teachers – to sort it out.

Two of the teachers, Mr Horsfall and Mr Lord, knew who'd done it. They must have worked out that in a one-on-one, I'd be able to take care of myself, even though I was quite a bit younger. So they took a big chance and on my third day, put me in the boxing ring with the cock of the school, one of the lads who'd beaten me up. I'm pretty sure they'd cleared it with Dad first but in those days the approach to discipline was a bit different.

Anyway, there we were, me and the school's main man. It was shit or bust and I waded in. I bust his nose and his lip and, from that day, I never had a minute's bother with any of the other kids. I was seen as the school hard man although, to be honest, that was never my style. I was more interested in playing sport and having a laugh. I tried to keep away from bother.

Our football master was called John Bateman. He loved his football. He recommended me to Yorkshire Amateurs, my first proper club. He was a lovely man. He never married and lived at home with his mam, but he kept tabs on me as I progressed up the ladder. Every week he'd get on his bike and ride across town to see me play for the Amateurs or, later on, for Leeds City Boys. He used to come and watch me at Leeds United, too. I never knew or I would have made sure he got tickets for the home games, but he wasn't that sort of bloke. He's dead now, bless him, and it wasn't until he'd gone that I realised how much he'd done for me and how he'd always followed my progress. I never had the chance to say thanks, but he's the man who put me on the first rung of the ladder that led all the way into the professional game.

The Amateurs ran sides at all age levels. I started with the Under-10s and was soon spotted by the City Boys, the top junior club around. Mike Healey and Doc Towers were the coaches. I played for both clubs until my mid-teens and as there were no club academies, the City Boys was the natural stepping stone into the professional game. Their ground was at Oldfield Lane in Armley, not far away from the jail, and it was a smashing set-up. I always played centre-forward as a kid; playing at the back never entered my head.

Mam mainly looked after my football because Dad was usually busy in the shop. She'd been a top sprinter in her time, running for Yorkshire and she's always loved her sport. Yorkshire Amateurs were based in Chapel Allerton on the other side of town, so Mam and I used to catch the bus into Leeds and another bus out to Chapel

Allerton for training twice a week and again for matches. We'd leave home at around five o'clock in the evening and get back after nine. All for 90 minutes' training!

The junior teams sometimes played on the playing fields at Temple Newsam House, a stately home on the east side of the city. So that meant two more bus rides. As a kid, you take things like that for granted; it's only when you have kids of your own that you realise how much time and effort – and love – is involved. And these days it does my head in when I hear kids moaning about not getting a lift or whatever. If the worst comes to the worst, they can always catch a bus. When I was fourteen, Mam and Dad decided I was old enough to do the journeys myself. And anyway, by then I was more involved with the City Boys, who were much closer to home than the Amateurs.

Every year City Boys used to have a big fund-raising raffle. Whoever sold the most tickets won a pair of top boots. I won them four years on the trot. Mam used to make sure we sold enough tickets through the shop to guarantee I picked up the prize. They were always my pride and joy and the first thing I did was to show them to my grandma. She lived about half a mile away with my Auntie Doreen, Mam's sister. My Auntie Molly lived just round the corner.

I used to go and see my grandma every day, and when I ran in with my boots she showed me how to polish them and really make them shine. After that I always used to go down to her house with my mucky boots in a plastic bag and give them a real good going-over. Sometimes she'd do it for me. We were very close and eventually she came along to see me play for Leeds United juniors and then the reserves in a couple of pre-season games. She was in a wheelchair by then and it wasn't easy manoeuvring her around, but she was chuffed to bits.

While I was at City Boys I played representative football for the first time, for Leeds Under-11s. We made it into the final of the Yorkshire Junior Trophy against Sheffield in April 1978. I don't remember too much about it, to be honest, although I can recall this little midfield man on the Sheffield side who seemed to be everywhere. He looked a decent player even then. His name? John Beresford, who made it into the pro game and clocked up over 500 games at left-back for Barnsley, Portsmouth, Newcastle, Southampton and Birmingham. Bez and I progressed through the junior ranks at county and England level together and turned pro at roughly the same time. We've been mates ever since those early days.

Later that year I was named in the Leeds Under-11 squad for a three-day tour of Tyneside. It was my first chance to sample the delights of an away trip! There was an Under-13 squad, too, and we all met up at the Wallace Arnold bus station in Leeds at 8.45am on the Thursday. We were left in no doubt about what was expected of us, thanks to the 'Notes on Behaviour and Clothes' in the tour brochure. It told us that we were representing Leeds; that our behaviour had to be in keeping with this; and that we had to be neat and tidy and reflect credit on the city. We had to wear our school uniform, if possible, and trousers (not jeans) and a shirt and tie when attending matches and for the evening meal. We also had to bring our sports equipment in a sports holdall, separate from the rest of our clothes.

It was a hell of a big deal for a kid of ten, who'd never really been too far away from base before. We stayed in a hotel in Whitley Bay and as soon as we checked in, the team manager gave us another dire warning about what would happen if we messed about. The coaches watched us like hawks all the time. On the last night we were taken to the cinema to steer us away from trouble in the hotel. We played three games against South Shields, Newcastle and North Tyneside.

Playing for Leeds City Boys also gave me a chance to discover how it felt to appear in front of a big crowd. We used to be the ballboys at Leeds United's home games, six games on and six games off on a rota system. It was fantastic. I used to stand near the tunnel and watch the players lining up. Then they came out to a huge roar, with fans chanting their names. And I was part of the action for 90 minutes, totally immersed in what was happening on the field. I must have done a decent job as a ballboy as well because I never got a bollocking for not paying attention.

But ballboy duties were always secondary. The real thing was being involved in a professional football match. I used to imagine it was me out there on the pitch with the crowd chanting my name. I savoured every second and used to think to myself, 'This must be what it's like to be a real footballer.' It was the first time I'd sampled the buzz of the professional game and only those of us who have been lucky enough to make the grade will know what I mean when I say there's no other feeling like it.

Years later, Stan Ternent, my manager at Hull, Bury and Burnley, used to say that scoring a 3ft tap-in was like making love to a beautiful woman. Perhaps even better. I wouldn't necessarily go along with that, Stan, but I know where you were coming from, if you'll pardon the phrase! And as I ran up and down the touchline at Elland Road, I convinced myself that one day I'd be out there for real.

Yet even though I didn't live a million miles from Elland Road and spent Saturday afternoons there on ball-boy duty, I was never really a Leeds fan. I used to support West Ham. God knows why. I must have liked the colour of their shirts. Their golden age of Bobby Moore, Geoff Hurst and Martin Peters had long gone, but as I was growing up they won the FA Cup twice, in 1975 and 1980, and had some decent players. Trevor Brooking was my idol, although I can't have followed his example too well – I don't think Trevor was booked in over 600 games for West Ham and England. There were other good players around, too. People like Mervyn Day, later a team-mate at Leeds, Billy Bonds, Frank Lampard, Alvin Martin, David Cross and Stuart Pearson.

But it was Leeds United, not West Ham, who came calling on 28 September 1980, the day of my fourteenth birthday. There was a knock on the door at eight o'clock in the morning. It was a Sunday, Dad was in the shop and I was still in bed. It was Geoff Saunders, United's chief scout. He wanted to get me signed up on schoolboy forms before anyone else came along. We'd had a whiff from City Boys that something was going to happen when I reached fourteen so seeing Geoff on the doorstep was no great surprise.

It was a moment of destiny for me. I'd grown up in a massive rugby league stronghold and, at first, I think Mam and Dad wanted me to follow in Harry Wilson's footsteps. I was good at both games and in addition to playing centre-forward for Leeds City Boys, I was doing well at rugby at school. One or two people reckoned I could make it as a pro and there were rumours that Leeds rugby league club might be interested. I loved my rugby, I still do, and I was always proud to be related to Harry Wilson, but deep down, when the crunch came, I knew I was always going to opt for soccer. I wanted to keep my looks, I suppose.

So when Geoff Saunders handed me the schoolboy forms, I signed them straightaway. Nowadays, a fourteen-year-old kid with a bit going for him would have someone looking after his interests, stalling the club a little to make sure he got the best deal, but in No.10 Parnaby Terrace there was just Mam, Dad and me. And I'd already made up my mind that I was going to be a professional footballer. From that moment, everything else went out the window.

2
MODELLED ON MADELEY

When I was thirteen and left Belle Isle to move on to Parkside Secondary School I didn't have to wait long to find a role model. On my first day, the teacher handed out our text books. They were old and battered and each book had a list of its previous owners inside the front cover. I couldn't believe my eyes when I read the name at the top of the list in my first book. Paul Madeley. I thought, 'Bloody hell, I never knew he'd been here', and immediately added my own name to the bottom of the list. From then on, that text book was a treasured possession; the only book I ever bothered about as my schoolwork took a back seat.

Madeley had been one of the stars of Don Revie's great Leeds United side of the sixties and seventies. He could play anywhere on the pitch and Jimmy Armfield, his manager for four years in the seventies, compared him to a Rolls-Royce. There weren't too many of those round Hunslet but, as far as I know, he was the only old boy from Parkside who'd made the grade in pro football – until I came along.

The school had a much richer rugby league pedigree, though. It was next door to where Hunslet's old stadium had stood and quite a few former pupils had gone on to turn professional over the years. Three of the lads from my era, Garry Schofield, Kelvin Skerrett and Andy Bateman, all moved into the pro game after leaving school. Garry played in the centre for Hull before completing a world-record move to Leeds in 1987. He became one of the game's all-time greats, winning a record 46 caps for Great Britain. Kelvin played for Britain as well.

It's a good job the sports stars did keep rolling off the production line from Parkside, though, because the school didn't have a lot more going for it. It must have seemed like the school from hell for most of the staff as they struggled to keep some semblance of order.

Quite often we'd look out of the classroom window and see a teacher being chased across the playing field by a group of lads and we'd immediately stand up, open the windows and cheer them on. Sometimes it was absolute mayhem and the staff were always fighting a losing battle. In the end, the school was shut down and replaced by South Leeds High School, next door to the South Leeds Stadium complex.

I never bothered with work at all. Sometimes I couldn't even be arsed to take my books to school. I rarely did any homework and didn't even turn up for some lessons – like religious education. I didn't see any point. I was going to be a footballer, wasn't I? Looking back, I realise how stupid I was. There was absolutely no guarantee I'd make the grade, but that's not how I saw it at fourteen. I'd signed schoolboy forms for Leeds United and my mind was tunnelled into playing professional football.

Sometimes, during school dinner breaks, I'd go down to Elland Road for training sessions with other lads of my age. Barry Murphy, United's youth coach, was in charge. I'd race out of school, sprint down to the ground, get changed and spend as much time as I could working on my technique – heading, first touch and so on. Then it was clothes back on and a quick dash back to school, around one-and-a-half miles away. And later on, when I was playing for United's schoolboy side, I was allowed to go out of school and spend whole days at Elland Road, working with the apprentices.

The other kids at Parkside looked up to me because I was big, a good sportsman and, above all, because I was the one who was going to play for Leeds United. And while they were constantly being chivvied into deciding what job they wanted to do when they left school, I knew exactly where I was going.

In the playground, I hung around with the tough crowd. I used to kid on that I smoked, but I never did. I was usually the look-out instead. I used to wear glasses, funny little National Health jobs, and one day a big kid who thought he was cock of the yard pinched them and ran round the playground waving them about. I put up with it for a while and then decided enough was enough. I grabbed him by the throat, threw him on to the floor and started banging his head on the concrete. Fortunately, the other lads pulled me off before I could do any real damage, but I remember I was shit scared afterwards. For a start, I could have hurt him, put him in hospital, even. And what if Leeds United had found out? I realised I needed to keep away from that kind of trouble from then on ... and I did.

That didn't stop me winding people up, though, particularly the teachers. I was always one of the ringleaders. I still am. Once in the chemistry lab, I set the Bunsen burner going on a vice handle before calling over the teacher to tell him the handle wouldn't turn. He grabbed hold of it, burned the skin off his hands and I was hauled up in front of the Head. I was nearly expelled for that one.

I never could make much of chemistry and didn't believe the teacher when he told us that a few drops of acid could make a hole in a piece of clothing. I decided to test it out for myself and, when his back was turned, I poured a load of acid on to his jacket, which was hanging on a peg. Ten minutes later, there was a massive hole in the sleeve.

In the end the chemistry teacher gave up and a few of us used to sit at the back of the class and play a football game we'd devised involving a couple of dice. We had our own mini leagues and knockout competitions and, every now and then, a huge cheer interrupted the lesson because Leeds had beaten Man United in the cup semi-final.

Sometimes we'd wait until the teacher wasn't looking and then tie a piece of string to his briefcase. Then, as the lesson progressed, we'd gradually pull the case to the back of the class and hide it. We'd be out of there before he realised it was missing. Sometimes we'd lock a lad up in a cupboard for the whole of a lesson. Most of the teachers didn't even notice.

Once some kids were chucking a few coins around during a lesson and the back of my head was on the receiving end of them. I picked the coins up and hurled them back, but I was off-target and they hit a kid called Andrew Ward in the mouth. He ended up losing two front teeth. This prompted another trip to the headmaster.

On balance, though, I don't think the teachers disliked me. I may have been a nuisance and a bit of a jack the lad, but I was never downright nasty and they put up with me, warts and all. Mind you, one of the games teachers once got more than he bargained for during a rugby league session. He was a total pillock, the sort who always used to join in the game and had to have the last word. Even though he was supposed to be the referee, he'd kick the match-winning penalty or grab the ball, sell a dummy and score himself instead of passing the ball on to one of the kids. Once, when I was clean through for a try and was about to touch down, he clicked my ankles from behind and I lost the chance.

I don't know whether he thought it was a huge joke or what, but he did that kind of thing to all the lads and, in the end, we got totally pissed off with him. One day, he decided to join in a scrum and got ready to pack down in the second row. I was in the opposition front row and I said to the hooker, 'Just keep my arm free.' When the scrum packed down, I smacked the teacher and bust his nose open. The scrum erupted and everyone was looking innocent, as if we didn't know how it had happened, but we all did, including the teacher. He couldn't prove anything, though. I left soon after, but I bet he didn't mess about in games any more.

It was an all-boys school, but fortunately there was a girls' high school nearby. The girls were at the top of the hill; we were at the bottom, and in between was a wood. Perfect! Kids from both schools would disappear in there at lunchtime. No wonder some of them fell asleep in afternoon classes.

I got out as soon as I could because I knew Leeds United were waiting. I've no idea what qualifications I left with. A few CSEs, I suppose. My mam went and picked up the certificates after I left, but I never bothered looking at them.

But although I couldn't be arsed with schoolwork, football was a totally different matter. While I was at Parkside I played regularly for Leeds City Boys and when I made it into their senior side, I was making a mark alongside some decent players. One of them was David Ripley, who was also a top cricketer and ended up playing at Northants for 17 years. A wicketkeeper-batsman, he moved on to the coaching staff in 2001 and we've stayed in touch. Dave was a more than useful midfield player: he had a great brain and was a good passer of the ball. I'd make the runs and he'd put the ball right in my path. I always thought he had a good chance of making the grade, but he was a bit short of pace and eventually fell by the wayside. Brian Deane, who had a 20-year career with 9 clubs and played for England, was following on behind. However, of all the kids I played with and against, only a handful went on to make the grade. It was to be the same story all the way into the professional game.

I played schoolboy football at various different age groups, almost always as a striker, against teams from all over the north – Manchester, Sunderland, Sheffield, East Northumberland, North Yorkshire, Humberside, Lancashire, Salford, to name but a few. On Monday, 13 October 1980, we played Liverpool Boys under the floodlights at Anfield, for the Leeds United Supporters' Club Cup. It wasn't the first time I'd played under lights – our game against Sunderland a couple of weeks earlier had been floodlit, too – but for a little nipper, travelling across the Pennines to play a fixture like that at Anfield really did feel like the real thing.

It was exciting, but scary. The Sunderland game may have been my first taste of floodlit football at a big stadium, but I knew what Elland Road was all about. I'd been out there as a ballboy, knew the feel of the place and it was my hometown club, after all.

But Anfield? Fucking hell! We'd all heard about the famous badge proclaiming 'This Is Anfield' in the corridor leading from the dressing room to the tunnel and we tried to be just like the pros we'd heard about and jumped up to touch it on our way out. Unfortunately we couldn't bloody reach it. The Liverpool captain was Gary Ablett, who had a long career playing in defence for both Merseyside clubs and Birmingham, but looking down the list of the 32 players on duty that night, I think only Ablett, Don Goodman and I had much of a pro career. The result of the game? No bloody idea.

My first step on the international ladder came in late 1981 when I was one of 31 lads called up by the English Schools Football Association for the north of England trials at Blackpool followed by the national trials at Lilleshall early in 1982. Little did I know I'd be seeing plenty more of Lilleshall's rehabilitation centre in years to come. I received a letter from Allan Clarke, the Leeds manager, congratulating me on my selection. There is no doubt that it is an achievement and an honour, he wrote.

We received strict instructions about what to bring with us to Stafford railway station, where we would be met by the coaches for the journey to Lilleshall. All the football kit plus a smart jacket or blazer for meals – as well as some soap and a towel. This time, there were quite a few lads who would go on to play at league level, including John Beresford, Darren Beckford, Frazer Digby, Tim Flowers, Paul Holland, Paul Moulden, Mark Seagraves, John Moncur and Dennis Wise. And I must have made a bit of an impression. I made the final training squad a few weeks later along with Beckford, Beresford, Digby, Flowers, Kevin Keen, Kevin Russell and Wise, but I didn't get in the side.

Soon afterwards, on 13 May 1982, I received another letter from Clarke. It read:

Dear Peter,

May I first of all apologise to you for the delay in writing this letter, but we are pleased to inform you that we would like to offer you an apprenticeship with this club when you leave school in 1983, subject to a medical examination.

We would be obliged if you would write a letter of acceptance within twenty-one days of receipt of this letter.

A meeting with you and your parents will be arranged to discuss the apprentice contract and also plans to further your education while pursuing your career as a footballer with Leeds United.

Kindest regards.
Yours sincerely,
Allan Clarke

Soon afterwards, we all went down to Elland Road for the official signing with Clarke and Martin Wilkinson, his number two. We were shown into Clarke's office. Wilkinson told my parents how the club would look after me and the other boys who were signing and what a great opportunity it was.

Mam replied, 'My son doesn't swear, you know.' It must have seemed an odd remark, but Wilkinson just smiled and said, 'Well, give him two weeks with this lot and you might find he's discovered a new vocabulary!' It didn't go down too well.

Martin was a lovely bloke. He always had time for the kids and their parents and he took time out to give Mam and Dad the lowdown. 'We're only signing six lads, so Peter has every chance. It's not as if we're taking on twenty and hopefully all six will come through and make it as professionals.' Five of us did.

The others who signed at the same time were Terry Phelan, John Scales, Mark Russell, Nigel Thompson and Lyndon Simmonds. Neither Phelan nor Scales made an impact at Leeds, but both went on to have a good career and played for Wimbledon in their FA Cup victory over Liverpool in 1988. Scales won 3 England caps and played for Newcastle, Liverpool, Spurs and Ipswich, while Phelan also played at the top level with Manchester City, Chelsea and Everton. Thompson also played a few games for Leeds and later for Rochdale and Chesterfield, while Simmonds made one or two appearances before also moving on to Rochdale.

Technically, I suppose, Clarke was my first manager. He was an England international, an Elland Road legend and had been a key figure in Revie's triumphant team of the sixties and seventies, but I was just a kid and he was a distant figure, involved with the first team and the struggle to keep Leeds in the top flight. I wasn't in awe of him as such; we just never really came into contact when I'd been down at Elland Road during my time as a schoolboy apprentice. Even if I walked past him in the corridor, the odds were he wouldn't speak, so I've no real idea what he was like, neither as a person nor as a manager.

And soon after I signed my apprentice contract, he was on his way after Leeds dropped out of the top division for the first time since 1964. His successor, as player-manager, was Eddie Gray, who'd been youth team coach. So he knew that I was making a bit of a name for myself at Elland Road. I'd played for the juniors, both up front and in defence, through the 1981–82 season, even though I was still at school, and Gray made sure the club kept me involved. I was invited to all the schoolboy coaching sessions, and whenever possible, was also allowed to join in the apprentices' training sessions, too. And even though I wasn't due to sign apprentice forms for another 15 months, he asked me to report for pre-season training ahead of the 1982–83 season. Welcome to the big time, Swanny!

I suppose I should have been shit scared. I was, after all, a fifteen-year-old schoolboy walking into the lion's den of professional football. But I wasn't. In fact, I can honestly say that at no time on my way to a professional contract did I feel overawed in any way. I just knew it was going to happen. Was it arrogance? Maybe. But isn't that just a part of professional sport?

Over the years, I've heard people say they've been stunned or overwhelmed to be offered professional terms or a new contract. That was never me. As far as I'm concerned, any pro who's shocked to be offered a deal doesn't believe in himself, so I wasn't being big-headed when I assumed I'd be taking the next step, just being honest with myself. As soon as I signed at one level, I started preparing to move on to the next one. In the long term, I was looking to buy a car, a house, to get married and have all the things that football could offer me. At that moment in time, I'd signed an apprentice contract and, even though I was still at school, I couldn't wait to get started.

3
PEACE BE WITH YOU!

Even though Leeds had dropped out of the top flight for the first time since 1964, there were still some big names at the club when I reported for my first day of pre-season training. How about Eddie Gray, the player-manager, for starters? Or Frank Gray, his brother, and Trevor Cherry, two more survivors from the Revie era? And, despite suffering relegation, there were four more internationals – Peter Barnes, Kenny Burns, Arthur Graham and Frank Worthington – still at the club, not to mention big-money signings like Paul Hart and Kevin Hird.

By and large, the senior pros were great with the kids. Barnes and Burns, in particular, were a different class and always ready for a laugh. Barnes was a bit of a hero. He drove a Ford Capri 2.8 injection, which soon became my dream car. I promised myself that I'd go out and buy one when I signed pro forms. Unfortunately, it never occurred to me that Barnes was on £1,000 a week and could afford a motor like that. My first weekly wage as a pro was £85 and I had to settle for a second-hand Mini Metro. Amazingly, I once collected a speeding rap in it. I was proud of that. I didn't think it could go that fast.

SWANNY

Frank Worthington was another larger-than-life character who'd arrived midway through the 1981–82 season in an effort to keep relegation at bay. Leeds was his fifth club after spells with Huddersfield, Leicester, Bolton and Birmingham. He went on to play for Sunderland, Southampton, Brighton, Tranmere, Preston and Stockport, as well as a spell in the States, before finally jacking it in with 757 league appearances to his name. Incredible!

Frank used to wear the most amazing outfits and thought nothing of reporting for training sporting cowboy boots and a Stetson. One day, he took me to one side and offered me a tenner to clean his jeans. I assumed he was on a promise. 'No problem,' I said. 'Where are they?'

Frank produced the jeans. They had a line of small mirrors running down the outside of each leg. He wanted me to polish the mirrors – not with soap and water, but with Windolene from the hardware shop down the road. It took me hours. I just hope the jeans helped him to do the business.

For the first few days of pre-season, we went to Roundhay Park on the outskirts of Leeds. Morning sessions were solid running, up and down hills and round the lakes in the park. Two laps of a circuit. We had a break for lunch and then started again in the afternoon. Sometimes we'd go on the track instead and run a few 800 metres but basically, the start of pre-season was all about running, running and more fucking running.

I sometimes saw senior players kneeling down and being physically sick on the climbs. The punishment was to go back down to the bottom of the hill and start all over again, so I soon learned that if I was going to puke, the best thing was to let it go while I was still moving.

The running was one-paced and had nothing to do with playing football; its aim was to build up stamina and it was the only kind of pre-season people knew at the time. They'd been doing it for years and nobody had ever questioned it. It wasn't until the study of sports science arrived on the scene that people began to realise just how outdated the old ways were.

The first proper pre-season I had was probably down at Plymouth thirteen years later after Neil Warnock had taken over as manager. It goes against the grain to say something good about Warnock, but he got it right that time. We built up in stages and while we used to run non-stop for the best part of an hour in my early days at Leeds, the longest stint in pre-season under Warnock was a 55-second sprint.

My last full pre-season, at Burnley in 1999, was physically much easier and entirely football-related. We did short sprints or we'd sprint 50 yards, walk 10 yards, then go again and sprint another 50. As a result, the players were far better prepared for the speed and intensity of a professional match.

In just a few weeks of that first build-up at Elland Road I felt I'd become part of the set-up. This was going to be my life. So it came as a massive shock to the system when early September came along and I had to go back to Parkside School for my final year. But I carried on playing for the juniors and also the city and county representative sides and, early in 1983, around twelve months after my England Under-15 trials, the FA were in touch again.

This time the letter was addressed to Mam and Dad and was signed by Bobby Robson, the England manager. He was inviting me to join the England Under-16 squad for a weekend of coaching and trials at Lilleshall ahead of the 1983–84 European Under-16 Championships.

Robson said I'd been identified as a player of international potential, adding: 'Naturally, I would like to think this opportunity to step on the first rung of the international ladder will have preference over any other games your son may have been involved in during this weekend.' He could say that again!

That weekend, in March 1983, was my first real experience of just how tough professional football was going to be and how I was going to be on trial, day in and day out. It was time to stand up and be counted. There were 29 of us and we were all on the books of professional clubs, ranging from Arsenal, Chelsea, Newcastle and Manchester City to York City, Scunthorpe and Orient. Yet, once again, only a handful of those players went on to play at league level for any length of time: Joe Allon, Darren Beckford, John Gannon, Paul Holland, Paul Moulden and me.

We trained in front of a panel of assessors and team selectors. At first, I looked around at some of the other kids and thought what incredible players they were. Some of them seemed to be capable of anything on the training ground, but it was a different story when the practice games began and the tackles began to fly in. All of a sudden, a lot of them didn't really want to know any more. Not me. I relished the challenge.

I may not have been the most gifted player around, but I could handle the pressure of playing for an England place in front of the selectors. And I was pretty certain I was going to be named as one of the strikers. Instead, I picked up a back injury towards the end of the weekend and missed out. Beckford, who went on to play over 300 league games, was chosen instead. I was devastated for a while, but was soon able to see the positive side and realise that I'd taken a big step on the road to the professional game. I may have suffered a setback, but I'd seen what was involved and I was even more certain that I was going to get there in the end.

I didn't have to wait long for a spot of good news. A week or so after missing out at Lilleshall, I was called into the headmaster's study again. For a change, Mr Muston was smiling. He'd received a letter from Leeds United:

We are writing to obtain permission for your pupil, Peter Swan, to be released from school in order to join our party who are travelling to Rome to take part in a football tournament.

The dates of the tournament are from Monday, 28 March until Sunday, 3 April. Hoping you are able to give the necessary permission.

Yours sincerely,
E. Gray, Player/manager

Permission or no permission, I wasn't going to miss out on that one. It was my first trip abroad and there must have been a bit of a panic about getting me a passport. I can't remember too many of the finer points, but the competition was held at a complex on the outskirts of Rome, presumably at AS Roma's training ground. There were four teams – Leeds, Internazionale, Udinese and Roma – and we were scheduled to play a round robin over the five days.

The first game was against Inter and I was named up front. I wasn't really fit because of the back problem that had ruled me out of the England Under-16s. I had to wear a corset with metal bars supporting my back, but I'd always dreamed about playing against one of the top Italian sides, so I wasn't going to throw up this first opportunity. I knew that I might never get another chance to play against Inter in my life.

But it was hopeless. I could hardly move during the warm-up and, as we lined up for the national anthems, I knew I wasn't going to last long. I tried to run it off once the game started but, after about twenty minutes, I struck a ball and felt this searing pain down my back and into my groin. That was it. But I'd been on the field long enough to sample Italian tactics for the first time. Even though they were only fifteen or sixteen, these lads were past masters at the art of nipping, shirt-pulling, poking opponents in the eye, spitting, the lot.

All in all, it wasn't the best of tournaments for me. My back was killing me and soon after we arrived I picked up some sort of bug and was forced to spend a day in bed. Even though I was a long way from my home and family, I didn't get a lot of sympathy. The lads were more interested in training, playing and messing about, so I just had to stick in there and get on with it. So there were some lonely moments ... and one massive highlight.

Halfway through the tournament we were told we'd be having the afternoon off. We were going to St Peter's to see the Pope. All four teams and officials were herded on to buses and driven off into Rome. We swept into St Peter's Square and, after about three security checks, were shown into our seats alongside the raised podium from where the Pope was going to deliver a blessing. We were sitting near to the entrance to St Peter's and I could see the massive square outside. There seemed to be a million punters waiting for a glimpse of the main man.

If I'd had a choice I wouldn't have bothered going but, looking back, it was one hell of an experience. We had to sit in the boiling sun for what seemed like ages, while these chaps were ranting on in foreign languages. But eventually Pope John Paul II gave his blessing, then climbed into his 'Popemobile' and was driven around between the podium and the special guests, stopping every now and then to shake people by the hand.

We were told that when someone shouted 'Leeds United Football Club' we all had to stand up. So we answered the call as the Pope's car approached us. He climbed out. I thought that, as I was there, I'd better see what all the fuss was about. So I made sure I was near the front as he walked by and thrust my hand out in front of me. He took my hand, looked into my eyes and said, 'Bless you.'

I was only sixteen and didn't give a shit about religion. I only had a vague idea who the Pope was, but I was genuinely moved. And I know this might sound like a load of bollocks but, from that moment on, my back started to get better. I didn't play again in

Italy, but I was fit again after a couple of weeks when most people thought I'd be out for a lot longer.

As time went by, I'd see pictures of the Pope on the telly in the pub and I'd tell people, 'Oh, I've met him, you know.'

'Fuck off!'

'No, I have, honest.'

To this day, I don't think people believe me. But now I have proof! One of the official photographers at the Vatican took a picture of me shaking hands with the Pope and sent it to the club. Jack Roberts, one of the staff who'd travelled with the team, kept it as a memento. When he died a while ago, everybody had forgotten about the picture. But when I started working on this book, I decided to try and find it. I contacted Jack's son, Alan, who was stadium manager at Sheffield Wednesday and who had once been general manager at Elland Road. He said he'd have a look through his dad's possessions. A month later, I had a call on the mobile. It was Alan. He'd found the picture.

When we returned from our Italian job, I only had a few months before I could finally get away from Parkside and move into Elland Road full-time. And after being around for so long on a part-time basis, I was very much one of the boys. Or make that one of the general dogsbodies, otherwise known as apprentices. OK, we did our training and played for the juniors and, if we were lucky, the reserves, but it seemed as though our principal role at the club was to keep the place clean and to look after the senior pros. It could have been a real chore, but put a group of lads into a situation like that and there are always going to be plenty of opportunities for a few laughs.

I was usually the frontrunner when it came to practical jokes. That was my style. I worked, trained and played with a smile on my face – and why not? I had the best job in the world and I was getting paid for it. It may not have been a lot, but it was enough to keep me in beer, even at that age.

SWANNY

During the summer, before the start of the season, we had to paint the turnstiles and the barriers and once the senior players reported back for pre-season, we had to clean up the dressing rooms after training and matches. If we made a mess of any of the jobs, we found ourselves on the receiving end of a bollocking or even a fine. We also had a few 'punishments' of our own if one of the lads cocked it up.

Sometimes we'd chuck him into the wicker hamper that was used to carry the players' boots on away trips. Then we'd turn the hosepipe on the basket until it was completely soaked before firing it off down the corridor that ran under the main stand. It would career away, bouncing off the walls and spraying water everywhere. Woe betide anyone who got in the way. Or else we'd pin the offender down on the dressing-room table, shave off his pubes, cover his cock and balls with masses of black boot polish and then top it off with a coat of Vaseline. It took days to get rid of it.

Most of the younger pros, who were a couple of years ahead of us, had a car, usually a bit of an old banger that they'd park in the car park behind the main stand, a respectful distance away from the top-of-the-range BMWs, Sierras and so on that belonged to the senior players. In those days, the training ground was part of the Elland Road complex, situated at the back of the main stand with the car park in between. The training ground was a good 10 feet higher than the car park, so no one up there could see what was going on down below. So sometimes we'd nick a set of keys and give ourselves a driving lesson, tearing round the car park for a while before returning the car to its parking slot.

John Scales, who lived in Harrogate, was a bit posher than the rest of us apprentices. He actually had a car of his own. And one day, Terry Phelan and Nigel Thompson took it for a spin and reversed it into the bottom of a floodlight pylon. There was a big dent in the boot. What to do next? After a bit of careful thought, we opted to park the car backed right up to the wall and hoped Scalesy wouldn't spot the damage.

Sure enough, when we'd finished for the day, he showered, changed, picked up his keys, said cheerio and pissed off out to his car. We waited with bated breath until we spotted him driving away, blissfully unaware that his motor was no longer the mint-condition vehicle he'd parked that morning. The next day, he was back, playing fuck about how some pillock in Harrogate had run into the back of his car and not bothered to leave a note.

One Friday, when Terry and I were looking for an early getaway, we were told to paint the players' tunnel. Leeds were going to be on *Match of the Day* on the Saturday night and they wanted everything to look good for the cameras. The tunnel was painted white with a blue stripe, the depth of a single brick, running from end to end along each wall. The white was straightforward and we polished that off in no time. But the blue stripe needed more care and was clearly going to give us some grief if we wanted to get away quick.

So I said to Terry: 'Right, get the brush ready. I'll tip the blue paint out of the can straight on to the wall. You slap the paint on as it comes out. Should be a doddle.' Trouble was, the paint came out of the can far quicker than Terry could brush it on and by the time we'd finished, all the blue had run down the white walls. It was a right mess and we had to hang around until nine o'clock before the white paint had dried enough for us to do the blue stripe properly.

Poor Terry was the unwitting victim on another occasion, but this time it wasn't a deliberate practical joke. I'd turned up for work that morning feeling pretty down because my grandma, the one who used to help me clean my boots, had died the previous day. She'd been laid out in the front room for family and friends to pay their respects and I told the rest of the lads what had happened when I reported for training. They did their best to cheer me up and, while all this was going on, I failed to spot that Terry wasn't around and hadn't heard about Gran.

I knew he was a religious lad so, after training, I asked if he'd like to come back with me to see my grandma. He said he would and we chatted away on the way back to the Parnabys. When we walked into my auntie's house, he can't have noticed that everything was hushed and the curtains were drawn. So I said, 'Right, she's in 'ere,' and opened the door to the front room. Terry breezed in and I could see the blood drain from his face.

We did manage to play a bit of football in between all the jobs and the jokes. We had a good youth team and reached the Northern Intermediate League Cup final in 1984. We played Newcastle over two legs in the final and this was our line-up in the first game at Elland Road. In goal we had Phil Hughes, who later played for Northern Ireland. The back four were Denis Irwin, John Scales, Neil Aspin and Terry Phelan, with Mark Russell, Lyndon Simmonds, Scott Sellars and Nigel Thompson in midfield and me and Tommy Wright up front. Waiting in the queue were the next generation, people like David Batty and Gary Speed. I reckon that lot went on to play over 5,000 league games between them. In the opposition line-up was a young hopeful by the name of Paul Gascoigne.

The Northern Intermediate League was a tremendous learning curve for all of us. All the big clubs were involved and we'd be up against teams just as strong as we were, sometimes stronger, week in and week out. They were tough, competitive matches. Just about all the players had been part of a small intake each season and clubs were very precise about who they would pick. Most of them went on to make it.

I'm convinced that the finishing school I went through at Leeds was far better than today's academy set-ups. Sometimes I'd be playing in the juniors on a Saturday and for the reserves in midweek. That wouldn't happen often today because usually the academy kids go right through to eighteen, playing only against boys of their own age and physique. The coaches seem to think that, unless a kid is really talented, he isn't ready to go in against the men until he's eighteen. That's a load of crap. If you're good enough, you're old enough ... and it was an environment that made me grow up fast. It was the same for a lot of other young players who went on to make the grade. It was sink or swim in a very hostile environment and a young player who could make it through that challenge was ready to move on to a higher level.

I played plenty of reserve-team football as an apprentice, still switching between centre-half and centre-forward, and in Kenny Burns, I was playing alongside an old pro who had done exactly the same thing during his early days at Birmingham City. At seventeen, Kenny played league football as a striker, before eventually settling into central defence. It was an education to play a few games alongside him at the back. I was sixteen; he was thirty-three, a former Footballer of the Year. I had a few junior games under my belt; he'd won twenty-one Scottish caps, played in a World Cup, won two championships and two European Cups. But to Kenny, I wasn't just some young kid hoping to make a name for himself. I was his mate and his colleague in the trenches. As far as he was concerned, it was all for one and one for all. Sometimes he'd take me to one side in the dressing room and talk to me about his partnership with Larry Lloyd at the heart of the defence for Brian Clough's Forest. He told me how they worked together to sort out the opposition and how they used to look after one another.

He once told me: 'Swanny, never retaliate straightaway. If someone clobbers you early on, walk away. Retaliate and you're booked, maybe sent off. So leave it, and wait.' He showed me what he meant in a reserve game at Blackpool. Midway through the first-half, one of their strikers came across me and took me out with a late challenge. I went down and had already started to get up and give him one back when I felt a hand on my shoulder. It was Kenny. I stayed down for a few seconds, then got on with the game.

Early in the second half, a long high ball was played up to the same striker and Kenny took him out. He ended up in a heap with his shirt and shorts ripped open. As the trainer ran on, Kenny turned to me and said: 'That's what I mean, Swanny. I've looked after you, now you look after your next centre-half.' He didn't even wait for the red card, but walked off the field, down the tunnel and soon afterwards moved on to Derby County.

I played regular reserve-team football for three seasons, sometimes up front but mainly in the back four. In August 1984 I signed my first professional contract and I was one of the players Gray was bringing through for the future. Some of his production line, like Irwin, Andy Linighan, Aspin, John Sheridan and Wright, had already made the first team. Now I was there, or thereabouts.

Nigel Thompson, my room-mate on the Italian trip and a team-mate since we had played for Leeds Under-9s, was called up for the first team in the last away game of the 1983–84 season. Managers often chuck kids in for a game or two if there's nowt to play for and Nigel struck lucky. I was pleased for him, but at the same time I felt gutted that it wasn't me. I was sure I'd be next in the queue but instead Lyndon Simmonds got the nod. It was so bloody frustrating because I felt I was ready and it wasn't as if the team was pulling up any trees. The waiting game continued all the way through into the 1985–86 season but in October, with the first team apparently going nowhere, Eddie left. The directors' patience had run out.

Eddie was always seen as one of soccer's gentlemen and his critics said he was too much of a nice guy to be a manager and that he didn't have the mean streak required to be a successful gaffer. I wouldn't argue with that, but it wasn't necessarily his biggest problem. I didn't play a first-team game for him at Leeds, but I sensed that although his teams went out wanting to play for a manager they respected and liked, they didn't really know what was expected of them.

Eddie had been such a naturally gifted player in a great side and he had been surrounded by players of similar quality. And he seemed to think his kind of quality came naturally and that everyone could all play like him. They couldn't and he never seemed to quite come to terms with that.

He was a laid back sort of guy, a fitness fanatic – he was still running half marathons well into his sixties – and he would never dream of asking a player to do something he couldn't do himself. He'd be the first on to the training ground and the last off it and if a player needed a bit of extra work, he'd be there to help. He later returned to Leeds for a short stint in charge in 2003. And earlier, as youth-team coach, he produced the nucleus of the side that reached the semi-finals of the Champions League in 2001. Players like Alan Smith, Harry Kewell, Jonathan Woodgate and Ian Harte were all nurtured by Eddie.

He will always be seen as a key figure in the club's history but, as a manager, the best he achieved in three years was seventh in his final season and he paid the price. The fans were furious and staged a huge demonstration following the first match after his dismissal. Was I sorry to see him go? From a personal point of view, yes. I liked Eddie and he must have felt OK about me because, four years later, he paid a club record fee of £200,000 to take me to Hull City. He also worked as an agent for a while and I was one of his clients. But, from a footballing point of view, I wasn't disappointed to see the back of him. I felt I was ready for league football but Eddie hadn't given me the breakthrough. So when he left, I reckoned I'd have a better chance of making an impression under the new man, whoever he might be. That's always the way when a manager leaves. If asked, players will usually say they're sorry to see the gaffer go – but the only ones who are telling the truth are the players he has selected on a regular basis.

4

FARTS AND ALL!

One way or another, 1985 was quite a year. I made my first-team debut for Leeds United, I was sent off for the first time – in a reserve game at Barnsley – and I met the missus. I need to get my priorities right here, so I'd better start with Rebecca.

We met on 11 May 1985. But if that Saturday hadn't been one of the blackest days in football history, we'd never have got together at all. A couple of days before, I'd been out on the piss in town and had bumped into a lass called Linda McGee. She'd been my first girlfriend in the old Belle Isle schooldays. We'd only been a couple of kids then and the relationship petered out but, on that Thursday, we were getting along fine and I arranged to see her again on the Saturday.

I was injured at the time and decided to go and watch Leeds play Birmingham at St Andrews. It was a dreadful afternoon. During the game, a teenager was killed when a wall collapsed as a group of Leeds fans ran riot and, as soon as we got back into the car afterwards, we learned the awful news from Bradford that, on a day when they should have been celebrating Bradford City's promotion from the old Fourth Division, over 50 fans were feared dead in the Valley Parade fire.

SWANNY

When I got home, I was in no real mood to go out clubbing, so I decided to give Linda a miss and joined my mam and dad for a night out in Barwick in Elmet, a little village on the outskirts of Leeds. Three of the lads at Elland Road, Tommy Wright, Dennis Irwin and John Sheriden, lodged there with a couple called Cath and Trevor, who had housed quite a few young pros at one time or another.

Cath was holding a charity evening and wanted the four of us to stick around for a while. I was thinking more in terms of a few beers in one of the village pubs. Instead, I hung around ... and I met Bex. She had a friend in the village and they'd decided to go along to Cath and Trevor's. And we've been together ever since. She must have been impressed by the pink shirt and black 'Staypress' trousers!

We hit it off straightaway and, if memory serves me right, she kept grabbing my hand and trying to get me to go outside. She has a different take on the evening. At the end of the night, I wanted to give her my phone number, but we didn't have a pen between us, so she fished some eyeliner out of her make-up bag, wrote the number on a piece of paper and stuffed it into her handbag. By the time she got back to her home near Wakefield, the eyeliner had run and she couldn't make out all the numbers. So next day, she and her mam sat down and tried to work out what the numbers might be and started to ring round all the options.

Meanwhile, back in Parnaby Terrace, I was blowing away, wondering why she wasn't ringing and why I'd never asked for her number as well. Eventually, the correct number slotted into place and we were in business.

I didn't tell her I was a pro footballer for two months. The season had ended and I had a lot of time on my hands, but when she asked me where I worked, I made out I was unemployed. I told her I just did a bit o' this and a bit o' that here and there. It sounds old fashioned, but I wanted her to love me for who I was and not for what I did. Eventually, when the time came for us to return for pre-season training, I had to come clean.

Soon afterwards, she asked me round to meet her mam and dad, Maureen and George. I was just a lad from a terraced house in Hunslet, so their four-bedroom detached house seemed like a mansion. They started showing me all the old pictures of Rebecca as a kid while the two of us were sitting on the floor with our backs to the settee. At one point, she leaned across to grab a photo and accidentally dug her elbow into my stomach. 'Wow, that's solid muscle,' she said.

'Aye, you could stand on it if you wanted,' I replied.

Instead, she pressed my stomach hard with both hands, really hard. And out came this massive fart. Nobody knew how to react so, after a couple of seconds, I said: 'Perhaps it's a good job you didn't stand on my stomach after all!' They put up with me from then on. Farts and all, you might say.

We'd been courting for a couple of years or so when Mervyn Day, the Leeds keeper at the time, pushed me into buying my first house. He'd been going on at me about it for a while, but I was more interested in spending my brass on nights out with the lads than thinking of settling down. He'd come into training with estate agents' brochures, pin me in a corner and talk to me about the housing market. Eventually he cajoled me into going to look at one or two places.

Bex and I were ready to get engaged by then, so I began to see there was probably a bit of sense in what Mervyn was on about. But when I finally opted for a place in Wrenthorpe, a village on the outskirts of Wakefield, I was stretching the finances to the absolute limit. I wasn't happy about that. There was a danger that my nights out were going to be restricted but, thanks to Mervyn, I was on the ladder early and I've never fallen off. Looking back, it was probably the best advice anyone ever gave me and, for once in my life, I listened and did as I was told.

I bought the house a while before we got married, but there was no question of moving in together. No bloody chance! Neither of our parents would have heard of it. So we had to wait until after the big day, 24 June 1989, at Stanley Parish Church, near Wakefield, followed by a reception at the Cedar Court hotel on the outskirts of town. Honeymoon? Hawaii. I'd made a point of not telling Bex where we'd be going, but I'd opted for a hotel called the Twin Towers. When I announced it to her in my wedding speech, all the guests started chanting 'Wem-ber-lee! Wem-ber-lee!'

We were both twenty-two and a lot of managers were keen to see their players married off even younger than that. They reckoned that if you had a wife, and a settled life away from the training ground, you'd be less likely to cause bother off the field. You'd rather be in front of the telly than out on the piss with the lads. They must have been bloody joking.

For me, drinking and nights out had been part of my life since I was about fifteen, long before I signed pro. Every Thursday I used to go out supping with my mate Jonno. I was a big lad for my age, so while there may have been one or two sidelong glances from pub landlords, I never had a problem getting served. Jonno, on the other hand, was only a little lad and I had to hide him in a corner until I got the beers in.

We'd go out and get completely smashed. And we carried on as I climbed up the ladder into the professional game. Thursday was traditionally the lads' night out where I came from and I didn't see any reason to change just because I was a footballer. I'd turn up for training the next day with a massive hangover and then just burn it off. When you're young you really can burn the candle at both ends, can't you? I'd go home and get my head down on Friday afternoon, have some tea, then sit down and watch the telly. Come Saturday morning, I'd be as fit as a fiddle.

I wasn't the only one, not by a long chalk. As an apprentice and young pro, it was common to see players arrive for training, or even on match day, stinking of drink from the previous night. Once John Sheridan reported for a home game looking distinctly below par, but he just got changed, went out, won the match with a penalty and collected the Man of the Match award. I used to see things like that and think, 'Why waste a night out when you can play like that afterwards?'

We got into a few scrapes, but I can't recall any real bother in the bars, either from fans or young hopefuls who fancied their chances against the United players. Mind you, Steve O'Shaughnessy, who was a year younger than me, once got more than he bargained for. After he made his second-team debut he organised a night out to celebrate and we went out to a bar called the Sunset and Vine.

He was playing the big 'I am' and when this really fit bird walked by, Steve said: 'Just watch this.' He grabbed hold of her arse as she went by and then turned away to lap up the applause. She just swung round and kicked him right in the bollocks. He went down like a bag of cement. He was white as a sheet and I'll swear he was on the floor for about twenty minutes. The big pro footballer who knew how to pull the birds!

The Leeds players were always being invited to charity events and that usually meant an opportunity for a night on the piss. Once, a crowd of us arranged to go to a big Children in Need do in Bradford. Mam and Dad were away and I was looking after their two dogs. I'd been on the ale all afternoon and, when I got back, I realised I should be taking the dogs for a walk. We used to walk them round a nearby cemetery. So I set off, let the dogs off the leash for a romp round and lay down on one of the cemetery benches. I woke up an hour later. No dogs. I staggered home and, thank God, the dogs had made their own way back. I fed them, got changed, called round for Jonno and set off for Bradford.

There were quite a few of the lads there, so we all helped with the auctions and the other fund-raising events and, somehow, I contrived to win a giant teddy bear in the raffle. There was a bit of drink flowing and, once the formalities were over, we all headed off to a club to finish the night in style. With me carrying the teddy bear.

I was well pissed by the time we left and Jonno and I were in fits as we tried to find a way of getting me, him and the teddy bear into the car. In the end, we stuffed the bear into the backseat and stuck its head out of the window at the driver's side. We'd only gone a couple of miles when Jonno said, 'There's a car behind flashing its lights.' I couldn't use my rear-view mirror because there was a bear's arse in the way and the wing mirror was blocked by the bear's head. Seconds later, the flashing light materialised as a police car. Two coppers climbed out.

They clocked the teddy bear and one of them said, 'Do you mind coming to sit in our car, sir.' He opened the door and I fell out into the road. I thought, 'This is it. I'm finished.'

'Have you been drinking?'

'Not really. Just one or two.'

'Have you been breathalysed before?'

'No.'

'Right, blow into this.' He explained what to do in more detail. I blew into the box and, surprise, surprise, the crystals changed from yellow to green. 'You've obviously had too much to drink. You'll have to come back to the station with us.'

I decided to go for the sympathy vote. 'Fair enough. But I play for Leeds United, you know, and I've just been to a charity event for Children in Need. We've raised a load of money.'

'You play for Leeds?'

'Aye.'

He looked at me more closely, seemed to recognise me from somewhere and said, 'Well, that's all right then. Why didn't you tell us before?'

FARTS AND ALL!

He chucked the teddy bear into the back seat of the police car, walked back to our car and climbed in behind the wheel. Jonno and I piled in as well and we were chauffeur-driven back home, with his mate providing us with a police escort.

But I didn't learn from my mistake. A couple of years later, after one of the stag nights before I got married, I was driving home with about six of us in the car. There may have been no giant teddy bear this time, but there were the same flashing lights, the same rigmarole from the cops, the same outcome from the breathalyser, the same plea for mercy in the name of Leeds United ... and the same result. I was a lucky lad.

Just before we got married I went on a night out with a few of the boys. I was living in the house on my own and told the lads beforehand that they might as well come back to my place. We went out and got well pissed and when we got back they all kipped down on the lounge carpet.

The next morning I got up first and went down to make a cup of tea. I walked into the lounge and there in the middle of the pink carpet we'd just had laid in our new home was a giant turd. I couldn't believe it. I shouted, 'What the fuck's that?'

Sheridan was the first to wake up. 'I don't know. It wasn't me.'

'Well, it certainly wasn't me.'

'It must have been the dog.'

'We haven't got a fucking dog!'

They came up with a few more excuses and no one would accept responsibility. We did our best to clear it up, but there was still a mark by the time we'd finished so a couple of the boys went out and bought a rug. We laid it over the stain and, for a while, I managed to make sure I did most of the work with the vac. Then one day, out of the blue, Bex told me she'd never liked the rug and it would have to go. She moved it away, saw the stain and I was left with some explaining to do. She wasn't impressed.

SWANNY

Drinking never took over my life, but there'd always be someone looking for a night out and they knew that Swanny would never say no. Sometimes, on a Sunday morning, I'd get a call from Noel Blake – who arrived from Portsmouth at the start of the 1988–89 season – inviting me to go to church. That meant the pub. I'd go out before lunch and come back on Tuesday afternoon.

Blakey would take me to some of the black bars in the Chapeltown area of Leeds. Often I'd be the only white man in the place and if Blakey went for a pee, I went with him. Just to be on the safe side. I never felt totally comfortable, but Blakey was a big unit in that community and there was never any trouble. We'd go out on a Sunday, sleep in the car that night, go training on Monday, carry on drinking through Monday, sleep in the car again and train on Tuesday. Then it would be time to go home.

A few years later, when I was going to sign for Port Vale, Bex discovered that Blakey was playing just down the road at Stoke. At first she refused to go because of what we might have got up to although, as it happened, I didn't see much of him while we were down there. He finished up playing over 700 games for 9 clubs in a 20-year career and, after heading up the Stoke academy, he joined the FA coaching staff in February 2007. By then, the sessions with Swanny must have been just a distant memory ... but they can't have done him any harm.

Once, some time after we got married, I went out on an overnight session with a couple of the Leeds lads. I'd clean forgotten that we'd asked Ronnie Sinclair, one of the goalkeepers at Elland Road, and his wife Claire round to our house for lunch on the Wednesday. I arrived home at lunchtime, ready for a lie-down, parked the car and as soon as I opened the door Bex slung our lunch at me, including the pans. There was food all over the place and Zee, our Great Dane, who was still a puppy, must have thought it was her birthday. She started licking it off the carpet. Bex stormed out of the house, got into her car and reversed straight into mine. The front bumper and number plate fell off.

She climbed out, picked up the number plate and hurled it through the lounge window before driving off. As she disappeared down the road, Ronnie and Claire arrived and saw me standing at the broken window. I shrugged my shoulders. They got the message and drove off again. I managed to get Bex back onside in the end, but it wasn't easy.

After I joined Hull in 1989, we'd always have a meal and a bottle of wine the night before a home game. I was the cook and my speciality was chilli con carne and pasta. Bex would come home straight from work in the cosmetics department at Boots in Leeds and the meal and the vino would be ready and waiting. It became a ritual for the rest of my career.

In this day and age, a player caught drinking after Wednesday night would be in real bother, but I suspect that managers didn't really mind in my day. They must have known what was going on, mainly because most of them had done it themselves, but as long as a player didn't get into trouble and produced the goods out on the pitch they were prepared to turn a blind eye.

That was probably the case with Billy Bremner, who'd succeeded Eddie Gray in October 1985 and who would eventually hand me my league debut soon afterwards. Billy arrived from Doncaster, where he'd won promotion from the old Fourth Division in 1984. He was totally different from Eddie. They'd both been great players, but from what I've been told, Billy was even better than Eddie. Gray played wide left and was a matchwinner on his day. He had real flair. Billy, on the other hand, was one of the top midfield players in the business for over 10 years and won 54 Scottish caps compared to Eddie's tally of 12. On top of his playing ability, Billy also had the leadership, enthusiasm and driving force that inspired his team-mates.

SWANNY

Billy lived for Leeds United. He'd been there from the start of the Revie era and was appointed captain in 1966 after Bobby Collins broke his leg in a European tie against Torino. From that day on, Billy led from the front and Leeds United was his passion. He seemed always destined to return as manager and, when he did, that passion still burned as fiercely as ever, probably even fiercer. For example, he was absolutely determined the club should revert to the all-white Real Madrid strip that Revie had introduced in the early sixties and he'd go ballistic about any little bit of colour on the sleeves, shirts or socks. For Billy, it was all white or nothing, the full Monty.

Yet while Billy tried to follow Revie's example of developing a family atmosphere among the players, he was never reluctant to involve people from outside the club – and not just the ex-players who used to join in the five-a-sides on a Friday. People who were passionate about Leeds United. He must have thought their feelings would rub off on the players and in some ways they did.

One of his best mates was Herbie, a little Jewish jeweller with a glass eye. He lived in Alwoodley, one of the swish suburbs in the north of the city. How they came to know one another I'll never know. Herbie had supported Leeds through the golden days and was absolutely devoted to Billy. He'd turn up for matches in his Ford Fiesta, which had a little figure of a footballer – all white strip, with Billy's No.4 on his back – painted on each of the front doors.

Sometimes the gaffer would bring Herbie into the dressing room and let him do the team talk. He'd go straight into telling us how much he loved Leeds United, how much he loved Bill and how proud he was of each and every one of us. After three or four minutes he'd start banging on the table and eventually he'd be so emotional, he'd start blubbing out of his good eye. By the time we were ready to go out, we were all nearly as bad as Herbie!

We reached the FA Cup semi-final in Billy's second season and played Coventry at Hillsborough. They won 3-2 after extra-time and went on to beat Spurs in the final. The night before the game, we stayed at a hotel near Sheffield and Bill invited Herbie along, too.

On overnight trips we always used to have a game of carpet bowls after our evening meal on the Friday night. It was a tradition that Don Revie had started in his time as manager and Billy revived it as soon as he returned. He used to partner everybody up, work out the odds and start a book before the action began.

On this occasion, Herbie had gone for a lie-down before dinner and, while he was asleep, Ian Snodin and Brendan Ormsby tiptoed into his room and spotted the glass eye in a dish by the side of the bed. They nicked the eye. And when the carpet bowls started later on, it became the jack.

The game was in full swing when Herbie came into the lounge and called Billy over. Billy and the rest of us tried to look very concerned as he wandered over to Herbie. They sat down with their backs to us. We knew there was only one thing Herbie could be talking about and before long we could see Billy's shoulders going up and down as he tried to stop himself from laughing. He turned round and called out: 'Has anybody seen Herbie's glass eye?' We all tried to look blank and said we'd no idea where it was. Then Snodin said, 'Never mind your eye, Herbie, come and have a game of bowls.'

'How can I?' he replied. 'I can only see out of one eye.'

'Come on, you'll be all right.' And we handed him the jack.

5

SWANNY FOR ENGLAND!

My first senior game for Leeds United and Billy Bremner was as a sub in a Full Members Cup-tie against Manchester City at Maine Road on 14 October 1985. The competition was pretty small beer, it was just a group game and only 4,059 fans turned up. We lost 6-1. I made another substitute appearance in the competition before finally making my Football League debut on New Year's Day 1986: Leeds v Oldham Athletic at Elland Road.

I played in the middle of the back four alongside Neil Aspin. Dennis Irwin and Gary Hamson were the full-backs. We had David Harle, Ian Snodin, Martin Dickinson and Scott Sellars in midfield with Andy Ritchie and Ian Baird up front. We won 3-1, but I can hardly remember a thing about it. Nerves? I've no idea, but for some reason it's just a blur.

I missed the next three games, but Billy called me up again on 1 February, playing up front against Stoke City at Elland Road. It was a game I'll never forget. We won 4-0 and I scored twice. The crowd was only 10,485 but, to me, they sounded like 100,000. It was one of the few games when I felt the hairs on the back of my neck stand on end. I was scoring goals for my hometown club, my parents, my sisters and girlfriend were in the stand and just to know they were there to see me score those goals was one of the best feelings I had in the whole of my career.

The Stoke centre-half was George Berry, who'd previously played for Wolves and had over 300 games to his name. He's always been a good lad, George. He'd have known it was only my second game, so he wasted no time in trying to wind me up. If I'd believed everything he said early on, I wouldn't have gone near him all afternoon. Either that or I'd have been carried off after twenty minutes. That's how a lot of experienced pros tried to unsettle a young lad and we all took it with a pinch of salt. I didn't respond.

Both of my goals came from left-wing crosses by John Stiles, the son of England World Cup-winner Nobby Stiles. John is now a stand-up comedian on the after-dinner circuit. And each time I climbed high above Berry and headed the ball into the net. Bang! There were pictures of both goals in some of the papers the next day and another one of me in the back of the net celebrating with the Leeds fans. My feet were a couple of inches off the floor and my arms raised wide. At the end of the game, Berry shook my hand and said, 'Well played, son. I hope I don't see you again too often.'

I played in just about every game until the end of the season and finished with 16 league appearances and 3 goals. It was a useful introduction to league football and also to the pressures that come with the territory. And it was just about the only phase of my career when I was affected by pre-match nerves. When the teamsheet was put up on a Thursday, if we were travelling away, or Friday, fringe players like me would all rush to see the line-up. If our name was missing, it was a real downer. If we were one of the subs, it was OK. If we were in the side ... fantastic!

Then, almost immediately, the nerves would kick in – slowly at first, just a little feeling in the gut. Then, gradually, as the build-up moved up a gear, the nerves would start to wind up. It was hard to eat, nearly impossible to relax. Eventually, on a Saturday morning, I'd be thinking, 'I just wish I wasn't fucking playing. Anything but this.'

In the last hour before the warm-up, I'd rather have been almost anywhere else in the world. I knew it wasn't going to go away. I could never decide whether to be sick or not. Quite a few players were physically sick before a game, some for the whole of their careers. I'd try to put on a brave face and the other players probably didn't really notice – perhaps because they were feeling the same way. Somehow I'd finally make it across the white line and it was incredible how all the nerves and the tension would disappear with the first touch. I knew all along that they would – but it took me over 12 months before I came to terms with the nerves and learned how to control them.

One of the people who helped me through was Bobby McDonald, who joined Leeds from Oxford, having also played for Villa, Coventry and Manchester City. He knew I was a confidence player, someone who needed to feel at ease early in a game. In one reserve game, when I was playing at centre-back and Bob at left-back, he made a point of passing the ball to me early on whenever he possibly could. Nice easy balls that gave me a few touches. And all the time, he was encouraging me, telling me it was going to be my night.

And that night it was. I can hardly remember playing better. Every pass, every tackle, every header was right. I felt as if I could play forever and wished the game would never end. And all the time, Bob was encouraging me, pushing me on. He was only in the side because he'd been left out of the first team. He could have sulked. Instead, he took the professional line and tried to help a young player.

I don't remember the opponents and I don't remember the result. I just remember a fantastic game of football. It was one of the best nights of my life and, at the end, I remember walking off the pitch thinking, 'Yes, I can do this.' I played a few first-team games with Bob as well and he'd always make sure I got an early touch. He'd call out: 'Go on, Swanny, go and play!' Great lad, Bob. He doesn't know it, but I've got a lot to thank him for. He still turns out for the Leeds United All Stars in charity games.

Billy Bremner had inherited a side that hovered around the top six without ever making the big advance and after his first season, when we finished fourteenth, Billy brought in his own players, moving out people like John Scales, Terry Phelan, Dennis Irwin, Tommy Wright and Scott Sellars, who all did well elsewhere. With hindsight, he would probably have been better off keeping some of those players and building a new team around them.

But he wanted to put his own stamp on the club. He brought in defenders like David Rennie from Leicester, Jack Ashurst from Carlisle, Peter Haddock from Newcastle, Brendan Ormsby from Villa and McDonald. For the midfield, he signed Mickey Adams from Coventry, John Buckley from Doncaster and Mark Aizlewood from Charlton, and he also signed a couple of strikers, Keith Edwards from Sheffield United and John Pearson from Charlton.

With players like Neil Aspin, John Sheridan, Andy Ritchie and Ian Baird surviving from the Gray regime, we had a decent side. No one would pretend we were full of top-class performers, but there was a great spirit and a belief in the cause and Billy could take a lot of the credit for that. And it was in that 1986–87 season, while I was on the fringe of the first team, that he took us to the semi-final of the FA Cup. We lost to Coventry after extra-time at Hillsborough. I played in the 2-0 quarter-final win at Wigan, who were in the old Third Division, but injured my knee in the build-up to the semi and, at one stage, it looked as if I'd miss out altogether.

Thankfully I managed to convince Billy that I was more or less fit and he named me in a 16-man squad. There was £1,500-a-man bonus for the whole squad if we won and a worst-case scenario of £750 if we lost. There were only two subs in those days and I was pretty relieved when I wasn't one of them. It meant I wouldn't have to take a chance with the knee and I'd still pick up a bonus. I went into training on the Monday after the semi-final and the knee started playing up again. So the club sent me to see a specialist and, a week later, he removed a load of scar tissue. I didn't play again that season, but at least I'd collected my losers' bonus.

The rest of the players shrugged off the disappointment of our semi-final defeat to reach the Division Two play-offs. We beat Oldham over two legs in the semi-final and faced Charlton, also over two legs, in the final. Both games ended in 1-0 home wins. There was no penalty shoot-out then and the replay took place at Birmingham City's St Andrews. The game went to extra-time before Leeds lost 2-1. So near, but so far and who knows how the story of Leeds United might have changed had Billy reached Wembley or won that play-off final?

Without holding down a regular place over the next three years, I was usually in or around the senior squad and learned how it felt to be a first-team player. I wasn't a star, but I had to get used to talking to the media, signing autographs before and after training and also when I left the ground after games. I nailed down a seat near the back of the bus for away games and sampled overnight stays on longer trips.

At first I didn't have a regular room-mate, but from early in the 1987–88 season, I shared a room with David Batty. Batts was a year younger than me and I roomed with him for twelve months or more. We got on well, but life was never straightforward when Dave was around. His mind was always active and he didn't seem to bother about getting any sleep. I'd always be the first one to nod off and, sometimes, I'd wake up at around five or six in the morning and hear a strange spitting noise coming from the other side of the room. It was Batts. He'd be sat in front of the telly where he'd drawn a target on the screen with toothpaste. He'd roll up some tissue until it made a straw and then fire toothpaste through the straw at his target. He wanted me to join in, but I'd got better things to do – like trying to get some kip.

Batts wasn't a drinker and didn't try to pull the birds, but he was as daft as a brush. In training he'd sometimes leap on somebody's back and bite their head until he drew blood. Crazy! To him it was just a bit of fun and he'd run away, laughing his head off.

At first I had my doubts about whether he'd make it. He had the talent but when he arrived in the first team he looked a bit lightweight. Bremner used to call him into his office every morning and make him drink sherry with a raw egg stirred into it. It was supposed to build him up. Dave would go in knowing what to expect and he'd come out a couple of minutes later looking as if he was going to puke. But plenty of people have been on the receiving end from Batty since then and probably wished that Billy had never bothered with his muscle-building concoction.

He was certainly a strong lad by the time he made it into the England team in 1991 and was just about the best tackler from about two yards out that I ever saw. Razor-sharp. I've spoken to people who played with him later in his career, pros who'd been around for a long time, like John Beresford and Lee Clark at Newcastle, and they both said that Batts was the best tackler they'd ever seen.

He changed a lot over the years. Once he got married and had kids, he became totally family orientated and hardly ever went out with the lads or socialised. He lives for his family. Every now and then he'll join us for a reunion and he lets himself go a bit. He's great fun then, joining in the jokes and the banter, but he's always glad to get back to the family and out of the goldfish bowl.

Apart from being his first room-mate, I can claim another place in the David Batty Hall of Fame. I set up his first league goal. And as he only managed 4 in 382 appearances, you might say I loom large in his legend. It was against Manchester City at Maine Road on Boxing Day, 1987. I dummied a City defender, let the ball run through my legs for Batts and he hit the jackpot. He had to wait nearly four years before hitting the target once more in a league game again, also against Manchester City.

There was another young kid making his way through the system around the same time. He'd been my boot boy after I signed pro in August 1984. His name? Gary Speed. I still changed for training in the away dressing room and Gary was there to make sure that my kit was ready in the morning, my boots were in good nick and there was a clean towel for me after I'd showered. It was a shit job, to be honest, but it was accepted as the way young footballers grew up. Everybody had done it in the past, so why change?

He was a grand kid and never a minute's bother. He was meticulous and well worth his £20 Christmas tip. If he forgot something I'd never bollock him because it would have been a genuine mistake. In some ways it wasn't easy for either of us. The previous day we'd been apprentices together and now I was the boss and he was the lackey, but I never pulled rank. There were one or two kids who caused a bit of bother. If we asked them to do a job they'd walk away and say do it yourself. Batts was a bit like that, although he was more mischievous than downright awkward and always had a smile on his face. Gary, though, was never a problem.

I used to look at him sometimes and think, 'This lad's got everything. The looks, the attitude, the skill, the commitment. He could go all the way, he really could.' Nice to know I'm right sometimes! He's become a big star and I'm absolutely delighted for him, but he's still the kind of guy who's always got time for his old pals. He's gone all the way to the top and I don't think he's upset too many people along the way. That takes a bit of doing.

In all, I played in 58 league and cup games between 1986 and 1989. Although Gray had seen me as a centre-half, I mainly played up front for Bremner and there were some good days. On 28 December 1988, two days after setting up Batts for his first goal, I scored against Middlesbrough at Elland Road. There was a Christmas crowd of over 34,000 and I went through, flicked the ball over the keeper and into the net. I ran on into the net and stood with my arms raised right in front of the Boro fans. I was pelted with stones and coins and they were killing me, but I just stood there laughing. What did I care?

During another game a few weeks later, I dived in among the flying boots to head in Ian Snodin's cross for the winner against Millwall at Elland Road. But there were some low moments, too – like the game at Stoke in December 1986, when I played in defence and lived to regret it. We got beat 7-2 after being 5-0 down at half-time. They had some top players in the side like Lee Dixon, who won 22 England caps at right-back after moving to Arsenal. Nicky Morgan was up front and scored a hat-trick. He seemed to hit the target every time he took a pop. As I was playing centre-half, it was one of the days when I didn't come out on top in the personal battle!

We were that bad in the first half that Bill was clearly going to have a struggle to find 11 of us wanting to go out for the second half. He just about had to push the lads down the tunnel. What does a manager say in those situations? All he can do is tell the players to push on, try and make something of it and at least win the second-half. Then we could hold our heads up high and face our fans at the final whistle.

So out we went – and in just about the first move of the half, I passed the ball across to our left-back, Ronnie Robinson, just inside the Stoke half. He didn't have a Stoke player closing him down and should have pushed forward towards their penalty area. Instead, he turned round and played the ball all the way back to Mervyn Day. It was the worst possible message we could have sent to our supporters. We were 5-0 down and passing the ball back from inside their half. They absolutely crucified Robinson from then on.

It was a nightmare, although we did a bit better in the second-half and when we pulled one back near the end, our fans chanted, 'One-seven, we'll only lose one-seven!' It was a humiliating day.

Earlier that season, I'd experienced a different kind of trauma when we played Bradford City at Odsal Stadium, home of Bradford Bulls Rugby League club. City had moved there because of the Valley Parade fire the previous year. I was playing up front this time and, with about twelve minutes to go, we were attacking strongly and I had a shot at goal that hit the post. It rebounded straight to me and I was just lining up another shot from the edge of the box when a young fan appeared from nowhere and tackled me. I recognised him as a lad who lived on the Parnabys and couldn't work out what was going on. Then I turned round and saw all the fans from the far end of the ground rushing on to the pitch. It was scary.

The Leeds fans had a bad reputation at the time and I didn't know whether they were coming on to attack the players. Then I saw what had happened. A portable snack bar had been parked at the back of the terraces and some Leeds fans had rushed it and set fire to the chip pan. They then pushed the van over on to its side and it had rolled down the terraces, forcing the fans to run for their lives. All we could see from the far end of the pitch was this big cloud of smoke coming up and we all thought straightaway that it was a repeat of the Valley Parade fire. We were told to leave the field. Eventually the ground was cleared and we had to go back and play the last 12 minutes in an empty stadium. It was a weird sensation and we got beat 2-0.

Because I was a local lad who put himself about a bit, I was popular with the fans for most of my time at Elland Road. You take the rough with the smooth, but even I had to admit some fans on the Kop were getting a bit over the top when they started chanting 'Swanny for England!' during one home game. The chant spread as the game went on and I couldn't work it out at all. It turned out that some mates from back home had started it for a bit of fun and a few more had joined in before most of the Kop got the hang of it and joined in as well. It didn't last long.

But I was on the receiving end from the fans, too. Once, when we were going through a bad time, we went to play against Oldham on their plastic pitch. It was an awful surface, we were struggling from the start and I made a silly backpass that led to a goal. The fans let me know straightaway what they thought and a few of them were on my back from then on. It didn't worry me at first, but when it had gone on for a few games, it started to get to me. I wasn't unhappy at Leeds, but I wasn't playing all that regularly and I could live without the boo boys.

I was beginning to wonder whether it might be time to move on when, in September 1988, with Leeds still just another Second Division outfit, Bremner left. It was a sad day for me. A player tends to like the manager who gives him his debut, the man who shows belief in him – not to mention the man who gives him his first pay rise. And Bill was a man I respected enormously. I'd have run through a brick wall for him.

But the bottom line is that apart from his second season when we reached the Cup semi-final and the play-off final, Leeds were not a lot better off after his three seasons in charge. He was the third manager in a row who'd been a player in the Revie era and I'm sure the board believed that was the way to bring back the good days. But in the end it didn't work and they decided it was time for a change of direction. So out with the old guard, in with the new, and within a few days, Sergeant Wilko was reporting for duty.

6
WILKO AND OUT!

Howard Wilkinson spent 8 years at Elland Road, won promotion to the top flight in 1990, lifted the championship in 1992 and reached the last eight of the European Cup the following season. He built a strong side around a midfield of Gordon Strachan, Gary McAllister, David Batty and Gary Speed and I suppose his record speaks for itself.

But from day one I couldn't make head nor tail of him. I couldn't get on with him at all and I wasn't the only one. I missed his first few training sessions because I was injured but a lot of the lads weren't happy. They couldn't understand what he was on about half the time. They said he seemed to talk in riddles; they just weren't on the same wavelength.

He arrived with a reputation for making players work hard, to run, run and run in training. And he was all that. But he'd also done a lot of research into sports science and was the first manager to introduce us to the value of vitamin tablets and drinks to supplement a healthy diet.

Most of us had never even heard of vitamin pills. We just used to laugh when he told us to take them, although now they're part and parcel of a player's preparation. Some of the lads did as they were told. Others, like me, thought it was a load of rubbish, went out for a few pints most nights and carried on as before.

When I was fit again, he didn't play me, so it wasn't long before I decided to find out where I stood. I knocked on his door, walked in and said, 'I've come to talk about my future.' He replied that if I wanted to look into the future, I'd be better off talking to Russell Grant, the astrologer. Russell would know more about my future than he did. I thought, 'What the fuck's he on about?' And, from that moment on I knew it wasn't going to work for me under Wilko.

Soon afterwards, we had a practice match. Before the kick-off, Mike Hennigan, Wilko's No.2, took me to one side. He said, 'We're looking for a centre-half – that's your position, go out and show us what you can do.' I had a really good game and, a few days later, Wilko and Hennigan called me over after training. Wilko said he was happy with the way I had played in the practice game. I replied, 'Well, I'm not happy with you. I don't want to play for you. I want to go.'

'What do you mean?' asked Hennigan.

'I just don't like him,' I said, pointing at Wilkinson, who turned round and walked away. Glynn Snodin, who'd followed his brother Ian to Leeds from Doncaster in 1987, was sitting in the dressing room when I walked in. He'd played for Wilko at Sheffield Wednesday. When I told him what had happened, he said, 'That's you finished, Swanny. You won't be playing for this lot again.'

That didn't bother me. I was so determined to get away that I handed in 7 written transfer requests in about three months. I'd knock on Wilko's door, slide the envelope underneath and walk away. After a while, he christened me 'Postman Pat'. And from then on, he kept trying to embarrass me in front of the rest of the lads, making jibes about my weight and calling me Postman Pat. To me, though, it was water off a duck's back.

WILKO AND OUT!

As it happened, Glynn's prophecy turned out to be wrong. I played 2 games for Wilkinson before moving on to Hull, where Eddie Gray had taken over as manager. I'd heard they were keen on me before the bust-up on the training ground. First, I played at Nottingham Forest in the fourth round of the FA Cup at the end of January 1989. We lost 2-0. Then, on 14 March, I was called up for a Second Division game ... at Hull.

Wilko told me he thought I'd be able to handle Billy Whitehurst, their centre-forward, better than anyone else. Now Whitehurst just happened to be one of the two hardest players I ever encountered. The other was Noel Blake, who hadn't missed a game all season for Leeds. Whitehurst v Blake would have been real red meat stuff, yet Wilkinson was leaving out Blakey and bringing me in to take on Whitehurst. It didn't make sense. If anyone could tame Whitehurst, it was Blake. I did OK, escaped unscathed from my close encounter with Big Billy and Leeds won 2-1.

A week later, Wilkinson called me into his office, two days before the transfer deadline. He told me Hull wanted to sign me, adding that I'd know that already because they'd tapped me up. They had, but I wasn't going to tell him because then he could have landed Hull in the shit for making an illegal approach. He wouldn't let go of it, but I stuck to my guns.

I was on £350 a week with Leeds at the time and after my meeting with Wilko I decided to ask Hull for £500, a ten grand signing-on fee and a club car. I drove across to Hull and told them what I wanted. They were prepared to negotiate on the wage, but a £10,000 signing-on fee was out of the question. A car? No chance!

I rang Leeds and asked for Wilko. His secretary told me he wasn't in. I said, 'Right, can you give him a message. I'm not signing for Hull.' He was on the phone straightaway; he told me to get my arse back over to Leeds. So I hopped into the car, drove back to Elland Road and walked into the main reception area. And who should be sitting there waiting to see the manager? Gordon Strachan, then at Manchester United.

It all clicked straight into place. Leeds had no money, they wanted to sign Strachan and they were going to use the money they got for me to finance the deal. All of a sudden, I'd found a bit of bargaining power.

I went into Wilko's office, where he was sitting with Bill Fotherby, the Leeds chairman, and another director. Bill was a lovely bloke who left Leeds in 2000, but he couldn't kick the football habit and went on to become chairman of Harrogate Town. Wilko asked why I hadn't signed. 'I've told them I'll settle for £400 a week, but there's no way they'll give me a ten grand signing-on fee or a car, so I told them to forget it.'

I was only a kid, but I'd heard the senior pros talking about their own moves. They always said that if your new club wouldn't pay a signing-on fee, the old club would find the money – because they were looking to move you out to sign a new player themselves. So I thought, 'Right, if Hull won't give me what I want, I'll see what Leeds can do.'

I said, 'You give me some money to go.'

I thought they'd tell me to bugger off, but instead they asked how much I wanted.

'Ten grand.'

'No.'

'Fine.' And I stood up and started to walk out. They offered five grand, but again I said no. The three of them talked among themselves and, in the end, agreed the money could be paid as a loyalty bonus for serving the bulk of my contract.

When I got outside, it suddenly occurred to me that we hadn't worked out how they would pay me. I asked the club secretary. He said they'd forward a cheque the next week. Nothing had arrived after a fortnight, so I rang the secretary again. 'Where's the money?'

'We sent it a week ago.'

'Well, I haven't received it.'

'We sent it to you at Hull City.'

I'd assumed it would be sent to me at home and hadn't really looked through the players' mail at Hull, but I rummaged through a pile of old letters in a corner of the office and there, lying under a chair, was a letter addressed to me. There was a coffee-mug stain on the envelope. Inside was a cheque from Leeds for £5,800. My payment of ten grand less tax, the cost of a club tracksuit and my club suit, which was three months old. A couple of my unpaid fines were also deducted.

Strachan moved in to Leeds the next day. He turned out to be one of the best signings the club ever made, leading them back into the top flight the following year and then to the championship in 1992, but the episode taught me for the first time that the whole business of football transfers is just a game.

I was always going to end up at Hull and, in a way, I was piggy-in-the-middle as the two clubs hassled over who would have to fork out the least amount of money to get me there. Either way, I didn't care. I was earning an extra £50 a week at Hull and thanks to the pay-off, I was now the proud owner of a Ford Sierra sports. I'd finally caught up with Peter Barnes! What's more, I'd got Wilko off my back. As far as I was concerned it was goodbye and good riddance.

No one can take away Wilko's achievement in winning the championship with Leeds and I respect that, but he was unable to take the club any further, maybe because he lacked real man-management skills. I've always felt the players were playing for the club, not the manager.

He went on to become technical director at the FA and as well as laying down a blueprint for a national academy, he also had two spells as England's caretaker-manager – first, following the departure of Glenn Hoddle in 1999 and again, after Kevin Keegan's resignation a year later. But I never felt he could really communicate with people. Perhaps that's why he has featured so rarely on television panels or other places where the game is discussed in depth ... an ex-England manager who also won a league title would seem to be the perfect candidate.

It was a wrench to be leaving Leeds; it was my hometown club and had been my first club. While all the haggling was going on, it had been a tense time and I didn't have a clue what the fee would be. I kept asking myself, 'What am I worth?' I had no idea. The word in the media was that Leeds were asking a six-figure sum and to me that sounded like a hell of a lot of money. When the fee was announced as £200,000 – a club record for Hull – I was staggered. For the first time in my career I could stand up and say, 'Right, I am somebody now, not just another player.'

That's why I'll always feel that Hull is my club. I supported West Ham as a kid and learned what pro football was all about at Elland Road, but my move to Hull turned me from a nobody into a somebody. I was the club's record signing. It was the first time I'd felt really wanted.

The Hull fans were a different class from the start. In terms of results, I didn't have the best of starts. We won only 1 of the 12 games I played at the end of that season, the first one, and we finished up just outside the relegation zone. The supporters never turned against me when they could easily have blamed the record signing because things had gone wrong. They were fantastic – they still are. I enjoyed almost every minute of my stay there and I just wish it had been a better time on the field for the club.

The fee wasn't scary. On the contrary, it gave me a kick up the backside. Maybe I'd been freewheeling a bit at Elland Road, but all of a sudden I was a star and the move gave me a real buzz. It also helped that Eddie Gray had shown faith in me. I was desperate to do well for him and keep him in a job. Sadly, it didn't work out that way.

The first problem I had to tackle at Hull was 6ft tall, weighed in at 13st and was called Billy Whitehurst. He was in his second spell at Boothferry Park after starting his career there with 47 goals in 193 league games following his arrival from non-league football. He'd been away to Newcastle, Oxford, Reading and Sunderland before returning to Hull in 1989 with his cult-hero status still intact.

Billy had been dubbed 'The Hardest Man In Football' and I knew from my experience against him in my final appearance for Leeds that he was not a man to take lightly. It was a no-holds-barred battle and once, after I gave him a bit of a dig, he rounded on me and said, 'Do that again and I'll smash you – either on the field or in the bar afterwards.' I thought, 'Fuck me, I'll be signing for this lot soon. How will I handle him then?'

I soon found out. On my first day as a Hull City player, I arrived early for training. It was a massive dressing room and I'd no idea where I was supposed to change, so I just sat down in the middle of a bench and started to strip off. Guess whose place I'd chosen? Nobody said anything to me, but I sensed the rest of the lads were trying hard not to laugh. I couldn't work out what I'd done wrong.

A few minutes later, Whitehurst came in. The conversation in the dressing room stopped. He walked over towards me, took off his jacket and hung it on his peg with me sitting underneath. He didn't say a word. I shuffled along the bench until I was out from under his jacket and considered my next move. I could either take him on, or try and make a joke out of it. I said, 'I hope you've forgotten what you said in the Leeds match! Anyway, pleased to meet you.' We shook hands and Billy said something like, 'Good luck. Enjoy your stay. Hope it goes well for you.' We were good mates from that moment.

Bill was a hard man on and off the field, but in training and matches he always gave 100 per cent. He'd be at the front of the sprints and would work his rocks off for the whole session. On the field he never let anyone down and I always enjoyed playing with him. But playing against him was an entirely different matter! He was a man I'd always want in my side.

He was the big man in the dressing room and his sidekick was Iain Hesford, the keeper. They could easily have made life difficult for me. I was the record signing and I'd come in from Leeds, the biggest club in Yorkshire. Hull had always been in their shadow. But once Bill and Hessie had worked out what sort of character I was, they made me feel part of the dressing room and I settled in very quickly. I've been at clubs where new signings have come in and thrown their weight around and been given a tough time by the old guard, but I managed to avoid that and felt easy more or less from word go. Unfortunately, Billy didn't hang around for too long and moved on to Sheffield United the following year. Apart from that first stint at Hull, he never stayed long at any of his clubs and was always looking for a move and a bit of cash.

Eddie Gray had seen me as a defender during his time at Elland Road and he played me at the back at Hull. I thought I was doing a decent job; I felt I could look myself in the mirror after each game and know I'd done as well as I could. But football is a team game and if we weren't doing the business on the pitch, then I had to take my share of the blame. In the short time I worked for Eddie at Hull, I felt as though all the lads were keen to do well for him, but it just didn't happen. After such a disastrous end to what had been a disappointing season, his departure was inevitable.

Hull named his replacement soon afterwards. Colin Appleton. Colin *who*? That's what I thought, too, but I was ready to give him a fair crack of the whip. We were due back at the beginning of July, but I decided to go in a week early and get a bit of work done in advance. And when I wandered into the dressing room I spotted this geezer in overalls, working on the skirting boards. He looked like Freddie Boswell from *Bread*, the eighties television sitcom.

I'd no idea who he was. I just assumed he was a joiner or the club's new odd-job man. I said, 'Hello, you OK?' He didn't look up but replied, 'Yes, fine.' And that was it. I changed, trained for an hour or so and he was still there when I got back. This time, neither of us spoke. I returned the following morning and the same thing happened. So on the Wednesday, I didn't bother saying hello. I thought if he couldn't be arsed, neither could I. Bollocks to him!

The rest of the players reported on the Thursday when the chairman, Don Robinson, introduced us to our new manager: the man in the overalls, Colin Appleton. He'd played for Leicester in the fifties and sixties and had captained them in FA Cup finals against Spurs and Manchester United. He'd started his managerial career at Scarborough and won promotion from the old Division Four in a previous stint at Hull, but it was a surprise when he returned to Boothferry Park after spells with Swansea and Exeter.

It was a weird pre-season. We hardly trained on grass. Appleton used to take us to the coast and we'd work on the beach instead. He never established any authority. There were some strong characters around – people like Whitehurst, Billy Askew, Hesford, Ken de Mange and me – and he couldn't handle us. Once, when we were training at a local cricket club, a couple of the boys went into Appleton's dressing room, nicked his underpants, grabbed a stump and hung them out in the middle of the square. He didn't say a word about it. Sometimes we more or less did our own thing. We'd respected Eddie Gray and worked hard for him but just didn't get the results. For Appleton, however, there was no such respect.

We desperately needed to get off to a good start, but there was no spark and not a lot of confidence. Sure enough, we staggered out of the blocks with 4 draws and a defeat in our first 5 league games. I started the season in defence but, bizarrely, after an opening draw with Leicester, I ended up playing in 4 different positions in as many matches: goalkeeper, defender, midfield man and striker. I was at the back for our second game, the first leg of a Littlewoods Cup first-round tie against Grimsby, and also started in defence in the league game at Bournemouth on the Saturday.

But our goalkeeper Hesford was injured in the first-half and although he struggled through to half-time, he obviously wasn't going to be able to continue afterwards. When we reached the dressing room, everyone started looking round to see who would volunteer to take over. There was no response. I had a vague idea about what might be coming next, so decided it was time for a tactical pee. When I returned, there was a green goalkeeper's jersey hanging on my peg.

We were 4-1 down at the time and ended up losing 5-4, so I couldn't have done all that badly, but I hadn't a clue what I was doing and suspect the scoreline was more down to Bournemouth taking their foot off the gas than to any brilliance on my part. In fact, any success I had was probably down to the Hull fans behind the goal, who kept telling me what to do!

The next game was the second leg of the Littlewoods Cup-tie at Grimsby and I was named among the substitutes. I went on in the second-half when Andy Payton was injured but instead of taking his place up front, I was told to bolster up the midfield. We lost on aggregate after extra-time. Then, for the home game against West Ham, I started at the back before moving up front when Whitehurst was injured. I scored our goal in a 1-1 draw. So 4 positions in 14 days; it must be some kind of record.

But the West Ham game also showed what a mess we were getting into, even though the season had only just started. Whitehurst had failed a fitness test the previous day, so Appleton called me in an hour before the game, told me he was going to move me up front and went through how he wanted me to play.

I said, 'Right, fine.'

I walked back down the corridor and into the dressing room, where Whitehurst was already changed, wearing the No.9 shirt. Appleton came in a few minutes later, took one look at the situation and started to read out the team. I was back in defence and Whitehurst was up front. It was a joke.

I said to Bill, 'You weren't playing ten minutes ago.'

He lasted about twenty minutes, but he'd made his point. He was the main man and the manager wasn't going to shunt him aside.

We failed to win any of our first 14 games, with 8 draws and 6 defeats. We were rock bottom and something had to give. On Monday, 30 October, after a 2-0 home defeat by Brighton, we were called in for a crisis meeting.

Appleton was sitting on a laundry basket. He had this habit of holding his arms out wide when he started to talk to a group of players. And he often said, 'Oooph', through pursed lips before getting underway. 'Oooph, this is a crisis,' he said. 'What are we going to do?'

At that moment there was a knock on the door and one of the directors came in. He said, 'Colin, can we have a word?' We assumed he'd be getting the bullet, but he was back ten minutes later. With his arms outstretched again, he said, 'Oooph, the chairman's resigned. He's gone. That could easily have been me.'

As he said that, the lid of the wicker basket collapsed and he fell backwards into the boots. The place erupted and while Appleton was trying to extricate himself, there was another knock on the door. It was the same director. He started saying, 'Colin ... ' but couldn't locate the manager, who was still in among the boots. Finally, Colin freed himself and was told the new chairman would like a word.

That was enough for Whitehurst. Never a happy man when he was sitting around doing nothing, he fished a tenner out of his wallet, called in one of the apprentices and told him to go and buy some pies from the shop across the road. The lad returned with his pies a few minutes later and we were all digging in when Appleton walked back into the room. This time he didn't sit on the basket.

We all knew what was coming next.

'Oooph, now it's me. First the chairman, now the manager.'

We all cracked out laughing. Appleton hung around for a couple of seconds, then turned and walked out. We never saw him again.

Tom Wilson, his assistant, took over for a couple of games, but we didn't have to wait long before Appleton's replacement was named: Stan Ternent, who'd been No.2 to Steve Coppell at Crystal Palace. We learned straightaway that life under Stan was going to be a very different kettle of fish.

He called a team meeting on his first morning and came straight to the point. 'Right, we're in the shit. If we're going to get out of the shit, we'll all have to piss in the same pot. If you don't want to piss in the same pot, come and see me and you can piss off. See you on the training ground in ten minutes!'

It was the kick up the arse we desperately needed.

7

THE DOG OF WAR

Stan Ternent was up front, in your face. He knew exactly what he wanted and anyone who didn't buy into it found himself on the outside looking in. The strong characters fell into line, the results improved and Hull eventually finished in mid-table. We won 14 and lost 10 of the 30 league games after Stan moved in. His philosophy was simple – and it never changed during my three spells as one of his players: if you were prepared to run through a brick wall for him, he'd back you all the way. Anything less and he didn't want to know. That was where I came from, too.

I got on well with Stan and he went on to sign me twice, for Bury and Burnley, later in my career, but we didn't get off to the best of starts. Tom Wilson, his No.2 who'd been caretaker since Appleton's departure, had picked the team for Stan's first game at Bradford City and named me up front with Billy Whitehurst.

Stan was sitting in the directors' box, supposedly to have a look at the players he would be inheriting on the Monday, but after about fifteen minutes, he appeared on the touchline. Up went the linesman's flag to indicate a substitution and my No.4 was held up. I couldn't believe it. I stormed off, had a shower, got changed, walked straight into the bar, and supped three pints, one after another.

As soon as the game finished – we won 3-2 – I walked up to Stan and said, 'Can I have a word?' He said he'd see me on Monday morning, end of conversation. Now somewhere down the line – don't ask me how – I'd discovered that Stan didn't like dogs. And it just so happened that we had a dog and a half back home in Wakefield. Zee, our Great Dane, weighed in at around 13 stone. So, on the Monday, I decided I'd take Zee across to training and get one of the kids to give her a run around while we were working.

I'd calmed down a bit from Saturday, but I was still simmering as I walked down the narrow corridor to Stan's office. Zee was out in front on her lead. I knocked on the door. Stan shouted, 'Come in,' so I opened the door, let the dog in and shut the door again. I could hear Stan yelling at the dog and, when I opened the door again, Stan was pinned to the wall with Zee's paws on his shoulders. She only wanted to play, but Stan didn't see it that way. He looked absolutely bloody petrified.

After a few seconds, I called off the hell hound, but made a point of telling her to sit outside on guard. Just in case. Stan sat down and we started to talk about Saturday, but I could see he was a bit wary, wondering whether I might set Zee on to him again at any moment. He explained why he'd taken me off and how he didn't think it would work with me and Billy up front. In the end, I accepted his reasons and the ice was broken. We still have a laugh about Zee when we meet up.

The atmosphere at the club was a million miles better under Stan and, to help things along, he decided we needed a bit of team bonding, as they'd call it today. So one morning, after he'd been around for a few weeks, he breezed into the dressing room and said, 'Right, you're doing well, lads. Time for a day at the races.' He fished into his pocket, drew out a wad of notes and handed the dosh to

Whitehurst. 'OK, Bill, you organise a bus and take the lads for a day at Cheltenham next week.' So far, so good.

The day before our trip, Whitehurst issued strict instructions. 'I want you all here at half past eight in the morning, suited up because I've ordered tickets for the posh enclosure.' We were all on time, but when the clock ticked round to 8.45am with no sign of Billy or a bus, we started to get a bit twitchy. Nine o'clock, no bus, no Bill. Ten o'clock, no bus, no Bill. We tried to contact him but no joy. It was obvious our trip was off, so we decided to cut our losses. After a few pints in the boozer, we went to the bookies in town and watched the racing from there ... in our suits, with our binoculars at the ready.

Whitehurst's status in the dressing room meant that no one was willing to take him on about it the next day, but we soon found out from Stan that although Bill's intentions had been honourable, he finally succumbed on the afternoon before the trip and put Stan's brass on a dead cert in the 3.30 at Huntingdon or somewhere. It went belly up, and so did our trip to Cheltenham.

I'd played at the back for Eddie Gray and in both positions for Colin Appleton, but Stan told me straight off that he wanted me to play up front with Andy Payton. By then, Payts had been around for three years and had developed into one of the most dangerous strikers in the division. We finished our first season together with 28 league goals between us – Andy notched 17 in 34 games and me 11 in 31, despite missing 15 games after the turn of the year with the first of many knee injuries.

It happened after 62 minutes of an FA Cup third-round tie against Newcastle at Boothferry Park. We lost 1-0. It seemed so innocuous at the time. I jumped for a ball, landed on my right leg and felt a little 'pop' in my knee. As I tried to move off, I crumpled. Jeff Radcliffe, our physio, came on, moved the knee around a bit and signalled for a stretcher. I thought, 'Hang on a minute, it can't be that bad,' and said I'd try to carry on for a while and run it off, but Billy Whitehurst was already warming up as I was loaded on to the stretcher.

The specialist had a look at the knee on the Monday morning and confirmed Jeff's worst fears. I'd torn the anterior cruciate ligament, in those days a career-threatening injury. I just felt numb. The specialist told me he had two options: he could allow the swelling to go down and then operate to replace the torn ligament, or we could hope the ligament would re-attach itself and, if I built up the muscles around the knee, I might be able to get away without an op. I went home in tears. When I told Mam and Dad later that my career could be over, Dad said, 'Look, can't you have my ligament instead?'

There was no op in the end because the ligament did, in fact, re-attach itself. I spent 5 weeks rehabilitating at the National Centre for the Treatment and Rehabilitation of Sports Injuries at Lilleshall in Shropshire, the first of many trips down there. Eventually I was fit to resume full training but, for the next 8 years, I never really trusted that right knee. If it had been my left leg I'd never have got through. That was my jumping leg and where I did all my twists, but the injury was always in the back of my mind. And when my knee collapsed again, while I was at Burnley in 1999, I knew there was only one possible outcome: I was out for 7 months.

This time I'd got away with 13 weeks as my mates battled to stay in the division. I finally returned, playing in defence, against Sunderland at Roker Park, because Richard Jobson was injured. We won 1-0, our third win in a row, I scored the goal and, with six games left, we were nearly out of the woods.

I played in 5 of those last 6 games. We won 4 and drew 1 to finish in a respectable fourteenth position. There was a genuine feeling among our supporters that we'd turned the corner and could have a bit of a go next season, but as Stan started to re-build the side, the seeds for another struggle had already been sown.

Towards the end of our escape, he signed Paul Hunter, a striker from East Fife, and two midfield men, Leigh Palin from Stoke and Gwyn Thomas from Barnsley. Then, in the summer, because of Hull's financial problems, he had to sell Richard Jobson, who moved to Oldham for £450,000 and helped them win the Division Two title in his first season. Stan used some of the money to bring in three defenders – Russ Wilcox from Northampton, Dave Hockaday from Swindon and David Mail from Blackburn. He also signed Tony Finnegan, another midfield man, from Blackburn. But none of his signings really came off. We'd been a close-knit unit during our great escape and while most of the new faces fitted in off the field, we never really got it together on the park.

Not that we had any idea of the trials that lay ahead as we embarked on our pre-season trip to Bulgaria in the summer of 1990. These days, Bulgaria is a member of the European Union and a popular tourist area, but it was a different story back then when the country was only just starting to emerge from the shadow of the Soviet Union. I think we were the first English club to go there pre-season and Yorkshire Television came along to make a documentary about the trip. It was called 'A Kick Up The Balkans' and John Helm, still a familiar voice as a commentator, was the presenter.

We stayed in Sofia and it was an absolute dump. Everything was grey: the cars, the buildings, the hotel, even the people. For our first pre-match meal there was just a bowl of fruit on the table so a few of us decided to go out and see if we could find something a bit more solid. We soon spotted a food shop on a street corner. There was a massive queue round the block and it turned out the people were waiting for the bread to arrive. When I reached the front of the queue there was nothing left.

The hotel had no facilities at all and, one day, Stan took us to the local swimming pool to let off a bit of steam and give us an opportunity to take a look at the local talent. It was a disaster. The water was cold and dirty, and all the women looked like men, with huge, hairy armpits.

I'd been appointed entertainments manager before we left so after a couple of days, I said to Stan, 'Look, the lads are bored silly. We've got to do something to let off steam. Can we have a drink?'

'OK, but don't be stupid and stay in the hotel.'

The beer was rubbish, but as it was only the equivalent of 3p a pint we weren't complaining. After we'd all had about 15 pence worth, some of the lads decided they wanted the entertainments manager to come up with something a bit more interesting.

'How about some women, Swanny?'

'Don't be bloody silly! Where am I going to find any women in this place?'

All eyes turned towards the reception area and the liftman, who'd already proved to be a bit of a Mr Fixit. He'd been able to get hold of levs (the local currency), sweets, even caviar, although why he thought sixteen Hull City players would want caviar, I've no idea. But if he could get hold of caviar, presumably a few birds wouldn't present too much of a problem.

He didn't speak any English, but using a bit of graphic sign language, I was able to get across the message that some of the lads wanted a woman. Could he help? No problem. The lads didn't believe me when I'm told them it was sorted, but it was my turn to laugh when, half an hour later, a couple of tarts wandered into the bar with a minder, who turned out to be their interpreter as well.

The four of us went upstairs and, through the minder, I explained what the lads wanted. Well, more or less, anyway. He told me we'd have to pay in English brass and, after borrowing a pen and paper, I took down a price list and went back downstairs.

'Right lads, there's the menu. Sort out who's going first.'

By this time, a lot of the boys had got cold feet, but about half a dozen decided to give it a go and I had to draw lots to see who the first couple would be. No names, no pack drill, but the first pair went upstairs soon afterwards, promising to be back in half an hour.

After about forty minutes, the next two in line decided the time had come to make a move. So we all went upstairs and they started banging on the bedroom door. The response was blunt and to the point: 'Fuck off!'

'You've had your go, it's time for someone else.'

'Fuck off!'

'Come on, do the decent thing.'

'We are. Fuck off!'

This went on for a couple of minutes but it was pretty obvious the first two lads had no intention of packing in. So we all returned to the bar, fired down another 15p worth of the local brew and staggered off to bed. We had a game the following afternoon, so we didn't want to overdo it!

Stan wanted us to have a bit of a work-out in the morning and had told us to report in the lobby after breakfast, wearing our tracksuits. Then, after our session and an early lunch, we had to be ready to go to the match, wearing our club suits. Sixteen players assembled in reception at two o'clock, fourteen of them wearing club suits. The other two, the lads who'd enjoyed themselves with the ladies the night before, were still wearing tracksuits.

'Where's your suits?' asked Stan.

'Suits?'

'Yes, your bloody suits. I told you to report in your suits.'

'Oh, we thought you meant tracksuits.'

'Well, go and change into your suits now. The bus leaves in five minutes.'

'Well, boss, there's a bit of a problem.'

It turned out that while the two players had been sleeping off their exertions in the early hours, the tarts and their minder had helped themselves to some gear, including their Hull City suits.

Stan went ballistic and fined them a week's wages on the spot.

On one of our afternoons off, I went for a walk round the market with Malcolm Shotton, one of our central defenders, who later managed Oxford for a while. We spotted an old woman with a stall full of cuddly toys and rugs that she'd made herself. Using sign language, I managed to find out what she wanted for the whole lot and she said she'd take the equivalent of 50p. I bought them all and took them back to the lads as presents to take home. She couldn't believe her luck.

Even better was a little kid who used to sit outside the Sheraton Hotel, begging. It was the only decent hotel in town, and was a different world from the dump we were staying in. We soon worked out that was where the best food would be. Steak and chips was back on the menu. There was a fountain in the reception area and a chap tinkling away on the piano.

Every time we went to the hotel we walked past the little lad and, towards the end of the week, I decided to do something about it. All the players had loads of Bulgarian notes that were completely worthless outside the country. We'd have just thrown them away when we got home. I knew the money had to be some good to somebody and thought of the little lad straightaway.

So on the last day, I collected all the spare notes, walked down the busy main road to the Sheraton and called the kid over. He held out his hand for a few coppers and when he saw my pile of notes, his eyes nearly popped out of his head. He walked backwards a couple of paces and bumped into one of the cars parked alongside the kerb.

I said, 'For you,' and held up the notes. He shook his head at first, then rushed over to me, grabbed the money, lifted up his jumper, stuffed all the money inside, dashed out between two parked cars and raced across the main street, somehow managing to avoid the traffic as cars screeched to a halt. I could imagine the scene when he got home: he'd probably get a battering from his dad for nicking all that money, but there was no way they would have given it back!

I mentioned what I'd done to one of our interpreters later.

'How much did you give him?' he asked.

'I think it was about 400 lev.'

'You mean that?'

'Yeah.'

'Do you realise you've given that boy the equivalent of his dad's earnings for five years?'

'Fantastic. If I'd known, I'd have got a bit more and split it between half a dozen of them.'

It was a great feeling. That kid probably lives in a mansion now and I can still see his face when I handed over all that dosh. If I bumped into him today, I'd know him straightaway.

On the field, the trip was a bit of a disaster. We lost our first two games, picked up one or two injuries and several tummy bugs and went into the last game with barely enough players to get a team together. In fact, John Helm was one of the subs – but there was no way Stan was going to send him on for a laugh. We needed some kind of result to avoid a whitewash. We drew and Helm vows to this day that we'd have sneaked it if he'd been brought on for the last ten minutes.

It should have been clear that our sub-standard pre-season trip was an omen. Once again we started off on the back foot by losing our first three league games and drawing the next four. And this time there was no recovery round the corner. Even after we'd finally scraped a couple of wins at the end of September, we failed to pick up any momentum – in fact, we were stuffed 7-1 at West Ham in the next game. What a farce!

We'd travelled down the day before but, to try and cut costs, we ended up staying in a cheap hotel about 20 miles west of London. West Ham is smack-bang in the middle of the East End, so we had to cross the city on the Saturday morning to reach Upton Park.

Sod's Law, central London was gridlocked and it soon became obvious we'd struggle to be there on time. We had to stop and ring the ground from a call-box to say we might be late and, at around two o'clock, the players were told to get stripped. Eventually, we arrived about twenty minutes before kick-off and went straight out on to the pitch to try and warm up as best we could. We went one up through Dave Hockaday after ten minutes, but West Ham equalised while we were still laughing about it and it was downhill all the way from there.

You can't blame a 7-1 defeat on bad travel arrangements, but the journey didn't help and the whole trip spoke volumes about how the club was more interested in cutting costs than making sure the arrangements were adequate.

We still managed to have a few laughs on the road, even though my bedroom life was never exactly a bowl of cherries. Why? Ken DeMange, that's why. Ken, a former Liverpool midfield player who'd also been at Leeds with me, was usually my room-mate ... and could he snore! I tried everything to shut him up and sometimes ended up giving him a huge shake, but he was a really deep sleeper and hardly noticed. He just turned over and kicked off again.

It was horrendous, but I finally did for him on one away trip when we were staying in motel-type rooms on the ground floor. There was a patio outside, so I worked out a plan of action and let a couple of the lads in on the game.

Once Ken was fast asleep and well tuned up, I gave my battle unit a call. They were down the corridor and into the room within seconds. We opened the patio door, crept back into the room and carried Ken's bed outside. It was bloody freezing. Then, just to make sure he'd feel at home when he woke up, we took the bedside cabinet, complete with his alarm clock and lamp, and placed them alongside the slumbering DeMange.

The lads tiptoed back to their rooms and I leaped into bed. I'd managed three or four hours' untroubled sleep when the banging started on the window. It was DeMange, wearing just his boxer shorts. He must have been on the verge of hypothermia. I made him hang on a while by pretending to be fast asleep, but no one could have slept through that racket and when lights started going on in the rooms around us, I let him back in.

On the field, though, things were going from bad to worse and, by the start of December, we were firmly entrenched in the bottom four. To make matters worse from a personal point of view, I was struggling with a heel injury as we prepared for our trip to Middlesbrough, one of the strongest sides in the division. Stan was desperately short of players and, even though he knew I was struggling, he called me in on the Friday and said, 'Look, Swanny, I really need you to play. We're desperate.'

'I've no chance, boss. I can't put my foot down on the floor, never mind take a tackle.'

'What about an injection?'

'Yeah, if it's going to work.'

So Stan, Jeff Radcliffe and me went to see the club doctor, who was working at the hospital in town. He assured me that it wasn't a ligament or muscle injury and there'd be no lasting damage if I played with a painkilling injection; he said it would be a bit like going to the dentist and the effects would start to wear off after about twenty minutes. 'Are you happy with that?' asked Stan.

I wasn't really, but I said, 'OK, I'll do it.' I waited outside and heard the doc explain to Jeff that the skin on the heel is thicker than anywhere else in the whole body. He said the needle would only penetrate far enough if it went in at a certain angle until it touched the bone. It didn't sound too promising to someone with a built-in fear of needles.

So off we went to Ayresome Park, Middlesbrough's home before they moved into the Riverside Stadium in 1995. When the rest of the lads went out to warm up, I was left behind in the dressing room, waiting for the jab. I was shit scared, to be honest, and I pleaded with Russ Wilcox, the skipper, 'Stay behind, Russ. I'm going to need some help here.'

And how! As the needle was going in, I started biting the pillow to make sure I didn't scream out. It was agony. Then all of a sudden, someone shouted, 'Fuck!'

'What's up?'

'The needle. It's snapped,' said Jeff. That's all I needed. There were three people round the treatment table and they all had to press on my heel until Jeff could see the end of the needle. Then he got his tweezers and pulled it out. I said: 'Is that OK? Am I sorted?'

'No, we haven't injected you yet.'

So I had to go through the whole business again, this time with Russ holding me down. I'd no time to warm up, so I just went straight out for the kick-off. And, sure enough, after about twenty minutes, the effect of the jab began to wear off. I called over to the bench, but Stan shouted back, 'Stay on, Swanny. Don't do any running. Just hold the ball up, bring people into play. The others will do your running for you. Just stay on!'

I hung on as best I could and I'd made it as far as the hour mark when I went for a low header. Simon Coleman, their centre-half, caught me in the eye with his boot. I went down. A few of the lads gathered round and someone said, 'Stay down, Swanny, don't try to get up.' But I'd been around long enough by then to know that meant bad news.

Jeff told me my eye had come half out of its socket and that I would need stitches. I got to my feet and started to trudge off the field. My heel was giving me absolute hell, I could hardly walk, never mind run, and now I was heading for the treatment room for stitches to my eye socket. The only consolation was that I was obviously done for the day, or so I thought.

I was lying on the couch after having my stitches when I heard the door open. I just knew it was Stan. I thought, 'God no, what does he want now?'

He put his arm under mine and started to lift me up. 'Come on, Swanny, just another fifteen minutes, give us another fifteen minutes.' I was like a zombie. I just let him lead me down the tunnel and out on to the pitch and yes, I gave him another 15 minutes until the final whistle. I was in absolute agony when I came off and we'd lost 3-0 after holding on for the first-half.

When Stan came in, he shut the dressing-room door, took one look at me and turned to the rest of the players. He said, 'That's what I call commitment. He hasn't let me down today, but some of you have gone out there and tossed it off. I want another ten of him playing for me because that's what it will take to stay in this division.'

In a way, Stan's words made it all worthwhile. They didn't take away the pain, but I knew he appreciated what I'd gone through. And I'm still going through it to this day. Over the next few years I had more than my share of painkilling injections and when I wake up in a morning I can feel the exact spot where the needles went in. Knees, ankles, Achilles tendons and, of course, my heel. Sometimes it takes about 20 minutes for me to get moving properly ... and every morning, I think of Stan.

Unfortunately for him, he wasn't around long enough to find out whether he was going to be given the commitment he was looking for. Results didn't improve and, just over a month later, he was on his bike.

8
WHERE'S PORT VALE?

Stan Ternent's departure early in 1991 marked the beginning of the end for me at Hull. I suppose I jumped ship. It wasn't a particularly nice thing to do, but Hull were struggling, my contract was coming to an end and I wanted to better myself. Every time I neared the end of a contract, all I could see was the signing-on fees, which meant a new car, a holiday for me and the missus and a chance to pay off a few debts. I never even contemplated staying at one club forever; I needed a new challenge and a kick up the backside sometimes. I reckoned it was dangerous for a pro to start feeling too comfortable in one place.

With my contract due to expire at the end of the season, I started to make a few noises about wanting to get away in the autumn. In November, I went public with a claim that I wasn't happy playing up front. In fact, I was more than happy as a striker, but I'd heard whispers that one or two clubs were keen on me as a central defender, so I wanted to let any potential buyers know that even though I was scoring a few goals, I wouldn't have any worries about switching into the back four if the right move came along.

So I told Stan I wanted to play at the back. He wouldn't hear of it. He said that, as long as he was at the club, I'd be up front with Andy Payton. I cranked up the dispute by slapping in a transfer request, which Stan rejected. The story soon broke in the local and national press, although I made a point of insisting that, even though I was unsettled, I'd continue to give 100 per cent for Hull in any position. That wasn't just bullshit, I really meant it.

But a disastrous December, in which we won only 1 and lost 4 of our 6 games could mean only one thing: Stan was on his way. Once again, Tom Wilson took over as caretaker and we waited to see who would be our fourth manager in less than 2 years.

I was recovering from another knee injury when Terry Dolan arrived at the end of January. I wasn't around on his first day because I'd been given permission to attend a funeral. The following morning I missed training to have treatment from Jeff Radcliffe. After my session, I started winding Jeff up and messing about in the treatment room. I was bollock naked and, as Jeff was trying to push me out of the door, I nipped past him and took refuge under one of the couches.

The door to the treatment room was at the top of a flight of steps and as I was lying under the couch, I could hear footsteps coming up the stairs. It was the new manager. And when Terry pushed the door open for a word with his physio, he was greeted with a bird's-eye view of my bare backside. When I saw who it was, I clambered out from under the couch, congratulated him on getting the job, shook hands and headed off to the dressing room.

It wasn't long before our discussions took a more serious course. I told him I still wanted to get away and Terry assured me that if the right offer came along he wouldn't stand in my way. He would have had two reasons for that. First, Andy Payton and I were knocking in the goals and were the club's two most saleable assets. If Terry needed money to re-build, he'd have to sell one or both of us. We both left before the end of the year.

Second, I was also a big character in the dressing room and he was probably a bit worried about how I would react if Hull didn't agree to let me go. I've always tended to kick off a bit if I don't get what I want and he would have realised that I could have been a problem for him.

All in all, though, I had a lot of time for Terry. I still do. He's a genuine bloke and I don't have a bad word to say about him. He respected that I wanted to go on and improve myself and I respected him for the way he came into a struggling club. He was straight and honest with everyone from the start. Sadly for him, he'll always be remembered by Hull fans as the man who took the club down twice – from Division Two in 1991 and then into the bottom division 6 years later.

He still gets flak from the fans. I don't know enough about 1997 to say what went wrong and why, but he never really had a chance in 1991. We were rock bottom after 4 straight defeats when he took over and while we managed an unbeaten run of 6 games in March, we still needed a miracle. Struggling clubs don't get many of those.

For me, Terry's only failing was his choice of No.2, a fella called Jeff Lee. He was the typical 'sergeant major' type of coach. I thought he had a limited knowledge of the game and made up for it by making a lot of noise. He seemed more interested in abusing and bollocking players than in encouraging them or bringing in new ideas on the training ground.

I suppose Terry saw him as a complete opposite to himself. Terry was quiet, thoughtful and rarely handed out a major bollocking. He left that to Lee, who ended up upsetting a lot of the senior players and losing their respect. In Hull's situation, that was the last thing Terry needed.

Even though I'd been telling the world I wanted to play in defence, Terry followed Stan's lead and played me up front with Payton. It made sense. In fact, he would have been mad to split up such a potent striker force. Andy and I shared 65 goals in 141 league games over two seasons, playing in a struggling side. In the relegation season, he scored 25 league goals and I got 12 out of our total of 57.

In all, Payts scored 230 goals in 610 games in an 18-year career with 7 clubs, including a spell north of the border with Celtic, so his record as a goalscorer speaks for itself. The downside was that he was just about the most selfish footballer I have ever come across.

He wasn't a team player. He'd never drop back into midfield, hold the ball up and spray it around. He reckoned that if he did that, he'd be missing the opportunity of being up at the sharp end when a chance came along. He didn't want anyone else to be in the box; that was his territory.

I was the target man and he was the predator. I took the knocks and he took the glory. I went up for the header, flicked the ball on and ended up in a heap with a bloody nose and Payts nipped in for the tap-in from six yards. And did he celebrate with me and say, 'Thanks, pal?' Did he bollocks! He was away, running to the fans, celebrating and lapping up the adulation.

He seemed to be only interested in two things: scoring goals and collecting his wages. I sometimes wondered if he even bothered about our results. I used to joke that if we lost 10-1, he wouldn't worry as long as he got the goal. He was usually one of the last into training and one of the first away and never really mixed with the lads. I've no idea what he was like away from the club because he never got close enough for anyone to find out. I never disliked him; how could I when I never had a chance to get to know him?

But as a pro, you put up with a player like that as long as he's delivering the goods. If Payts was scoring goals, we had a better chance of winning games and collecting our bonuses. Managers knew what a selfish player he could be, but they still paid good money for him because he was a decent bet to finish a season with twenty goals.

We worked hard together in training and in the end our partnership was almost instinctive. Payts knew that when I went up for a header, the central defender probably wasn't going to make a complete clearance even if I didn't win the ball outright. So he lurked five or ten yards away. He knew also that if the ball was on my right-hand side, I'd flick it left and vice versa, so he was moving before I made the challenge and I lost count of the number of times I finished up on the deck with Payts in on goal. In the end, I stopped bothering about whether or not he appreciated what I was doing; I just got on with my game.

But his goals meant he was a massive favourite with the fans. I was once chatting to a group of punters before a Hull game and one of them was full of Payton. 'What a great player,' he said. 'And what a great lad!'

I said, 'Hang on a minute. He's a good goalscorer, but a great lad?' I tried to explain about Andy's shortcomings as a team player, but I might as well have been talking to a brick wall.

I linked up with him again at Burnley in 1998, but this time I was playing in defence. He'd done the rounds at Hull, Middlesbrough, Celtic, Barnsley and Huddersfield by that stage and everybody at Turf Moor knew all about him. He was never one of the lads ... but in 5 seasons at the club he'd supported as a kid, he scored 81 goals in 178 league games, so on balance, no one was complaining. Certainly not the fans. They absolutely loved him.

They still do. When Hull played at Burnley in the 2007–08 season, I covered the match for Radio Humberside and Payts was down to make the half-time draw. He received a great reception from both sets of supporters. A bit different from my welcome when I'd made the draw during Burnley's game against Plymouth, another of my former clubs, a few months earlier. I had no problems from the

Burnley fans, but as soon as my name was announced, a chorus of 'Greedy Northern Bastard!' rang out from the away end. More of that little lot later.

Even with Payts and I knocking in the goals, Hull were relegated. And as soon as the season ended, it was time to start working seriously towards a move. Although Hull had let other clubs know I was available, the only whiff of interest I heard about came from an unofficial source, a chap called Don, who used to run the players' bar at Boothferry Park. He did it for years and, at the end of the season, he used to give the players the proceeds for a night out. When Hull moved to the KC Stadium in 2002, they made him a life member. I see him at all the home games.

Don claimed to be a big pal of John Rudge, the Port Vale manager, and after every home game he'd sidle up to me in the bar and say, 'You know Rudgie wants you, don't you?' I couldn't work out how Don knew Rudge and I thought he was just having a laugh, but he insisted that he spoke to the Port Vale boss regularly and said that Rudge was keen on me as a centre-half.

So when I learned that Port Vale really were interested, I had a lot to be grateful for. And I did him a favour in return. He was always grumbling because the players' bar was looking a bit down on its luck, so I pulled Russ Wilcox aside one day and told Don we'd give it a coat of paint. We even put some of that Artex stuff on the ceiling, which was a hell of a job. There was more on the carpet than the ceiling by the time we'd done. But we managed to get the job finished in a day and wrote our names and the date in a corner of the ceiling. I suppose the signatures were still there when they finally knocked the old place down. Even though I was likely to be moving, I'd been given my quota of two main-stand tickets for the new season, so I gave them to Don. He was chuffed to bits. He said it was the first time anyone had done anything for him after all those years.

WHERE'S PORT VALE?

My ex-gaffer Eddie Gray was wearing his agent's hat by the time we reported back for pre-season training and he told me there were four clubs interested in me: Sunderland, Bristol City, Wolves and Port Vale. Sunderland were the first club to get in touch and, on the face of it, it looked like a good move. They were a big club, Sunderland was a soccer hotbed and all that. I assumed the money would be good, too. But I wasn't going to be rushed and Eddie fixed a day for us to talk to all four clubs.

When the big day came, I set off to meet Eddie feeling pretty confident I'd be signing for Sunderland. In fact Bex had already received a few details from estate agents up there and we'd worked out what we could afford. So soon after I left, she jumped in the car and headed north to look at a few houses.

I linked up with Eddie and we spoke to Sunderland on the phone. It wasn't the best offer in the world by a long way. So he put them on hold and said we'd better go down and talk to Port Vale. On the way, Eddie called Jimmy Lumsden, the Bristol City manager, who was an old buddy from his Leeds days. Jimmy confirmed that Bristol were still interested. He asked Eddie to give him a call when we knew what Port Vale were offering.

We arrived at Vale Park and I waited in the corridor outside the manager's office while Eddie spoke to Rudge. I couldn't hear too clearly, but I had the impression things were going well. After a few minutes, Eddie emerged and said he was going to speak to Bristol City. Lumsden told him they could match what Port Vale were prepared to pay, so Eddie went back in for more negotiations with Rudge.

This time, Rudge said Vale might be able to find a bit more money and mentioned that Bill Bell, his chairman, owned a car showroom. We'd be able to have our choice of any second-hand motor from the forecourt. It looked as if a deal was moving forward when Rudge's secretary came in and said there was a call for Eddie. This time it was Wolves, wanting to know how things were coming along.

Eddie took the call in another room and, when he returned, Rudgie was not best pleased. I heard him say, 'Hang on a minute. You've come down here to talk to us and you're spending half your time talking to other clubs. If we can't get something sorted now, forget it.'

So Eddie came outside again. 'Look, say what you'd be happy with and I'll go back in and tell him that's our final figure.' We agreed on a wage and a signing-on fee and Eddie told Rudge that if Vale could match those figures, we'd stop talking to anyone else and sign for Vale. Then he added that there was no way Port Vale's £300,000 signing was going to drive around in a used car. It was a new one or nothing.

I was still outside, but after a couple of telephone conversations, I was called in and Rudge said, 'OK, we've done a deal ... and we'll give you a new car. What about a Rover?' That sounded good to me. I didn't really have too much idea about Rovers, but with £650 a week, a signing-on fee of £52,500 over three years and a brand-new motor, I wasn't going to argue about what particular model might be involved. As long as it was white – for some reason, I was heavily into white cars at the time. We shook hands on a deal. Rudgie gave me a couple of pairs of boots before I left and I stuffed them into a carrier bag. Eddie and I hit the road north feeling pretty chuffed.

When I got home, Bex was waiting. 'Have you signed?' she asked.
'Yes.'
'Fantastic. I've found us a house as well.'
'Whereabouts?'
'Just south of Durham. Near the A1, so we'll be able to get home quickly.'
'I don't think we'll be going there, love.'
'Why not? Is it too much?'

'No, no problem with the price. It's just that I've signed for Port Vale, not Sunderland.'

'Port Vale? Where's that?'

'I've no idea. There's no such place. I just know it's a hell of a long way from Durham.'

'You mean you've signed for a club and you don't know where it is? Are we going north, south, east or west?'

'It's somewhere near Stoke-on-Trent.'

'Where's Stoke-on-Trent?'

'About an hour and a half away down the M1.'

'Why have you gone there?'

'The money, of course.'

However there was still one major obstacle to be negotiated before my move to Port Vale could be completed: a medical. Even though I'd played regularly since coming back from my cruciate injury, I knew I was by no means certain to come through a rigorous examination if Vale really scrutinised my right knee.

I was told to collect all my medical records from Hull and drive down to Vale for the check-up. Jeff Radcliffe gave me a big file with a history of all my injuries and then said, 'And here, you'd better take these as well, Swanny.' He handed me all the x-rays that had been taken of various parts of my anatomy during my time at Hull. I thought, 'Brilliant!' and jumped in the car. I stopped half a mile or so down the road and held up the x-rays to the light. I wasn't bothered about my heel, my cheekbone and all the other bits and pieces that had been damaged over the years. I was only interested in the x-rays of my right knee.

There must have been half a dozen of them, each one an item of incriminating evidence. There was only one thing to do. Once I'd reached the M62, I opened the passenger's window every five miles or so and chucked one of the x-rays out on to the hard shoulder.

Everything went well at the start of the medical although I knew they'd eventually want to look at the knee. Sure enough, I was asked which knee was involved.

'The left one.'

'OK, we'd better do a scan.'

The knee came through with flying colours. Crazy! It couldn't possibly happen today, of course. Sometimes players go through a two-day medical before they sign. I'd have struggled to survive two hours.

Even though I'd made a bit of a song and dance about wanting to get away, I was sad to leave Hull. I'd had some good times and made a few mates and, in a way, I enjoyed being around dilapidated old Boothferry Park, which had definitely seen better days by the time I left. Fans used to tell me there was once a time when it was one of the best grounds in the country. It had seating in the main stand and behind both goals in the days when many clubs only had one seating area.

But by the time I played there, the away end had become a supermarket, part of the popular side was closed because the terraces had crumbled and the whole place was run down. To make matters worse, on match days there was a horrible stench of piss from the gents' toilets in the corridor under the main stand. There was no escape from it, and if it was bad for the fans as they walked down the corridor before climbing into the stand, imagine what it was like for the players in the dressing rooms.

During my stay, the club never really threatened to fulfil its potential. Hull is a big city and, for the first 104 years of Hull City's history, it was the biggest city in Europe never to have had a club in the top flight. The people there are sports mad, but there was always a feeling that soccer was second best in a rugby league stronghold. OK, Hull FC and Hull KR have been top clubs for years, but that didn't mean Hull City could only ever be a second-tier club at best.

Over the years there had been occasions when they'd looked well placed to make it into the top flight, but they'd never taken the final step. And I have to say there were times when they weren't given the support when they really needed it.

When I signed for Hull in 1989, I felt there was real potential and a big opportunity for the club to move forward. But obviously the fans didn't see it the same way because throughout my stay, crowds rarely got above 10,000. That was never going to be enough to put together a side capable of sustaining a promotion challenge.

It's easy for supporters to go along when a team is successful, even if they are playing in one of the lower divisions, but the time a club really needs its support is when things aren't going quite so well. The fans won't like me for saying this, but they weren't there when they were needed and eventually, in 2001, the club went into administration. For a while it was touch and go as to whether it would even survive.

Thankfully, the move to the KC Stadium changed all that and, after back-to-back promotions in 2004 and 2005, they were averaging around 15,000 in the Championship. With the right financial package in place after the takeover by Paul Duffen, in June 2007 the club's infrastructure finally seemed to be built on solid foundations.

Even so, I don't think many people expected 2008 to be the year Hull finally reached the Promised Land. By that stage I'd been working as BBC Radio Humberside's Hull City pundit for nearly five years and I have to admit that, at the start of the season, I was worried they might struggle again. They'd only just survived the previous year and I thought they would be happy to settle for a mid-table finish.

But I'd reckoned without the Dean Windass effect. Phil Brown had brought Deano in on loan after he succeeded Phil Parkinson as manager in January 2007. He was nearly thirty-nine, but his goals had helped Hull to stay in the Championship. In June, he moved in from Bradford City on a permanent deal as Brown's first major signing. A manager's first buy is a massive thing because it shows what his intentions are for the club. Bringing in Windass demonstrated to the fans that Hull were no longer happy to settle for second best.

He was the local boy who'd come home at last, the talisman. He loved Hull City, he was a larger-than-life character and he gave everyone connected with the club a big lift. And the team developed a winning blend as the season progressed. If they had a blip, it tended to last for only one game, and they didn't get twitchy with the finishing line in sight.

With about ten games to go, people started to ask me if I thought they could make it. I always said yes. I was starting to feel deep down that they would. They saw off Watford in the play-off semi-finals and a goal from Windass – who else? – was enough to win the final against Bristol City. No wonder Hull City Council are thinking of naming a street after him!

That victory was the biggest thing that's ever happened to sport in Hull. Both rugby clubs have played at the highest level and won trophies, but for the football club to finally reach the Premier League was enormous. Over 100,000 people lined the streets for their victory parade and they had sold more than 20,000 season tickets by early June.

I was thrilled for everyone at the club: for Phil Brown, his No.2 Brian Horton and his coach Steve Parkin; for the players and, above all, for the fans. And I knew how lucky, honoured, even, I'd been to be able to follow their team's progress, week in and week out, through my radio work.

Everyone seemed to be caught up in the euphoria, even some of the local media. They were talking about how 'we' had finally done it, about what 'we' were going to do next season, about how 'we' would be going to Manchester United, Chelsea and the rest. But hang on a minute ... *We*? It's the players and the fans who will be in the front line. The media will just be there to do what they have always done: cover the action and try to let everyone back home know what's going on. And, let's be honest, if Hull had lost at Wembley, 'we' might easily have become 'they'.

For me, the play-off final was just a fantastic day and I was glad I had my two boys, George and Harry, along to share the experience. As we were walking down Wembley Way before the game, fans kept stopping me and asking if I'd pose with them for a picture. I signed a few autographs. The atmosphere was amazing and I really felt part of it, but when I finally reached the stadium, my mood changed. All of a sudden I felt absolutely gutted that I could no longer be out there playing. Memories of my only previous experience of a play-off final came flooding back. It had been on 30 May 1993, the day when Port Vale lost to West Brom and I was sent off. It still hurt 15 years on, and, standing outside the new Wembley, I just wished I could have gone out there and set the record straight. Thankfully, Hull did the job for me.

9
JOKER IN THE PACK

'**S**wanny! In my office! Now!' If only I had a tenner for every time John Rudge said that. And nine times out of ten, it meant a bollocking. Usually a fine. In the end, he just used to shout, 'Swanny!' and I knew what was coming. But what the hell! From the summer of 1991, I had three great years at Port Vale. A smashing set of lads, super fans, a couple of Wembley appearances and a promotion.

I became good mates with Robbie Williams, Vale's celebrity fan. And Phil 'The Power' Taylor, the 11-times world darts champion, who was another Vale supporter. I first met Phil when he was the celebrity guest at a game against Stoke. He presented me with the Man of the Match award. Darts wasn't too big at that time, but he'd recently picked up his second Embassy Professional World Championship title and did a lap of honour with his trophy at half-time.

We stayed in touch after I left Vale and soon after I retired in 2000, I spotted him at a charity dinner. I went over to his table for a chat. As I approached, he stood up, shook hands and introduced me to the people on his table – and anyone else who happened to be listening – as the best centre-half ever to play for Port Vale!

Rudgie was brilliant. I liked him a lot and, even though I caused him a bit of grief, I think he thought I was OK, too. He knew the game inside out and had a real talent for finding young players, turning them into good pros and making a bit of money for the club. Two classic examples were Robbie Earle and Darren Beckford, who both left just before I arrived. Rudge signed Earle as an amateur and, after playing over 300 games, he joined Wimbledon for £775,000.

Beckford, who was with me at the England Under-15 trial at Lilleshall 8 years earlier, arrived from Manchester City after playing just a handful of league games. He went on to top 200 appearances for Vale before switching to Norwich for £900,000.

Rudge was a bit like Dario Gradi at Crewe in that he hung around at one club for a long time and was well respected throughout the game. He may have had to work to a shoestring budget but, for most of his 15 years at the club, Vale punched above their weight.

By and large, he had a good relationship with his players, although he sometimes had problems handling what I would call 'characters'. Me, for example. He knew I liked a laugh and a joke and sometimes he tried to join in, but he never quite knew how far to go or whether we were laughing at him, rather than with him. Sometimes he had to beat a hasty retreat to stop things getting out of hand, but he is a good man and a good manager.

I'd played as a striker for almost two seasons before I signed for Vale and did well, but although Rudgie used to chuck me up front sometimes, he never really saw me as a centre-forward. He'd paid £300,000 for me as a defender, so if he'd started playing me up front, people might have questioned his judgement. Fair enough.

He had a bit of money to spend after selling Beckford and Earle, so I wasn't the only new signing. Martin Foyle arrived from Oxford for £375,000 and Rudge also signed another striker, Keith Houchen from Coventry. Keith was already a bit of a legend on account of his spectacular headed goal for the Sky Blues in the 1987 FA Cup final against Spurs, the year Coventry knocked out Leeds in the semi-final. They still keep digging out the video clip.

At first, Vale put me and Houchie up in digs in Burslem, not far from Vale Park, in a house run by a couple called Chris and Reg. It was a great big rambling old place. Chris and Reg were a lovely couple, a bit like Cath and Trevor who used to look after the young pros at Leeds. They already had one of the lads staying there when Houchie and I arrived: Tim Parkin, a defender. He'd been lodging with them for a while after moving from Swindon. His missus wasn't keen on living in the Potteries and was happy for him to stay over with Chris and Reg during the week.

Because he'd been around the digs for a while, Tim was the blue-eyed boy of the household and we soon spotted that he had a bit more on his plate than me and Houchie, along with one or two more fringe benefits that weren't handed out to the new boys. And Tim knew the score, no doubt about it. He wasn't going to be the one to tell Chris and Reg that it should be fair dos for all.

So, after a couple of days, I said to Keith, 'I've had enough of this. Time to teach him a lesson. I'll go into his room tonight before he turns in and hide under the bed. I'll give him a couple of minutes with the light out and then leap out. It'll scare him to death!' Houchie went along with the plan and after tea, he pointed out Tim's bedroom, which was on a different floor from ours.

At around half past ten, I made a big play of being knackered. I said, 'I'm off to bed, lads. See you in the morning,' headed off upstairs and slipped into Tim's room. The lights were out and I slid under the bed and waited for him to arrive. Nothing happened for about half an hour and I began to wonder what was going on. Tim was usually the first to hit the sack.

Finally, after another ten minutes, the door opened, the light went on and I watched in disbelief as two pairs of slippers came through the door and across the carpet. It wasn't Parkin, it was Chris and Reg. Houchie had stitched me up something rotten!

What could I do? If I'd leapt out then, I might have given one of them a heart attack or I could have caught Chris putting her nightie on. All I could do was stay put. It was a nightmare and if I'd been caught, I'd have been in big bother just a few days after signing. As usual, I soon saw the funny side of it and struggled not to crack out laughing.

After what seemed an age, the light went out, there was a bit of shuffling and some mumbled goodnights. I hoped that would be as far as it went. And, sure enough, before long the sound of gentle snoring told me the coast was clear. I rolled out from under the bed, crawled across the floor, opened the door as silently as I could and made my escape.

A couple of days later, Houchie and I went round to the car showroom to collect our club cars. Mine was a white Rover, as promised. Houchie's was red. On the way to the training ground later in the week, I was following a red Rover down a hill. There were some traffic lights at the bottom. I assumed Keith was in the car in front and, as the traffic slowed down for the lights, I got up close behind him and gave his rear bumper a bit of a nudge. We moved forward a couple more times and on each occasion I did the same thing. It didn't cause any damage. But all of a sudden, the car in front jerked to a halt, the handbrake went on and the door opened. A complete stranger climbed out. He was an off-duty copper. Fortunately, when I explained the background, he saw the funny side of it.

Houchie and I were both house-hunting, so we worked as a team. He was looking to rent a place north of Stoke for six months to give him time to find somewhere to buy in Cheshire. I wanted to buy

Top: Proudly lifting my first trophy …
as captain of Hunslet Carr Primary School
Rugby League team.

Above: As a young lad with my sisters
Janice and Diane (*left to right*).

Left: Me, aged three, with my mam in
Blackpool.

Above: I've always loved a good bit of fancy dress. Here you can see me donning a sexy St. Trinian's costume – you've got to love the hairy legs – and a rather fetching nurse's outfit. That's my mam in the crazy pumpkin costume!

Below: Having a pint down the local with my best mate, and partner in crime, Jonno.

Above: The day I met the Pope, aged 16. (I'm the young lad stood just to the left of the Pope, shaking his hand.)

Below: Celebrating my goal against Middlesbrough at Elland Road, 28 December 1988. This picture was taken minutes before the Boro fans started pelting me with stones and coins!

© Andrew Varley

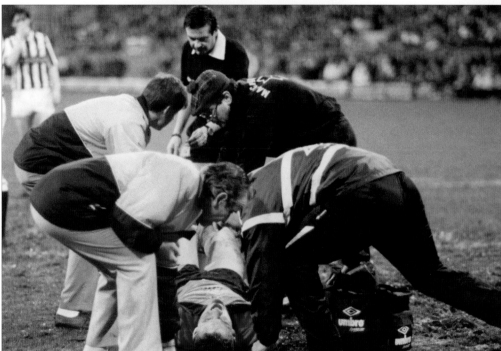

Above: Newlyweds cutting the cake.

Below: Being stretchered off after the first of many knee injuries. It didn't feel that bad at the time, but it turned out I had torn the anterior cruciate ligament, a career-threatening injury in those days.

© *Mail News & Media Ltd*

Above left: The long road back. I was out for 13 weeks with this injury (I wasn't so lucky later in my career).

© *Mail News & Media Ltd*

Above right: Ouch! Colliding with Barry Venison of Newcastle United at Boothferry Park, 3 November 1990.

© *Mail News & Media Ltd*

Below: In action against Bristol City with my team-mate and fellow striker Andy Payton, 16 February 1991. Payts was one of the most dangerous strikers around at this time, but he was never really a team player!

© *Mail News & Media Ltd*

The game from hell against Middlesbrough. I was struggling from the off with a heel injury. Then, 60 minutes in, I took a boot in the eye. My eye was hanging out the socket, and I had to have stitches. But that didn't stop Stan Ternent dragging me back on for the final 15 minutes.

But there were some good times as well ... I'm seen here celebrating with Gareth Roberts (*right*) and Wayne Jacobs (*centre*), having just scored the third goal for Hull City against Sunderland.

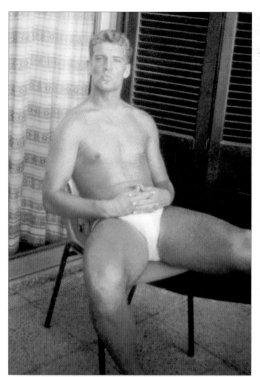

Above left: Bathing beauty!

Above right: Fooling around pre-season with my great friend and Port Vale team-mate
Keith Houchen.
© Stoke Sentinel

Below: Lying in wait for my team-mates. Vale manager John Rudge gave us a day off
from training to spend a day doing battle on the paintball field.
© Stoke Sentinel

straightaway and was targeting somewhere south of the town with easy access to the M6 or the A50 across country to the M1. Chris helped us by scouring the estate agents. The digs were awash with house details and every day after training, we'd set off. We took it in turns, north for Houchie one day, south for me the next.

Once we went to look at a place Keith fancied out in the country. It was built into a hillside on three levels with a garden at the bottom. I stayed in the lounge, on the top floor, while he and the estate agent looked round the place and eventually they emerged to inspect the garden three tiers below. The top floor was linked to the garden by a flight of steps and, while I was watching them out of the window, I noticed a leather pouffe alongside a chair in the lounge.

It weighed a ton and I started to wonder how far I could get it to roll down the steps towards the garden. I opened the French window leading to the stairs, picked up the pouffe and set it going down the steps. Houchie and the estate agent were deep in conversation three floors below with their backs to the house. I didn't expect the pouffe to go too far, but my aim was true and it picked up a fair bit of speed as it gathered momentum.

With about ten steps to go it was barrelling along at a fair old lick and still they hadn't noticed. I remember thinking I wouldn't want to be on the receiving end of it, but, at the very last moment, they seemed to hear a noise behind them, turned round and leaped for safety. The pouffe hurtled between them and bounced into a hawthorn hedge at the bottom of the garden. Houchie knew exactly what had happened and was laughing his head off. When the pouffe had finally been extricated from the hedge, I was able to convince the bemused estate agent that it had all been an accident.

On my own home front, I found two or three places that I thought were ideal but Bex knocked them all back. In the end, after Houchie had found a place to rent, I moved in with him for a while. Finally, Bex and I plumped for a four-bed detached house on a

Wimpey development in Stone, a village around ten miles south of Stoke. It was close to a couple of convenient watering holes, the Three Crowns pub and Little Stoke cricket club.

Our first house guest was Houchie, who by that time had also found a place to buy, but was still waiting for all the paperwork to go through. He stayed for about three months. Sometimes we'd go for a pint after training but, if the weather was half decent, we used to nip up the road to Alton Towers, a few miles east of Stoke. It was half price in the afternoons and, if we jumped a few queues, we could manage to fit in all the rides before dark. We were a couple of big kids.

It didn't take long for me to fit into the dressing room. There was loads of good banter flying around from day one. A few of the boys would always be game for a joke and there was no shortage of people looking for a night out.

The only person I couldn't get a handle on was an old geezer called Gordon. He was well into his sixties and, once or twice during my first few weeks at the club, he came wandering into the dressing room before training. He'd sit down next to me, strip off, wrap my towel round his waist and amble off into the sauna. We'd go out to work and when we got back, I'd find a wet towel in my place on the bench. He never really spoke to anyone and, apart from a few 'all rights' from the players, no one bothered him either.

I didn't like to rock the boat at first but, after three or four wet towels, I decided to find out what was going on. I pulled a couple of the lads to one side and asked, 'Who the fuck's that? Every time he comes in, he uses my towel. Look!' I showed them the wet towel.

'Oh, it's only Gordon. The gaffer knows him. He comes and cleans the lads' cars. In return he gets a couple of stand tickets for himself and the wife. Rudgie lets him have a sauna every week. He's harmless enough.'

'Maybe. But why does he have to use my fucking towel every time?'

'No idea.'

This went on for a few weeks. Normally, I'd have tackled Gordon about it, but as I was a new boy and he was a pal of the boss, I didn't want to upset him. One morning, though, things came to a head. I'd picked up a bit of a niggle and couldn't train. After a spot of treatment, I went back into the dressing room and waited for the lads to come in from training. My towel was missing and Gordon's clothes were hanging on the peg next to mine. He was obviously in the sauna. I thought, 'Right, I'm going to sort him once and for all.'

I got hold of a pair of scissors, snipped off one of his shirt sleeves, cut both his trouser legs off at the knees and cut the toes off his socks. For good measure, I got some Super Glue from the office and stuck his shoes to the ceiling.

The lads returned from training as Gordon was emerging from the sauna with my towel round his waist. He said hello to one or two of them and then started to get dressed, socks first. When his toes popped through the end of the first sock, the lads could hardly believe what I'd done.

I was killing myself. Gordon tried to laugh it off at first, but when he put his shirt on and then discovered his trousers had been snipped as well, he was nearly in tears. He asked me if I'd anything to do with it. I just shrugged, said I knew nowt about it and carried on reading my paper.

'I'm not having this!' he shouted, walking out of the dressing room and into Rudgie's office. Five minutes later, the gaffer appeared. He came straight over to me. 'Right, Swanny, what's going on?'

I just burst out laughing.

'What's so bloody funny?'

'Just look at the ceiling.' They were standing right under the shoes. Poor Gordon started crying. Rudgie put an arm round his shoulder and they went back to his office. I must admit, I started to feel bad about it then and after Gordon had gone home, I heard what was to become a familiar cry for the first time. 'Swanny! In my office! Now!'

'Was it you?'

'Yes.'

I tried to explain about the sauna and the towel, but I could see I wasn't getting anywhere.

'Look, you're way out of order. And you're going to have to buy him some new clothes, all right?'

'OK. How much?'

'It's 240 quid.'

How Rudgie had come up with that figure I'll never know, but I paid up.

A couple of days later, after news about Gordon, the sauna and the scissors escapade had spread round the club grapevine, I decided I needed to do a bit extra in the gym after lunch. All the lads had gone home and, as I walked out of the players' entrance, I could hear this voice shouting, 'Had any good bollockings this week, Swanny? Picked up any fines?' I recognised the voice. It was Bill, one of the maintenance staff, but I couldn't see him anywhere.

He carried on cracking jokes about the episode with Gordon until I finally spotted him, standing on the flat roof of a building behind the main stand. He must have been doing some repairs and had climbed up there on a ladder. He was laughing his head off about me, Gordon and the sauna. I decided he wouldn't be coming down for a while. I wandered over to his ladder, picked it up and carried it across to the other side of the car park.

'What are you doing?' I leaned the ladder against a nearby wall.

'You're not fucking laughing now, are you? See you in a couple of hours.' And off I went to the gym. When I came back, Bill was still up there. I put the ladder back, had a shower, got changed and drove away. Next morning, Rudgie came into the dressing room. 'Swanny! In my office! Now!' It was another fine. This time I couldn't help feeling that the gaffer could see the funny side of it, but rules are rules and all that crap.

On the field, I didn't have the happiest of starts. Rudgie paired Neil Aspin, my old team-mate from Leeds, with Dean Glover at the back and I was on the bench in four of the first 10 games. I missed a couple more with a foot injury and it wasn't until the end of September that I played the first of 4 consecutive games. The foot was a persistent problem that wouldn't go away and, while I was just about fit enough to start games, I missed a lot of work on the training ground.

But the injury didn't prevent me from making a return trip to Anfield 11 years after my first appearance there for Leeds City Boys. It was a Rumbelows Cup third-round tie and we'd been drawn against Liverpool after beating Notts County over two legs in the second round. We'd been exempt from the first round. Liverpool weren't at full-strength, but even so, we faced a pretty formidable line-up in front of Bruce Grobbelaar in goal. The back four was Harkness, Hysen, Molby and Burrows. McManaman, Tanner, McMahon and Walters were in midfield with Rush and Saunders up front.

Rudgie decided to play me in attack to try and ruffle a few feathers. We did well. We were level on at 1-1 at half-time and although Rush put them in front in the second-half, we were having a bit of a go at them going into the last quarter. And when John Jeffers, a former Liverpool player, got away down the right I sensed we could be in business.

I was ahead of my marker when his cross came in and found myself with only Grobbelaar to beat from six yards. In front of the Kop! Glory beckoned. The name of Peter Swan was about to go up in lights. It was a bit of an angle, but I wasn't going to miss a chance to make my name as the man who equalised for a Second Division side at Anfield. Then disaster struck.

I don't know how it happened. I must have taken my eye off the ball for a split second, but instead of side-footing my way to fame, the ball hit my heel and skewed back across goal. I was starting to wish the ground would swallow me up ... when I saw the ball was heading straight to Martin Foyle, who was following in behind me. Grobbelaar had already committed himself to cover my shot so he was out of the game and Foyle was left with the simplest of chances to equalise from my perfectly placed 'cross'.

Afterwards all the press boys wanted to talk to me. 'That was a great ball back in. So unselfish. Why didn't you have a shot yourself?'

'Well, I saw Foyley was in a much better position, so once the keeper had committed himself, I just knocked it back into the middle.' They bought it hook, line and sinker.

Rudgie gave us a team talk before the replay. He'd written the Liverpool side in team formation on the blackboard. He started to go through them, one at a time. They were household names, top-class performers, but the gaffer insisted on pointing out their individual weaknesses.

After a while, we started to laugh. Rudgie couldn't work out what was going on until someone said, 'We watch 'em on telly every week, boss. It's not their weaknesses we're worried about, it's their fucking strengths.' He laughed, rubbed the team off the board and said, 'OK, just go out there and play!' Liverpool took full advantage of the wide-open spaces of Vale Park in the replay and rolled us over 4-1. We didn't get anywhere near them for 90 minutes.

I hadn't really been fit to play because of my foot. Rudgie admitted before the game that it would be a gamble to play me, but as long as the medics said there was no risk of long-term damage, he would take a chance. The following day, however, I was sent for a scan in an effort to sort out the problem once and for all. It revealed a stress fracture and it meant I would be out of action until Christmas.

We were in mid-table when I finally returned to the starting line-up at Barnsley on Boxing Day. We drew 0-0, our fourth successive draw, then failed to win any of our next 13 matches. By the time we finally recorded a win, against Plymouth on 28 March, we were rooted to the bottom of the table.

In the end, we had to win our last two games to have any chance of staying up. And we blew it big style in our final away game at Cambridge. We lost 4-2 after being one up at half-time. What's more, I got myself sent off for dissent. I was playing up front, but had tracked back to help out the defence when Robbie van der Laan went up for a cross in the box with their midfield man, Tony Dennis. Vanders won the ball fairly, but Dennis went down in a heap and Paul Alcock, the referee, awarded a penalty.

I'd never really lost it on the pitch before, but there was no way that was a foul. It was such a crucial game and I just snapped. I had a real go at the ref, called him all the names under the sun – and a few more for good measure – and collected the inevitable red card.

It didn't stop there. Instead of going into the dressing room, I hung around in the tunnel and, when the ref came off after the defeat that virtually confirmed relegation, I let go again with both barrels. I thought I heard him say something back at me and that incensed me even more. I tried to get hold of him, but he nipped into his dressing room before I could reach him. Instead, I vented my fury by kicking a hole in his door before I was grabbed from behind by two coppers. They hauled me off to our dressing room.

Rudgie was furious and immediately hit me with a fine of two weeks' wages. He told the press that, while he could understand my frustration at what was a bad decision, players had to learn to control themselves. Soon afterwards, I received a letter from the FA saying that I'd be charged with bringing the game into disrepute for the incident in the tunnel after the game.

I requested a personal hearing, which was fixed for the end of May, but the club decided to get the first one in and fined me a further 50 per cent of my weekly wage for my part in the tunnel incident. So I'd been done for £1,500-plus and suspended for two games before the official hearing.

A few days after the Cambridge game, an FA official came to see Rudgie at the club, presumably to talk about the incident. I suppose the gaffer might have been in line for a bit of a bollocking for not keeping his players in order. I'd jarred my knee on the Saturday so I wasn't training and, after treatment, I had to stick around to wait to hear from Rudgie what the FA man had said.

I wasn't in the best of moods because of the fall-out from Cambridge and my knee and I could think of a million better ways of spending the morning than hanging about at Vale Park. However, relief was at hand. It must have been the day the beer was delivered to the social club, because there were loads of empty barrels around, so I decided to show Rudgie and the FA top brass what I thought about the whole business.

First, I piled all the barrels on top of one another outside the gaffer's door, which opened inwards. I also got hold of a washing line from the laundry, strung it out across the corridor outside the office, nipped into the dressing room, grabbed all the lads' underpants, pegged them on to the line and smeared a few pairs with melted chocolate.

Then I found a suitable vantage point. After a while, I heard Rudgie's door open. There was a clatter and a few muffled oaths before they started to dismantle my pile of barrels – only for the FA man to be greeted by a line of underpants when he finally emerged. They eventually cleared a route through the mayhem, the FA man left and within seconds of his departure, the inevitable cry of,

'Swanny!' rang out. I protested my innocence, but all the other players were out training and I was the only person around, so the case for the defence was less than convincing. Another few hundred quid was added to the tally.

But even with all the fines and the bollockings, I just couldn't stop myself. I was young and didn't care about the consequences. With hindsight, I was just a big, daft kid at heart, but that was my nature. It still is, to some extent. I'll still have a laugh with anyone. I'd have behaved like that in whatever job I did, but football gave me so many opportunities for practical jokes and silly pranks and I just couldn't resist.

Our last game of the season was against Grimsby at Vale Park. After our defeat at Cambridge, we had no real hope of survival, but if we won and the three teams above us – Oxford, Brighton and Plymouth – all lost, we would sneak out of the mire. It was a hell of a long shot, even though Grimsby were safe and had nowt to play for. I wasn't fully fit, but I said I'd give it a go and Rudgie played me up front. I didn't last the 90 minutes and we lost 1-0. Relegated at the end of my first season. A few days later, I saw a specialist about the knee and he confirmed that I would need an exploratory operation.

The FA hearing on 28 May rounded off what had been a less than perfect month. One of the Vale directors said he'd come along with me and we listened to the prosecution evidence. It didn't sound too good and things took a distinct turn for the worse when, halfway through the proceedings, the director nudged me and said, 'Sorry Swanny, I've got to go back to work. You're on your own from here.'

I did my best to plead a case for mitigation, but I was given a further two-match ban for bringing the game into disrepute. Then the chairman said that as I'd already been clobbered by the club, they'd be lenient and only fine me £500. *Lenient?* I couldn't believe it, but there was no way they were going to budge. To make matters worse, when I called in at Vale Park the following day there was a letter waiting for me from Cambridge. Enclosed was a bill for £200 for repairs to the referee's room door.

So I headed for a summer break with a sizeable hole in my bank balance and a knee operation looming. Because of the suspension, I'd miss the first four games of the following season, so my part in the pre-season build-up would be more or less meaningless. It was a nightmare situation for a professional footballer.

10
JUST WILLIAMS

These days Robbie Williams is instantly recognisable across the planet, from Stoke to Stockholm and from San Francisco to Sydney. But it was a different story when I first met him back in the summer of 1992. Rob was a member of Take That, an up-and-coming boy band from the Potteries. They'd had their first top-ten hit in May, and the following year would rocket to superstardom with three number ones, but Rob could still sit in the stand at Vale Park without too many problems from the punters.

He was just an ordinary kid. When he was out with me, Bex and our regular Saturday crowd, all he wanted was to be one of the gang. And when the two of us went for a few pints or a night out together, we'd go out of our way to find places where he was already known or where he wouldn't be instantly recognised. As I mentioned before, he enjoyed being with me because there was never any hassle. That's how I liked it, too.

Mind you, we had some right old escapades together! Like the Sunday I was invited to be guest of honour at a kid's birthday party. Bex and me knew Annette, the little lad's mam. Her house was on a village green and the kids were all football fans. The idea was for them to have a game on the green before coming inside for their tea. The food was all laid out on a table in the dining room and, after singing 'Happy Birthday', they'd be introduced to a real footballer. Me.

I'd fixed up to have a few beers with Rob at lunchtime and Bex dropped us off at the Darlaston Inn, a pub on a roundabout outside town. After we'd had a couple of drinks, word got round that he was in there, so we decided to move on. I gave Bex a call, she picked us up and we all headed off to another pub. Bex and I had something to eat while he played the fruit machine. When it was time to set off for the party, Rob and I were well away.

When he went for a pee, I had a quiet word with Bex. 'What shall we do? Take him to the party as well or drop him off first?'

'You'd better ring and find out if it's OK to take him.'

So I called Annette, who was giving the party. 'It's Swanny. I'm on my way. Is it all right if I bring a mate along?' She probably thought it would be one of the lads from Port Vale.

'Yeah, that's fine. See you soon.'

I'd arranged to use the back door so the kids wouldn't see me arrive. Bex dropped us off and Annette was just adding the finishing touches to the tea when we walked in. She recognised Rob instantly and did a double take. I said, 'Hi, Annette, this is Rob.' She put down the jelly like a flash and said, 'Come and have a drink!'

Rob was a bit peckish and asked if it was OK to have a bite before the kids came in. Again, no problem ... until he tripped up on his way to the table and landed headfirst in the jelly and custard. The table gave way and, for a few seconds, it looked as if the whole tea party would end up on the floor.

But Annette played a blinder and somehow managed to pull off a damage-limitation exercise. Virtually all the grub was rescued. Rob, on the other hand, wasn't in such a good condition, with bits of sandwich, cake, jelly and custard all over his face and shirt. 'Come on,' I said. 'You'd better go and get yourself washed down.'

News that Rob was in the house had spread by this stage and a few mums had abandoned the football. Two of them said they'd take him upstairs and clean him up. They were gone for quite a while and I was beginning to wonder what the clean-up operations might include when they came back. Without Rob.

'Where is he then?' I asked. 'He's my responsibility. His mam'll kill me if he's done a runner.'

'Oh, don't worry. He decided to have a lie down in the bath, we couldn't lift him out and he fell asleep.'

I sent a quick SOS to Bex and she was round in no time. We left Rob for a while and then nipped upstairs, woke him up, hoisted him out of the bath and cleaned him up. Bex took him home while I joined in the party. And everyone lived happily ever after. Except the mums, who'd heard Robbie Williams was at the party and dashed round to meet him ... only to discover he'd been whisked away.

Sometimes we used to go to a casino near Hanley, one of the five towns that make up the Potteries. Rob enjoyed a gamble and told us how once, when Take That were on tour in America, the bouncers wouldn't let him into the gaming rooms because he was too young. He called it 'Casinos R Us' because he felt like a little kid staring through a toyshop window at the forbidden fruits inside. So near but so far. Instead he had to play the slot machines.

There were no such problems back home in the Potteries. Once when he came with us he lost 50 quid in no time. He stalked away and sat sulking for a while. To him £50 was a drop in the ocean, but that didn't mean he enjoyed losing it. On another night, five of us all went along together. Rob, me, Bex and my sister Diane, and a young lass called Sam. I didn't really know her, but she seemed nice enough. We played the tables for a few hours but, when it was time to go home, we couldn't find Rob anywhere. Or Sam.

I said to Diane, 'Where is he then?'

'I don't know.'

'Well, you're supposed to be keeping an eye on him.'

'Why me? I'm just here for a bit of a gamble.'

'Either way, it's four in the morning, we've lost Robbie Williams and guess who's going to have to tell his mam tomorrow?'

We searched high and low, inside the casino and outside in the car park. The staff were getting decidedly twitchy about going home to bed by the time we'd completed the search. They said they were locking up. There was only our car left in the car park and still no Rob, no Sam. Bex said we ought to ring his mam. 'At four o'clock in the morning? You're joking. She'd kill me. There's a good chance he's gone home anyway.'

Then we heard a rustling noise and the lid of one of the giant waste bins in the car park started to open. Rob's head appeared first, then Sam's. They climbed out, laughing their heads off. They said they'd decided to hide in the bin for a while and could see us all panicking out in the car park. I took that explanation with a pinch of salt. The important thing was we'd found them in one piece.

The whole world knows that Rob liked a drink. So did I. In fact, I was out on the lash just about every day and getting pretty good at it. At one of our sessions, Robbie said, 'Right, Swanny, I'll match you drink for drink.' We kicked off with lagers and then started adding shorts. I was struggling. Things were moving when they shouldn't have been and the old double vision was setting in. But Rob seemed completely OK.

We'd arranged for Bex to come and take us up to Stone cricket club and, when we arrived, we decided to have a game of darts. I could hardly see the board, but Rob seemed OK as he made his way over to the mat for the first round. After he chucked his opening arrow, he just kept on going and fell flat on his face, though. Got him!

I thought he'd be out for the count, but instead, he got to his feet, sat down on a stool, gathered a few of the lads round and said,

'Right. Give me a name, give me a place, give me a country, give me an animal.' He named a few more things and we all chipped in. He started tapping his feet, nodding his head and miming to himself. Then he broke into a song with every one of our words in the lyric. Incredible! We gave him a round of applause and he went and served behind the bar until it was time to go home.

Once, in the Three Crowns, he started chatting up a bird in the bar. I happened to know she was married to a copper. I said, 'Come on, Rob, leave it. Let's go.' I'd got Bex's car with me and it was obvious we were going to have a bit of a session. So I decided to drive to the cricket club up the hill from the pub, leave the motor there and walk home. We had a few pints, but I could see he wasn't settled.

'What's up?'

'I need to go back to the pub and see that bird.'

'You're mad. I've told you, her husband's a copper.'

'I'm going back.'

'Well, I'm not driving.'

'I'll drive.'

He took the keys, got behind the wheel and switched on the ignition. The car was parked on a slope and we moved off. Moved isn't really the word to describe what the car was doing. Jumping, more like. He drove across the outfield, managed to negotiate the exit and started bouncing down the road.

'Have you passed your test?'

'No.'

'Have you driven before?'

'No.'

'Shit!'

The pub wasn't far off, but it was downhill all the way and there was a mini roundabout between us and our destination ... and there was no way Rob was going to leapfrog that. 'Push your left pedal to the floor,' I said. He did. 'The middle one is the brake. Push it down now!' We were in free wheel, the bouncing had stopped and we were slowing down, but not enough.

I grabbed the handbrake and slowed the car to a virtual halt as we approached the roundabout. Somehow we got round it and reached the pub car park. He leaped out and ran into the pub. I suspected I wouldn't have to wait long before I saw him again. I was right. Seconds later, the door opened and Rob came out headfirst. I was already on the phone ordering a taxi.

He had no idea about money or how much anything cost, but once, after he lent me 40 quid on a night out, he kept banging on about making sure I paid him back. I promised I'd have the money next time, but clean forgot to go to the cash machine in advance.

'Where's my 40 quid?' he asked straightaway.

'I forgot. We'll go to the cash machine now.' I drove into town. When we reached the bank, he handed me his card and said, 'Can you check my balance while you're there?' He gave me his pin number. I collected my money and my own balance, printed out a balance for Rob, got back in the car and handed him the print-out of my balance. We drove off.

'Swanny, what does £760 DR mean?'

'It means you're 760 quid overdrawn.'

'You're joking.'

'You know your problem, Rob. You should have been a footballer like me. Here, have a look at my balance.' I handed over the other print-out.

'Bloody hell! And you only play for Port Vale.'

'Aye,' I said. 'The problem is you've got my real balance in your other hand. £760 DR!'

We kept the house on in Stone after I moved on to Plymouth in 1994 and for a while after I joined Burnley a year later. And Robbie would sometimes call round to see us. He'd wander in and light a fag. I'd say: 'You can't do that!'

'Why not?'

'Never mind why not, outside!'

He'd stand outside the door, puffing away and trying to hold a conversation with me inside the house.

George, our first son, was born soon after I joined Plymouth and when Rob came round a while later, he asked, 'Where's George?'

'He's in bed, he's only a bairn, you know.'

'Can I go and see him?'

'Aye, of course.'

So we went upstairs, crept into George's room and watched him sleeping peacefully.

'Can I pick him up?'

'No, he's asleep.'

'I won't wake him.'

'Just leave him alone.'

'I want one of these.'

'How do you mean?'

'I love kids, I always have. I'd love to have one.' It was true. He was always really happy with kids around and enjoyed playing games with them.

We lost contact for a while when it was first revealed that he was having problems with drugs. I decided it would be better for him to make the first move if he wanted us to get together. And I didn't hear anything for around eighteen months. But when he made his comeback tour, we bought tickets for his date at a club in Leeds called Town and Country.

We'd only got the tickets at the last minute so we were sitting right at the back, a fair way from the stage. As we hadn't seen him for a while, we didn't let him know we'd be there. We were just happy to go and enjoy the concert. For the last two songs, the backstage team turned on the lights throughout the club and Rob was looking round the audience as he started to introduce his penultimate number. Bex suddenly said, 'He's spotted you!'

Too right! 'Swanny!' he shouted, and pointed in my direction. About a thousand pairs of eyes turned and stared. I waved back to acknowledge him. He said, 'See you after! For a drink!' The concert ended ten minutes later and we started to walk down the steps and out towards the exit.

All of a sudden, I realised I was playing the Pied Piper. There was a queue of fans lining up behind me, all waiting to see where we'd go to meet Rob. We walked straight out of the club, jumped into a taxi and set off. Bex said, 'What are you doing? We're supposed to be meeting Rob.'

'No chance.'

'Why not?'

'We haven't spoken for eighteen months. We can't just go for a drink now as if we've been meeting every week.'

I told the driver to go the Parnaby Tavern, the nearest boozer to my mam and dad's. After a while, the driver looked in his mirror and said, 'Who's all that bloody lot?' I looked round and saw we were being followed by a line of taxis, all full of fans hoping to keep a tail on the couple who were going to meet their Robbie.

The Parnaby Tavern has probably never seen anything like it. Bex and me walked in, I ordered a pint of Tetleys and a Guinness for the missus and we were just starting to sit down when what seemed like hundreds more people piled in. They looked a bit baffled. With the best will in the world, the Tavern was not exactly the setting for a pop superstar to meet his mates and nobody could quite work out what was going on.

When we'd finished our drink, I managed to order another taxi without anyone hearing what I was up to. We were going round to my mam and dad's and I wasn't going to be followed by all that lot. So when the landlord said our taxi had arrived, we raced out of the pub, jumped into the cab and set off into the middle distance.

All the other cabs had long gone, so there was no way the fans could follow us. And after driving round for a while, we were dropped off in Parnaby Terrace. How everybody else got back into the middle of Leeds is anybody's guess, but now I know how the superstars must feel when the paparazzi are on their trail!

A couple of days later, the phone rang at home. It was Rob. 'Where were you? Why didn't you come back for a drink?'

'We haven't spoken for eighteen months so I'm not going to jump at the drop of a hat. I don't work like that.'

So he invited us to two of his next gigs, in Sheffield and Hull. Before the Hull gig, he told me, 'I'm thinking of getting engaged.'

I'd seen in the papers that he'd been going out with Nicole Appleton from All Saints. They'd met on *Top of the Pops* and I assumed it would just be a bit of a fling.

'Who to?' I asked.

'Nicole.'

'You're joking! You hardly know her and All Saints are always off on tour. When did you last see her?'

'A week ago?'

'Where is she now?'

'Germany. On tour.'

'And what do you think she'll be up to on tour in Germany?'

'Oh, she's not like that. Anyway, she's got her mum with her.'

'So what. She won't just be sitting round like a nun. Think what you get up to when you're on tour.'

'No, I tell you. She's sharing a room with her mum.'

'How do we know her mum isn't at it as well?'

'Right, I'll ring her.'

He gave Nicole a call, chatted for a few minutes and then asked if her mum was there. He spoke to her for a while, too. 'There, I told you,' he said.

A couple of months later there were stories in the papers that they'd split up. I called him up. 'Yeah, I know,' he said. 'Don't start ...'

SWANNY

Once he sent us tickets for a concert at the Manchester Arena. Bex and I went along with John Beresford, another ex-pro who's been my best mate for years, and his missus, Bridget. This time we were in the VIP seats with some of the lads from Manchester United – Teddy Sheringham, Dennis Irwin, Gary Neville, Ole Gunnar Solskjaer – and a few more big hitters from outside the football world as well.

Rob was into his third song, walking across the stage, when he spotted me. 'Swanny!' he shouted. I acknowledged him and, as I did so, I noticed Geri Halliwell peeping out from behind all the technical equipment at the back of the stage. She and Rob were pals at the time. She'd no idea who I was, but because Rob had shouted my name, she decided to wave as well. So I gave her a wave back. That was a signal for a dig in the ribs from Bex. Afterwards I had to convince her that I'd never met Geri in my life.

Later we went backstage and we soon worked out that none of the Manchester VIPs could understand why a little-known ex-Port Vale player, now with Burnley, had been be singled out for preferential treatment by Robbie and a Spice Girl.

Another time he rang to ask if I fancied a game of golf. I didn't even know he played golf. He said he'd had a load of lessons and knew what he was doing. He was in London at the time, but we arranged to play at one of the clubs near Stoke a couple of days later. Tee off at midday. It was absolutely pissing down on the morning of the game and the phone rang at around eleven o'clock. It was Rob. I assumed he was going to call it off, but no, he was well up for it. 'And I've brought a couple of caddies,' he said.

'Caddies?'

'Yeah, two women I know in London.'

'Hang on a minute, Rob. Golf is golf, women are women and, for me, the two don't mix. I'm not going round a golf course with a couple of bloody women caddies. Bollocks to that! Tell 'em we'll see 'em for a drink afterwards.'

'No, no, no, you don't understand. One of them is my girlfriend and she's brought a mate along to caddy for you.'

'Rob, I've told you there's no way I'm playing golf with two women caddies. Let's make it another time.' And I put the phone down.

He rang back a few minutes later. 'You weren't joking, were you?'

'No, Rob. I wasn't joking.' I thought that was the end of the matter, but he called again a few days later and fixed up to go for a drink on the Sunday. Straight off, he started talking about our golf match. 'You'll never guess who your caddie was.'

'Rob, I don't give a shit.'

'No, Swanny. If you knew who your caddie was, you'd have said yes.'

He just wouldn't let it go and kept switching the conversation back to it all the time. To be honest, I was intrigued by that stage and pretty keen to know who the mystery lady was, but there was no way I was going to ask outright after all the bullshit that had gone on before.

Finally he picked up his phone, dialled a number and said, 'Swanny's here now. I'll put him on.' He handed me the phone. It was a woman.

'I've heard so much about you, Swanny. That's why I wanted to come up and caddy for you.'

'Well, I'm sorry, love ...' And I explained all about women caddies to her, adding, 'I told Rob we could all have had a drink afterwards, but he said it was caddies or nothing.'

'Another time, maybe.' She rang off and I passed the phone back to Rob.

'Did you recognise her voice then?'

'No, I didn't recognise her voice. What are you drinking?'

'You must have recognised her.'

'Rob, for fuck's sake, let's forget it. What are you drinking?'

'Well, I'm going to tell you anyway. It was Patsy Kensit.'

All of a sudden I developed a whole new attitude towards women caddies.

11

IT COULD BE HEARSE

My first season at Port Vale had not been one of the best. Even though Rudgie had paid £300,000 for me, I'd been in and out of the side for the first 10 games and then, when I'd started to hold down a regular place, I picked up the foot injury that sidelined me for 9 weeks in mid-season. It was stop-start all the way and 33 league appearances – 6 of them as a sub – was not what I'd been looking for.

Relegation hurt. Leeds had been relegated after I'd signed schoolboy forms and Hull were relegated after my third season. The last thing I wanted when I joined Vale was to have to go through another relegation. There were times when I started to wonder if I was some kind of jinx. I'd been a pro for 8 years and never really tasted any success. I was hugely determined to put the record straight when we reported back for the 1992–93 season.

The same feeling ran through the squad. At the end of December 1991, we'd been in eleventh position in the old Second Division. Now we were starting a new season in Division Three. We'd let ourselves and the fans down; this time we were going to give them something to shout about.

SWANNY

We'd always been a close bunch. We played together, trained hard together and went out on the piss together. Every Wednesday there was a night out at Maxine's nightclub in Hanley and there would always be 12 or more of us involved.

And as the countdown to the new season continued, I cemented my position as prankster-in-chief, scoring a major success after Paul Kerr, one of Rudgie's summer signings, crashed his Mercedes on the way into training and put it off the road for a few days.

Paul had a mate who hired out cars for weddings and funerals, so he gave him a buzz and asked him if there was anything he could borrow while his motor was being repaired. The only available option was a hearse. You can imagine the reaction when Paul swept into the car park the following morning.

For me this was far too good an opportunity to miss. I immediately pulled Keith Houchen and briefed him with my plan. After training, we'd nick Paul's hearse, one of us would lie in the back and we'd go for a drive round Burslem. Houchie seemed a bit reluctant at first – mainly because he wanted to be in the back while I drove – but as it was my plan, I pulled rank and he agreed to go behind the wheel. Once Kerr was safely in the shower, we nicked the keys, Keith hopped into the driver's seat and I climbed into the back and lay down.

Anybody walking past the hearse would have been higher than me and could have seen me lying there, but to other car users, the window of the hearse was above eye level and the vehicle looked empty. We'd decided in advance that we'd make our move if we had to stop at traffic lights and after a few minutes, Houchie called out, 'Right, Swanny, we're coming up to some lights. They're just going to red.'

I waited for a few seconds before I heard the call: 'There's a car drawn up alongside. Two old biddies in the front.' I lifted my shoulders slightly until my head was in full view and then turned and looked at the two old dears. As I did an eyes front and lowered my shoulders, the lights turned to green and off we went. We left a trail of chaos behind us.

The car containing the old biddies hadn't moved and the traffic was piling up behind it. Houchie stopped a bit further on and looked in his mirror. The lights had gone to green twice and still the old biddies' car hadn't moved. A big queue was building up. We resisted the temptation to try the same trick at the next lights, motored serenely back to the ground and handed the keys back to Paul.

Kerr was a midfield player who'd moved in from Millwall and he soon became identified as our Brain of Britain. I didn't really take to him at first. He was a southerner and always seemed to want the last word in team meetings but, like me, he enjoyed a night out and before long we were good mates.

After he finished, he went into insurance and, at one stage, was working for the PFA as a financial adviser. He had an incredible memory. I once went into the away dressing room and Paul was in there with 10 apprentices sitting on the floor in a circle around him. They all put a fiver into the middle and then one by one, gave him their telephone number. When they'd finished, he said, 'Right, I'll read out the numbers and if I get anyone's wrong, I'll double the money and give him a tenner.' He got every single one right. I've no idea how he did it.

At the end of July, we went on a pre-season tour to Holland. We played in a competition with three other sides, a round-robin job, and made it into the final. We were there for less than a week and played a game on each of the first three days. So the morning after our final group game, Rudgie said: 'Right, lads, you can have a day off. You're free to do what you want, but remember, we've got the final tomorrow morning, so look after yourselves.'

We were based in a small town about 20 miles outside

Amsterdam, so I called the lads together and said, 'Anyone fancy a mystery tour? I'll hire a minibus.' There were 16 of us in all, but only 8 or 9 decided to give it a go, partly because Rudgie was floating about and I hadn't been able to let on where we were really going. After I'd cleared the general idea with the gaffer, I made the necessary phone calls, the bus arrived and we climbed aboard.

At first, we headed off in the opposite direction to Amsterdam, but a couple of miles down the road, I tapped the driver on the shoulder and he went into Plan B mode. He stopped, turned round and we hit the road to Amsterdam, making sure not to drive past the hotel.

It was a boiling hot day and when we arrived, we sat at one of the outside bars and had a couple of beers. Then a couple more and a couple more, and before long some of the lads decided it was time to have a look at what was on offer in the Red Light district, just round the corner.

I gave strict instructions that if we split up, everybody had to be back at the bus for five o'clock and we set off. One or two of the boys went missing as we strolled past the tarts' booths, but most of us made it to the canal running alongside the Red Light area. We were having a look into the murky waters when John Jeffers got too close and I gave him a nudge. In he went.

I was off balance after pushing him and Kerr seized the chance to fire me into the water as well. When someone tried to pull me and John out, we hauled them in. So in the end, there were four or five of us in there, being watched from a bar by a group of Vale supporters who'd come along for the trip. Apparently, the bar owner was keeping an eye on us, too, and said to the supporters, 'Your fans, they are crazy, absolutely crazy!'

They replied, 'They aren't the fans, they're the players!'

It was pretty obvious that Rudgie wasn't going to be too impressed if the tour organiser returned to the team hotel soaked to the skin, so I managed to persuade one of the supporters, a great big fat guy, to swap clothes with me. One or two of the other players did the same and when we got back to the hotel we managed to cover the tracks of the lads who were still wet and steered clear of the gaffer for the rest of the evening.

The next morning, I stuffed my borrowed clothes into a carrier bag and when we went out to warm up, ran behind the goals and handed them back to the fan who'd bailed me out. He gave me my wet gear back in return.

There'd been a fair bit of banter with the fans the previous afternoon and during the game, they started singing, 'Swanny, he couldn't score in a brothel!' I was a bit worried they might repeat it at our first home game, with the missus sitting in the stand, but fortunately, that particular chant was a one-off.

I missed the first two league games through suspension then slotted into the back three between Neil Aspin on the right and Dean Glover on the left. We were a good unit in a good side. We only won one of our first 8 games, but then won 4 on the spin and we were away. We lost only twice in 19 games and hit the automatic promotion slots, behind Stoke of all people, in mid-February. We stayed there until the final week of the season. For me, the only real hitch came off the field and involved Houchie, five bikes and an MoT Centre in Leeds.

Houchie had decided to give his missus and youngster a bike for Christmas, but didn't know where to start looking in and around Stoke. As it happened I was back home in Leeds that weekend. When I went into the Parnaby Tavern for a pint, I asked if anyone could help. I was told to have a word with Rod Rowson, a chap who lived nearby.

I spoke to Rod, who said he had a mate who ran an MoT centre on Kirkstall Road in Leeds. He sold bikes as a sideline. Rod said he'd have a word. A few days later, I got a call saying there were a few bikes we could have a look at. So Houchie and I drove north after training, found the MoT centre and were shown into an upstairs room. It was just like Halford's. There were bikes of all shapes and sizes and in every price range. So I bought two, one for me and one for Bex, and Houchie bought three. We loaded them into our cars and drove back to the Potteries.

At the first opportunity, Bex and I went off for a ride and then put the bikes in the garage when we got home. As we went through the front door, we heard the phone ringing. I picked it up.

'Hello.'

'Mr Swan?'

'Yeah.'

'West Yorkshire Police. We believe you are in possession of two stolen bikes.' I thought it was one of the lads winding me up and told him where to put his stolen bikes. Instead, I got full chapter and verse.

'On 17 November, you were seen driving a white Rover into an MoT Centre on Kirkstall Road, Leeds. You were followed by Keith Houchen, another Port Vale footballer, driving a red Rover. The two of you were later seen leaving the premises with five new bicycles. We have been surveying these premises for some time and believe those bikes to have been stolen. You have seven days to bring the bikes into the Police headquarters in Wakefield, where you will be questioned by detectives.'

I called Houchie straightaway. He'd had a similar call and we decided it wasn't a wind-up. So we gave it a few days and then headed north again on the day before we were due to play Stoke in a televised FA Cup first-round replay. We returned the bikes and were shown into an interview room.

A detective came in and said, 'You realise we were serious when we said seven days, don't you? This is the sixth and if you hadn't reported today, we'd have come down and arrested you in the dressing room before the game tomorrow night.'

We managed to convince him we'd no idea the bikes were stolen and lived to ride another day.

We secured local bragging rights by beating Stoke and reached the third round before losing at Newcastle. And we were also doing well in the Autoglass Trophy. It was the forerunner of what is now the Johnstone's Paint Trophy for clubs in the lower divisions and a lot of people saw it as a Mickey Mouse competition. Fair enough, I suppose, but with a Wembley final at the end of the line, it suddenly grew in importance for players and fans when we were drawn against Stoke in the southern area semi-final.

Mickey Mouse or not, over 22,000 people turned up for our 1-0 win at their place that secured us a place in the area final over two legs against Exeter. We won the first leg 2-1 at home, drew 1-1 in the second leg, and all of a sudden, it was Wembley here we come! The date? 22 May. The opposition? Stockport County. The problem? I was struggling desperately with a double hernia and would need surgery in the summer. It was by no means certain that I would be fit for the final.

During the last few weeks of the season, I hardly trained at all and needed a painkilling injection in my stomach before every game. I had to lie on my back on the treatment table and the needle was inserted until it touched the pubic bone. I wasn't totally happy about it, but I was assured there would be no lasting damage. And fair dos, there wasn't.

I was determined not to miss my first trip to Wembley and the last few league games that could mean promotion. I told Jim Joyce, our physio, that I'd do anything to keep playing and he suggested using an oxygen chamber. Robbie van der Laan had a similar problem and he came along, too.

SWANNY

The chamber was like a big dome with space for about half a dozen people inside. Patients climbed in wearing an oxygen mask, sat down and, once the door was shut behind them, the air pressure inside the dome was reduced and we were able to breathe pure oxygen through the mask. The theory was that breathing oxygen improved circulation and speeded up the healing process.

We had the treatment three times a week for a couple of weeks and it seemed to be working. So the chap who operated the chamber asked us to tell Rudgie to send down any other players who might benefit. There was a young kid who was struggling with a long-term problem, so he came along at the start of our third week.

He was a cocky little devil and we thought we'd wind him up a bit by saying that while he was in the chamber, it was vital not to take off the mask. We said that if he did, the pressure would force his eyes out of their sockets. Believe that and you'll believe anything, we thought.

On his first day, there were five of us in the chamber in all: me, Vanders, a couple and this kid. And after a while Vanders and I started messing about, having a bit of a pretend fight. We could see the young lad starting to panic and, all of a sudden, I turned, grabbed his mask and pulled it off his head. He let out a piercing scream and sat there with his hands clasped over his eyes. The attendant heard the commotion and came running up to see what was going on. He had to bring the pressure levels back to normal before he could open the chamber again, but eventually we all climbed out. The young lad was still in a real panic.

We explained that it had all been a hoax and, after a while, he started to see the funny side of it. Then he got home and told his mum. She was straight on the phone to Rudgie and we were hauled in the next morning. This time we got away with a lecture on how the young lads looked up to us and how we should behave more responsibly.

IT COULD BE HEARSE

I did everything I could to keep going in the last two or three weeks of the season, but after our penultimate match – a 1-1 draw at Exeter that kept us in second spot behind Stoke – Jim Joyce told me I'd have to take a break. I pleaded with him and Rudgie to let me play, to keep the injections going for one more game, but they weren't having any of it.

At the start of that final week, we were second. Bolton were two points behind, but they had a game in hand. They won it and moved a point in front of us. So going into the final game at Blackpool we were third and out of the top two for the first time in 20 matches. We won, but so did Bolton and we were condemned to the play-offs with 89 points, easily enough to win automatic promotion most seasons.

We were drawn against Stockport in the play-offs so, including the Autoglass final, we faced 3 games against them in a couple of weeks. I was ready to play through the pain barrier, but Rudgie decided against using me in the 2 play-off games. However, he told me that if we reached the final, I'd be in the side. We drew one-apiece at Edgley Park and won the second leg, thanks to a single goal from Martin Foyle. So we were on our way to Wembley ... twice! For the Autoglass Cup final on 22 May and the play-off showdown against West Brom nine days later. And there was no way I was going to miss either game.

The town had gone mad when we reached the Autoglass final and we ended up taking something like 20,000 fans with us. Not bad for a club with an average gate of around 7,000. I hired a 52-seater bus to bring my folks and a load of friends down from Yorkshire. Since I was a nipper I'd dreamed of playing at Wembley and now I was going twice in nine days. It was going to be the best nine days of my career and, finally, a chance to find out what success really felt like. Yet I came within a whisker of chucking it all away in a drunken haze.

SWANNY

Three weeks before the Autoglass final, we'd won 1-0 at Plymouth. Houchie was in the travelling squad, but wasn't going to be involved on the Saturday, so the night before the match he went out for a drink with some mates. They met up with a couple of blokes from London in a club and he ended up promising them tickets for the Autoglass final. The whole episode had slipped his mind when, a few days before the final, he got a call from one of these lads saying they'd meet him the night before the game for a drink. He could hand over the tickets then.

I was rooming with Houchie, who wasn't in the side for Wembley, and he asked me if I wanted to come along. Final or no final, I agreed and when they rang to say they'd arrived, we slipped out down the fire escape, jumped into their car and drove off to a nearby boozer. I had a few pangs of conscience as I walked into the pub, but they soon evaporated with the first couple of pints and a game of pool.

We left the pub at around 1am. By prior arrangement, together with a bung of 20 quid apiece, the two night porters had agreed to leave the staff entrance at the back of the hotel open. We slipped in undetected and, if we'd stopped then and there, there wouldn't have been a problem next morning. Instead we hit the complimentary sherry. There was a carafe in each room and guests were invited to have a tipple as an aperitif before their evening meal. Houchie managed to 'borrow' a second carafe so we demolished the first and were well into the second before I finally got my head down at six o'clock.

I failed to make breakfast at 9.30am, but managed to report on time for the brisk morning walk we had to loosen up. I stayed right at the back, but a few of the lads picked up the scent and couldn't believe what I'd been up to. I bumped the pre-match meal as well and had to send out for some mints and bars of chocolate to kill the smell and get a bit of food inside me. The drive down Wembley Way was just a blur. I didn't even see the Twin Towers and, in the dressing room, I nearly fell off the bench when I was putting my boots on. To make matters worse, it was a red-hot day and I was already dehydrated from the booze before we even got going.

I managed to get through the pre-match presentation ceremony and finally the game started. After about 20 minutes, I went up for a header with Kevin Francis, Stockport's 6ft 7in centre-forward, and when I landed, both calves cramped up. I went down. Jim Joyce ran on: 'What's the problem, Swanny?'

'I've got cramp in both calves, but I can't be treated for that after 20 minutes. Rudgie will spot what's going on. So tell him I've gone over on my ankle as I've landed, say I'll be OK.' Then he got a whiff of my breath.

'What *have* you been bloody doing? What's going on?'

I couldn't work out whether he was going to tell Rudgie. If he had, I'd have been hauled off straightaway, collected a massive fine and almost certainly never have played for the club again. But Jim kept quiet. After about half an hour, I started to feel better and got through the game, but I knew the cramps might come back at any moment. We won 2-1 with first-half goals from Paul Kerr and Bernie Slaven, who'd joined us from Middlesbrough just before the transfer deadline at the end of March. And the Man of the Match? Peter Swan.

Most of the players knew I was pissed, but nobody let on to Rudgie. And if he'd spotted anything, he probably had no idea how bad I was. It wasn't as if he didn't know I was a drinker and none of the players said anything afterwards. Why should they? We'd won and there was a win bonus of around £800 waiting for them in their next pay packet. It might have been a different story if we'd lost.

However, there was no way I was going to stage a repeat performance the following week. Vale had reached the semi-final of the FA Cup in 1954, at the time only the second team from outside the top two divisions to do so, but the play-off final was the biggest match in the club's 117-year history. We stayed in the same hotel and this time I was in bed early and up for breakfast, the morning walk and the pre-match meal. I was really buzzing.

Even though we'd done well against Albion in our two league games, we knew it would be tough. They were strong in all departments and they had a big threat up front in the shape of Bob Taylor, who'd been on the staff at Leeds with me. He had 34 league and cup goals to his name. However, including the play-offs and Autoglass final, we'd won 7 of our last 8 games and we fancied our chances.

It was tight and still goalless at half-time, but we'd been the better team. We still were until the hour mark ... when I was sent off for a professional foul on Taylor.

The ball was played over the top for Bob to run on to. Three of us were going for it at the same time – Neil Aspin on the left, Bob in the middle and me on the right. I could see the ball spinning through the air and sensed that when it bounced it would spin away from me towards Neil, but I couldn't be sure. So I committed myself to catching the ball on the half-volley and clearing it away beyond Neil. I went in on the slide, missed the ball and took out Bob instead. As I expected, the ball spun away towards Neil ... but not before Bob had gone down when he appeared to be clean through on goal.

The referee was Roger Milford. He hadn't sent anyone off all season. He did now. A straight red. And I started the longest, loneliest walk of my career. I felt as if I was on a conveyor belt, walking backwards. There were nearly 70,000 people in the ground, something like 40,000 of them supporting West Brom. Most of those fans were at the tunnel end and I had to run the gauntlet of their abuse as I made my way to the dressing room.

What really hurt was the sound of some fans laughing at me. It seemed I was just a joke to them. I wanted to sprint down the tunnel and get away from it all, but I wasn't going to give them the added satisfaction of seeing me run away and managed to keep walking. When I reached the dressing room, I slung my kit on the floor, jumped in a bath and lay there, alone.

Trevor Wood, the reserve keeper, came in to ask if I was OK. What could I say? I knew I'd let my team-mates and the Port Vale supporters down. I was devastated, totally gutted. Trevor handed me a can of Castlemaine XXXX and went back out. I drank the lager, had another and climbed out of the bath. I couldn't hear any sound from above so I hadn't a clue how we were doing. After I got my gear on I walked out of the dressing room with no idea where I was going.

I spotted the team bus at the far end of the tunnel and went and sat on my own at the back. I stayed there for a couple of minutes, then walked back down the tunnel to see what was happening. As I reached the end of the tunnel, the final whistle blew and the huge roar from the West Brom fans told me all I needed to know: we'd lost 3-0.

I went back into the dressing room and sat with my head in my hands until the boys came back in. Nobody said anything, not even Rudgie. I left them to it and went to meet my folks in the players' lounge. They were just as upset as me, probably more. When Bob Taylor came in, I congratulated him and wished him well. We had a bit of a laugh about the sending-off. Or Bob did, anyway.

After what seemed an eternity, it was time to get back on the bus. I joined the queue to climb on board, but instead of making my way to the back, where I always sat, I slumped in a seat right at the front. I didn't feel as though I could face anyone. I'd let them down big-style. It was my decision to make that challenge and it was a decision that had probably cost us promotion.

The bus made slow progress away from Wembley. I just stared out of the window. At one point I realised I was crying. I didn't care. After a while, I was conscious that someone was standing in the aisle next to my seat. I looked up. It was Paul Kerr. He had a bottle of champagne in his hand, one of the bottles we were going to sup to celebrate promotion. 'Here, Swanny, have some of that. And get yourself to the back of the bus where you belong.'

I still felt uneasy, but followed him to the back and gradually the banter started again. I was on the receiving end, but it was all good-natured enough. We used to have a Madness tape on the bus for away trips and a few of us would be up and down in the aisle, doing Madness impressions, on the way home. Why change because we'd lost at Wembley? Kerr put the tape on and some of the lads got up.

The motorway was choc-a-bloc, mainly with coach-loads of West Brom fans, but for some reason, most of them didn't seem to be celebrating when they should have been going wild. Instead it was the Port Vale team coach that was rocking to the sound of Madness. The Albion supporters we passed couldn't believe their eyes. For a party piece, a few bare backsides were waved in their direction as we drove by.

I went to the Three Crowns when we got home, but I wasn't in the mood. Everybody did their best to console me, but I knew I'd let a lot of people down, not least myself. At the time, I was only the third Englishman to be sent off at Wembley, but at least I was following in some illustrious footsteps. The first had been Kevin Keegan, who'd 'walked' after clashing with Billy Bremner during the 1974 Charity Shield game between Leeds and Liverpool. The second was Lee Dixon, the Arsenal and England full-back, who beat me to it by eight weeks when he saw red in an FA Cup semi-final against Spurs. So I knew that the press boys would come looking for me and decided to make myself scarce for a few days. Robbie van der Laan said he'd come along for the ride.

IT COULD BE HEARSE

Our first port of call was Leicester Races. A while earlier, I'd met Nick Cook, the Leicestershire and England cricketer. He was keen on the gee-gees and owned a racehorse himself. So I gave him a call and explained the situation. Nick said his horse was running the following day, so Vanders and I packed a suitcase apiece and set off.

We had a great day out at the Races and, the following day, I rang David Ripley, my old mate from Leeds City Boys days, who was Northants' wicketkeeper by that time. Like Cook, he was only too happy to have us around for a couple of days, so we headed east to the County Ground, Northampton, where they were playing a four-day game against Worcestershire.

On the first day, we divided our time between the members' enclosure and the bar as Northants piled up a big score and reported back for duty early on the second morning after a night out on the town. The game was being sponsored by Carling, so we were tucking into our first pint of the morning when Dave invited us to join in the warm-up.

Now it just so happened that Northants' overseas player that season was Curtly Ambrose, the West Indian paceman who was just about the quickest bowler in the world at the time. Curtly was wandering around with a bat in his hand as I ambled on to the field. 'Come on, Swanny', he said. 'Chuck a few down for me.' I was only wearing shorts and flip flops, but he said that wasn't a problem. So I threw a dozen gentle long hops in his direction. 'Thanks', said Curtly, 'That's fine.' And he handed me the bat. 'I'll just turn my arm over now.'

I'd had a skinful the night before and the first pint of the morning had topped up the level a bit, so I was in no fit state to tackle the world's most dangerous bowler. He gave me half a dozen deliveries and I didn't hit one of them. To be honest, I never even saw them. The only way I knew he'd let one go was when it hit the boundary board behind me.

SWANNY

The following day we moved on to Hull to watch a testimonial game for Gareth Roberts, the Hull City midfield man, and we then headed north to the Lake District. Keith Houchen had his own motor boat moored on Lake Windermere and was having a couple of days up there with some mates. He invited us along and we linked up at a hotel on the shores of the lake.

Straight off, Houchie asked if we fancied doing some water skiing, but there was no way he was dragging us into that. He wouldn't take no for an answer and produced a couple of dry suits. We thought he was taking the piss. We'd heard of wet suits, but *dry* suits? He assured us we could wear these things over our day clothes and, provided all the zips and seals were fastened, we'd stay as dry as a bone.

As we were chatting, a bloke came skiing into the jetty wearing one of the suits, leapt on to dry land and took off his suit. Sure enough, he was completely dry underneath. 'Right, we'll have some of that!' I said, and Vanders and I got kitted up, making sure the zip at the back of the suit was securely fastened.

We weren't going to make a fool of ourselves by trying to ski so instead we hired a couple of those big doughnut tyres and were towed up and down the lake for twenty minutes, banging into one another and having a real laugh. When we returned to dry land, the suits were unzipped and we stepped out totally dry. Houchie's mates had been watching the action and decided to have a go themselves, asking us to zip up their suits.

I looked at Vanders, he looked at me, we nodded in recognition. Instead of fastening the zip right across the back of the suits, we left a couple of inches open before shouting, 'OK, off you go, lads! All zipped up.' The boat set off and the rest of us headed off back to the hotel for a pint. When Houchie's mates hadn't joined us after half an hour or so, I began to feel the first twinges of anxiety.

So, as casually as I could, I asked Mark, Houchie's mate who'd explained how the dry suits worked, what would happen if they weren't zipped up properly. 'Oh, the suit would flood in no time. You'd drop to the bottom like a stone.' I whispered to Vanders, 'God, we might have killed them.' We waited anxiously for the next twenty minutes or so, all the time looking out of the window to see if they were coming through the hotel grounds. Then we spotted them. Their heads and shoulders were completely dry, but from the chest down, they were dripping wet, soaked to the skin.

The next day we headed home. Vanders packed his bags for a summer break and I went into hospital for a hernia operation.

12

LISA

I met Lisa soon after I joined Port Vale. I wouldn't say it was love at first sight, but it wasn't far off. Soon we were seeing one another nearly every day. I told Bex about her from the start.

We got together thanks to Tony and Jill Fagg, our next-door neighbours in Stone. Tony was a dentist and Jill was a nurse at North Staffs Hospital, on the outskirts of Stoke. She worked in the unit treating kids with cystic fibrosis. There was never enough money and she was always trying to organise charity events. She asked if I'd be prepared to help, so one day after training, I met her fund-raising team and I told them I'd do anything I could.

While I was there, I went to talk to some of the youngsters on the ward. Lisa was one of them. She was only eight or nine, a lovely little kid with a gorgeous smile. I chatted to her parents for a while and, as we spoke, it became obvious that Lisa didn't have too long to live.

That really hit me. I didn't have any kids at the time, but I could see what her mam and dad were going through. I felt I had to do something to help both them and Lisa, so I started popping in to see her on a fairly regular basis.

As part of her treatment, she had to have physiotherapy four or five times a day. She would lie on her tummy and a physio, a nurse or one of her parents would slap her up and down her back to bring up the phlegm on her chest. That helped her to breathe more easily.

One day, I was visiting the ward while Lisa was having her physio. I said, 'Do you want me to do that?' Her little face lit up. I asked the nurse if it was OK and she said that as long as her parents were happy, there wouldn't be a problem. The nurse showed me how to cup my hands so I could do the treatment properly and next time I visited, I took my turn as her physio.

I tried to visit every day after that. In fact, I reached the point where I felt guilty if I didn't call in. I couldn't just drive past the hospital on my way for a pint or a game of golf; I felt I had to pop in and make sure Lisa and the others were OK, even if it was only for five minutes or so. When Lisa saw me, she'd call out, 'It's my boyfriend, he's come to see me!'

After I'd been going for a few months, her mam and dad took me to one side. Lisa's last wish was to visit Disneyland, but she wouldn't have been strong enough to fly to America. Instead, her parents wanted to take her to EuroDisney. They didn't have enough money to pay for the trip.

'How much do you need?' I asked.

'About £800. That's for Lisa, us two and a carer. It doesn't sound a lot, but there's no way we can raise it quickly.'

'Leave it with me.' The next day, I walked into the dressing room and called the lads together. 'Can you give me 40 quid apiece tomorrow morning?'

'What for?'

'There's a little girl called Lisa in North Staffs Hospital. She's dying. Her mum and dad want to take her to EuroDisney. It'll cost them £800.'

The following morning, every single player arrived with £40 in cash. Sometimes, trying to coax money out of footballers can be like getting blood out of a stone. They'll claim they already help this charity or that charity, or simply say they don't want to get involved, but not this time. I went straight round to the hospital in the afternoon and handed over the money. Lisa's parents were absolutely made up.

I called in to see Lisa after her trip to Paris and she'd had a fabulous time. She brought me back a little Mickey Mouse as a souvenir. I still have it today. Soon afterwards, I had a call from her mam to say Lisa had died. I went to her funeral the following week.

Lisa has had a tremendous effect on me. She taught me what life is all about. If I felt I was getting nervous in the build-up to a big game, I took a minute or two out to think of Lisa. I said to myself, 'What are you getting all stressed up about? You're fit, you're healthy, you're doing a job you love and you're well paid for it. You've got everything going for you. Not like Lisa.' And I was able to see life and football in perspective.

I've talked about Lisa to my sons George and Harry. And when I do bits of coaching, I always try to get the message across to the players: of course football matters, but it isn't a matter of life and death and anybody who thinks it is should spend some time with kids like Lisa.

I carried on visiting the hospital after Lisa died and inevitably there were some traumatic times. Like the little lad who'd once been the mascot at a Vale game. The church was packed out for his funeral and I was standing outside, listening to the vicar's address. He started talking about how the little fella had loved Port Vale and how his favourite player was Peter Swan. I found it hard to believe that I had brought joy into that little boy's life and my first feeling was guilt. I asked myself why I hadn't started visiting the hospital earlier instead of spending so much time enjoying myself.

And for the rest of my career, at four different clubs, I always found time for visits.

Until I met those kids, I never really appreciated the impact a footballer can have on a youngster's life. Players should never turn a blind eye to it. They don't realise what joy they can give by just popping in, saying hello and spending a few minutes with children who are having a bad time. That's all it takes, a few minutes. I always used to hammer on about it to my team-mates.

Perhaps it's understandable that players at smaller clubs don't see themselves as stars compared with the Premier League millionaires, but they are big names and heroes to youngsters who support those clubs and they should do everything they can to help little kids who haven't got a lot going for them.

I'd been disappointed to miss out on promotion and had been desperately upset about letting everyone down after being sent off at Wembley, but thanks to Lisa and the other kids I was able to put it into perspective. And I was particularly moved by a letter I received from a Vale fan soon after the Wembley defeat. It was from Peter Haynes of Hanley, who wrote:

Dear Peter,

It is ironic that two of the players rated most highly for their character, generosity of spirit and true sportsmanship by everyone who has had the good fortune to know them even slightly should share the unenviable distinction of being sent off at Wembley ... you and Kevin Keegan.

I believe that you placed your entire career in jeopardy by playing with your injury throughout the Autoglass final and again, eight days later, in the play-offs, but that in itself says everything about you.

You have given more to Port Vale than anyone should expect from any player. You have lived up to the standards set by some of the great players from the past – players like Tommy Cheadle, the late Stan Turner and Reg Potts, who were members of the side beaten by West Brom in the semi-final of the FA Cup at Aston Villa in the 1950s.

Thank you for what you have done for football here in North Staffordshire, but thank you even more for what you do for the unfortunate children that you never let down.

Have a good rest and return again next season to bring pleasure and excitement into so many lives in your own unique way.

Sincerely,
Peter Haynes

No wonder I was so eager for the new season to start! But, for the second year running, my build-up wasn't ideal. I hadn't been able to have the double hernia op until June because of the play-off final, so I was a bit behind the game in pre-season. And once again I was going to miss the first couple of weeks through suspension.

It was so frustrating. I desperately wanted to give something back after being sent off at Wembley. To the players and the fans. Instead, I was going to miss the first three games. And, for just about the only time in my career, I let my frustrations boil over in training. I lined up with the reserves in one of our last practice matches. I was marking Bernie Slaven. Just for a bit of fun, I tripped him up as he went past me. Normally we'd all have had a laugh about it, but this time Rudgie didn't see the funny side.

He turned on me: 'That's why we didn't get promoted; because you took a stupid decision like that.' It was the first time he'd referred to the Wembley red card. I thought it was history by then and, for some reason, I lost it. Next time round, I really clattered Bernie, we squared up and I threw a punch. He took a kick at me and we had to be pulled apart. We used to sit next to one another in the dressing room and normally enjoyed a fair bit of banter, but not on that day. We didn't say a word to each other and a couple of days passed before we cleared the air.

These things happen at every club and are usually kept in-house, but instead word leaked out and before long there was a story going round town that we'd had a punch-up because I was having a fling with Bernie's missus. A fling? I'd never even met her.

I told Bex straightaway. She came to the first home game and, afterwards, Bernie took her to one side. He told her his wife hadn't been down from Middlesbrough since he'd signed for Vale late the previous season. I've no idea who started the story; presumably it was just someone hearing about the dust-up, putting two and two together and making five.

As it happened I always got on well with Bernie, although I never rated his taste in aftershave. He used to slap on some stuff called Joop and it was bloody awful. If you followed the scent around the club you'd eventually find Bernie. But he was a strong character and with 119 goals in the bank in over 300 appearances for Middlesbrough – not to mention 7 Irish caps – he gave us a bit extra up front.

We had a good squad. Paul Musselwhite was in goal with Neil Aspin, me and Dean Glover at the back. Allen Tankard, Kevin Kent, Darren Hughes, Dean Stokes and John Jeffers were in contention for places on the flanks. In central midfield Rudgie could choose from Ian Taylor, Robbie Van der Laan, Paul Kerr and Andy Porter. And Martin Foyle, Bernie and Nicky Cross gave us plenty of fire power up front. As the season developed, the gaffer brought in players like Joe Allon from Newcastle and David Lowe from Leicester to provide a few more goals.

It was probably the best team I played in. We were solid at the back, but we could really play going forward. All the midfield players were creative and we caused real problems. And even though there had been one or two changes in personnel, there was still a tremendous spirit right through the squad. And some larger-than-life characters. Like Robbie Van der Laan.

Rudgie had signed him from FC Wageningen in Holland in 1991. From Vale, he went on to have a few years in the top flight with Derby and he later played for Barnsley. His dad used to fly over from Holland for just about all our games.

Vanders had long, blond hair, drove around in a flash Italian sportscar and was known in all the local clubs. He was my regular drinking partner and sometimes we'd struggle to make the weight at the checks every Monday and Friday. We all had to troop into the physio's room on a Monday morning and stand on the scales. We were fined if we'd put on weight over the weekend.

Jim Joyce used those old-fashioned scales with a balance on the top. The trick was for one of us to distract him so he'd fail to notice that the player on the scales was only standing on one leg. Or immediately after Vanders had been weighed, I'd start talking to Jim before he had time to make a note of the weight. By the time we finished chatting, Vanders would be long gone, Jim had forgotten his weight and I'd supply him with the incorrect info. Easy.

There was a fancy hotel near the ground that had its own health club with a steam room. We were both members and sometimes we'd stop off on the way into training on a Monday morning and sit in the steam room for half an hour to lose some weight. Either that or we'd turn up early at the ground and go straight into the sauna to sweat off a few pounds. One morning, Vanders set a new all-comers record by losing 5lb. That must have been a hell of a weekend!

One night Vanders and I were out in a club. A couple of girls started taking the piss, claiming they were Stoke fans. We took no notice and, after a while, they took the hint and turned away. But someone had spilt a drink on the bar earlier and Vanders decided it was time for us to give them a bit of their own medicine. He started flicking the spilt beer at the girls' backs.

It didn't do their dresses any favours and eventually they stalked out of the club. When they'd gone, someone told us one of the girls was Rudgie's daughter. We thought he was winding us up, but after training the next day, Rudgie came into the dressing room and said, 'Right, day off tomorrow lads – except for Swanny and Vanders. Extra training for you two.' So it had been his daughter after all.

Andy Porter was another good man to have around. We called him 'Goober' for some reason. He was daft as a brush. Once, before a game at Grimsby, we were all lined up ready for the kick-off when the ref noticed we had only 10 men. No Andy Porter. We waited for half a minute or so until he came running out of the tunnel. He'd let out a fart during the pre-match kick-in, got more than he bargained for and dashed off to change his shorts. We were playing in all-white!

He used to spend most of the game laughing and joking. If someone made a bad pass or miskicked, he'd see the funny side of it. In one game at Stockport, a cross came in from our left and I flicked it on for Neil Aspin, who was on the right-hand corner of the box. It was on his left foot, not the strongest in the world. As he lined up the shot, his right foot knocked the ball forward and when the swinger came down, he missed it altogether. I started laughing, so did Goober and we were laughing all the way back to our own goal as Stockport counter-attacked. They ended up hitting the bar with Goober and I in stitches.

I returned from suspension for the trip to Plymouth at the end of August and missed only 4 more matches all season. There was a special atmosphere running through the club from the start; it

OFF YOU GO!

PORT VALE defender Peter Swan (5) turns away in despair as Bristol referee Roger Milford brandishes the red card. *Picture: PAUL WEBB*

I've had the honour of playing at Wembley twice in my career. Twice in nine days in fact! First in the 1993 Autoglass Trophy final against Stockport (*above*), then, again in the Division Two play-off final against West Brom (*below*). I was the third Englishman to ever be sent off at Wembley – to this day it is one of the biggest regrets of my career.

© *Stoke Sentinel*

Saluting Bernie Slaven's second goal for Port Vale against Cardiff, 6 September 1993.

Above: At home with Bex and George.

Below: Giving the thumbs up at a press conference with Plymouth boss Peter Shilton. As the club's record signing at £300,000, I was big news.

© Dave Rowntree

Inset: I didn't have an easy time at Plymouth and I didn't have many mates. But there was one fan, a guy called Tom Brown, who did everything he could to make me feel welcome. Here I am with his young lad, Alistair, and baby George.

Above: Starting afresh at Burnley, 1995. I am pictured here signing injured midfielder Steve Thompson's plaster alongside (*left to right*): Jamie Hoyland, Mark Winstanley and keeper Wayne Russell.

© Lancashire Telegraph

Below left: Another collision. This time in a game against Charlton not long after I joined Bury in the summer of 1997.

© Andrew Yates/ MEN Syndication

Below right: Mean machine. Playing a bouncer in *Off the Bone*, a film made in and around Burnley.

Back at Burnley. I am pictured here with my two boys, George and Harry, at Turf Moor.

Above: In my last season as a pro, at York, we played Manchester United in a pre-season game. Here you can see me challenging England midfield man Paul Scholes. © *York Evening Press*

Left: With Helen Chamberlain, my good pal and presenter of Sky One's *Soccer AM*.

Below right: Doing a spot of commentating for Radio Humberside with Mike White (*left*) and my great mate David Burns.

Above: Nearly 30 years on and I still can't resist a bit of cross-dressing! Here you can see me out on the lash in Magaluf with two of the lads from New Wheel FC (*from left to right*): Dave North, Mark Bird and me.

Below: This time it's a cowboy outfit, a Christmas bash in Blackpool and the YMCA with New Wheel mates Gavin Ansley, Dean Largent and Ian McKenzie.

With my darling wife Bex. Getting married to her is still the best thing I ever did.

seemed everyone wanted to put the record straight after the previous season's near-miss.

Sometimes a team collapses after losing a play-off final and struggles the following season. We didn't. We were never going to. In fact, we knew we'd go up. We didn't have the best of starts, with just 1 win from the first 7 games, but we strung 5 successive wins together after that and lost just 4 out of 33 matches between 14 September and 19 April. We reached the fourth round of the FA Cup, going out to Wolves after beating Southampton, then in the top flight, in a third-round replay.

It may be an old cliché that winning is a habit, but it's true. Two years earlier, when we were relegated, we sensed that even if we played well, we might lose. This time we were confident we'd win, even if we were below our best, and we went into our last 5 games knowing that if we won them all, we'd be promoted. We did. We beat York 2-1 at home, won 1-0 at Swansea and won our last home game 3-0 against Exeter.

Just like Bolton a year earlier, we had a game in hand on Plymouth and Stockport, our two main rivals for the second promotion slot behind long-term leaders Reading. That game was at Cardiff on the final Tuesday of the season. We won 3-1 to go into second place above Plymouth and we set off for our final match at Brighton determined not to blow it and face the play-offs once again.

Rudgie always liked us to stay in a nice hotel and this time he'd excelled himself. There was even a pianist playing a grand piano in the lounge as we went through for our evening meal. Nobody else took much notice of him, but after a while I spotted that even when he had a break, the piano music continued on automatic pilot. He'd obviously pressed a switch under the keyboard and then wandered off for a pint.

We were coming to the end of our meal, so I told the lads I was going for a pee and I'd see them in the lounge. I strolled across to the piano, sat on the stool and pretended to play. After a couple of minutes a few of the boys came out of the restaurant and stopped dead in their tracks at the sight of Swanny tinkling the ivories in the corner.

One of them turned back into the restaurant and shouted, 'Hey, come and look at Swanny! You're not going to believe this.' The first to appear was Rudgie, who must have been out of his chair like a flash and was clearly fearing the worst. The rest of the lads soon followed and they all stood in disbelief. I gave them two more numbers from my 'repertoire', stood up, bowed and milked the applause. As I walked across to join them in the lounge, the piano chimed up again ...

The incident summed up how relaxed we all were about the most important game of our season. And the decider turned out to be a stroll. Brighton were mid-table with nothing to play for and we were in control from the kick-off. Martin Foyle and Dean Glover gave us a two-goal lead at half-time and we never looked like losing. And when we were 3-1 up with just a few minutes left, I was finally granted my wish of being allowed to take a free-kick. I'd been chipping away all season that I should be given a chance with a direct free-kick. The only problem was that this one was 40 yards out!

We celebrated with our fans afterwards and when we got back to the dressing room, someone asked how Plymouth had got on at Hartlepool. They'd won 8-1. So yes, we'd needed that win. There was a big plunge bath in the corner and it wasn't long before everyone was in there, Rudgie included. Stan, our kit man, was given an early bath, too, but we had to be careful with him as he was responsible for the booze on the journey home.

After a four-hour drive, the coach pulled up outside The Place, a club in Hanley. Rudgie joined us for a couple of drinks and then left us to it. We were having a laugh at the bar when Lisa, Robbie Van der Laan's ex-girlfriend, came over and asked me for a dance.

We tripped the light fantastic for a few minutes and we'd just rejoined the lads when, out of the corner of my eye, I spotted her new boyfriend heading in our direction. Clearly he was not a happy man. He didn't waste time with words, he just head-butted me. I'd seen it coming and was moving away so he didn't make much of a contact, but as I stepped back, my knee caught the edge of a settee and I collapsed in a heap amid the cushions. As I lay there, the music chimed up: 'There may be trouble ahead, but while there's music and moonlight and love and romance ... let's face the music and dance.'

There was trouble ahead all right. The lads weighed in on my behalf and a free-for-all kicked off in a big way. The bouncers arrived and started chucking people out left, right and centre. I ended up with a fat lip and a split nose and explanations to make to Bex and Mam and Dad, who'd made the trip south to Brighton to see us clinch promotion.

Yet even though Vale were back in the old Second Division, I knew I wouldn't be going there with them. Towards the end of 1993, I'd started making noises about a new contract. When I'd signed over two years earlier, I was on top money. Since then new players had come in who were earning more, so I believed I had a reasonable argument.

But talk of a new contract was just a smokescreen really. I'd had three happy years at Port Vale, but sentiment didn't come into it. I needed a new start, a new challenge, a new car, a new salary and a new signing-on fee. Rudgie knew the score and when I told him I wanted to talk about a deal, he just said, 'If you want to leave, you can go.' He'd probably had enough hassle from me by that stage. Another three years and he'd have had no hair left at all, so I was transfer-listed at the end of October.

SWANNY

The previous season I'd had a tip-off that Newcastle were interested in me. They were in the old Second Division at the time, but were really flying towards promotion under Kevin Keegan. But I had 18 months left to run at that stage and Rudgie didn't want to know. Leicester were also sniffing around, but again it was 'no go' from the gaffer.

But once I was listed, it was open season. West Brom were first in with a bid of £250,000, which Vale turned down. They wanted their £300,000 back. I heard that Leicester also made another enquiry, but nothing happened and I just got my head down and helped Vale towards Division One.

Towards the end of the season, though, things started to move again with four clubs said to be interested: Burnley, Bolton, Notts County and Plymouth. Bolton and Notts County were in the First Division while the other two were in Division Two, but I didn't mind which division I played in. For me the move was going to be about money.

Two of us at Vale would be out of contract when the season ended, me and Ian Taylor. Ian was another example of a player Rudgie had picked up for nothing and was one day going to sell on for a lot of money. He'd scored 13 goals from midfield in 42 games and the big clubs had been having a look at him all season. Vale rated him at £2m. That seemed a lot to me, although he was obviously going to make the club a fair bit of brass eventually.

Ian was on £250 a week and, one day, when we were in the dressing room together, he said, 'They've offered me a new contract. I'm going to sign it.'

'How much?'

'They'll double what I'm on now.'

'Don't sign.'

'Why not?'

'Look, it says in the papers that Sheffield Wednesday want you.

LISA

If you go there, or to any Premiership club, you'll be on 1,500 or two grand a week. If you sign here, you'll be tied to your new contract and you won't be able to get out of it. Talk to the PFA, but don't sign.'

'I've no choice. I'm struggling for money. If I sign, I'll be OK.'

'Look, if you're short of money, I've got a bit on one side. I'll lend you some until you get away.'

So he called in the PFA and a clause was inserted in his new contract that if a club came in with a bid of £1m or more, he'd be allowed to leave. Soon afterwards, he gave me a call. He'd signed for Wednesday and wanted to thank me for helping him out.

I was chuffed to bits for him and also delighted he'd come to me for advice. He knew he could talk to me in confidence and that our conversation would go no further. That kind of respect from my fellow professionals was always important. Unfortunately, my own move was proving far less straightforward.

13

GHOSTBUSTER

I seemed no nearer a move by the time we reported back for pre-season in July. There was still talk of interest from Notts County, Bolton, Burnley and Plymouth, but none of them had agreed a fee with Vale. Nowadays, because of the 1996 Bosman ruling, I would have been free to walk away to the club of my choice, but that didn't apply then.

So I threatened to stay away. I was out of contract and I believed Vale were deliberately stalling by holding out for a fee of £350,000. In the end, I reported for pre-season as usual, but decided to call in our regional PFA rep, Vince O'Keefe.

Vince wanted to bring all the parties together, but I said I wasn't having that; all I wanted was a move. There were a few of the lads in the dressing room and they dived for cover as I grabbed a sweeping brush and started swinging it around my head. I said to Vince, 'Where's that bald-headed bastard Rudge? You're the PFA man, go and find him and get this sorted!' The lads were killing themselves. The influence of the union paid off. The following week I talked to Burnley and Notts County.

As our first baby was nearly due, Bex and I had more or less

159

decided to stay up north and Burnley were starting to look like favourites. While we were still thinking things over, I decided to go to the pictures with a mate. As I was walking out of the front door, I called back to the missus, 'Give us a shout if anyone rings.' She rang when I was on my way home.

'You've had a call from Peter Shilton.'

'Where's he?'

'Plymouth.'

'Plymouth? We're not going there.'

We talked it through when I got home. Even though I was more or less committed to Burnley, we decided that I'd speak to Shilts. I'd ask for a £70,000 signing-on fee and more than Burnley were offering. He'd obviously say no, but at least he couldn't claim I'd snubbed him. He rang the following morning. I told him what I wanted.

'Give me a couple of minutes,' he said. 'I'll ring you back.' Five minutes later, he called and said, 'OK, we'll do that.'

I thought, 'Fucking hell, what have I done?' I looked at the missus and said, 'Sorry, love, we'll have to go.'

As she was only about six weeks away from having the baby, I went down with my dad to have a look around and sort out the contract before signing. It seemed a lovely place. John McGovern, Shilton's No.2, took us out for a meal that night and the following morning I went to Home Park for the signing. It was going to be staged at a press conference.

I couldn't believe it when I walked into the room. It was packed with television crews, radio reporters and newspapermen. All that lot for me? I wasn't a big-name player, but I hadn't appreciated that, in football terms, Plymouth is pretty isolated and the club has a high profile in its catchment area. As the club's record signing at £300,000, I was big news.

The press conference started and the cameras rolled as I went to sign the contract. Problem. We'd agreed the signing-on fee should be paid over two years; the contract in front of me divided it over three.

So I turned to Dan McCauley, the chairman, and said, 'I can't sign this. We agreed two years, not three.'

He told me not to worry and said I should sign it then. We'd sort everything out later.

'No chance. I'm not signing that. Come on, Dad, we're off.'

As I stood up, the pressmen started asking what was going on and, for a while, there was total chaos. Outside in the corridor, McCauley and Shilton told me to stay where I was. They said they'd go and get the contract re-printed and come straight back. Eventually, we returned to the conference with the new contract, but I sensed they were gutted that I'd spotted the mistake. It wasn't exactly the best of starts for me, either. I believed they'd tried to pull the wool over my eyes from day one.

But I signed, talked to the press and posed for pictures. Then I said to Dad, 'Right, job done. Let's go.' I was delighted. OK, I didn't want to be down there, but the money was good and that's all I was interested in. I could put up with anything for two years. Or so I thought.

The first issue was what to do about Bex and the baby. Did she want to stay in Stoke and have the baby there, with me travelling up and down whenever I could? Or did she want to come down to Plymouth? We opted for Plymouth and I started house-hunting. First off, Shilts took me to see this massive place and said the club would pay the rent as part of the re-location package. Five bedrooms, indoor pool, gymnasium, all open plan, electric gates, everything.

Shilts lived a few doors away and said it would be ideal. I thought so, too ... but in my case, I was thinking in terms of parties. It would have been perfect for some great nights when the lads from Stone came down. I rang the missus and said, 'I've found this fantastic place, it's got everything, even a bloody gym! Come down at the weekend and have a look.' I was sure I'd cracked it.

Instead, Bex walked through the front door, took one look at the place and said, 'No chance. This isn't a home, it's far too big. There's no way I'd be comfortable here when you were away.'

So she went back to Stoke, I went back to the drawing board and the clock was still ticking towards the arrival of the baby. I spent every night looking at houses until eventually I found what we were looking for. A three-bed detached in Widewell Road, Roborough, on the outskirts of the town. It was in a nice little cul-de-sac and had a massive garden, which was perfect for both us and the dog. This time Bex said yes.

While she was down there, we made a hospital appointment for her to see a doctor to make sure everything was OK with the baby. We handed over all her notes from the hospital in Stoke. However, we were wasting our time: the doctor was foreign and didn't seem to understand a word of English. We tried to explain she'd had all the tests and that the baby was now due in three weeks. We pointed at the date on a chart.

But after examining her, he shook his head and pointed at another date two weeks later. I went out and found a nurse and said, 'Look, the doctor doesn't understand what we're saying. Can you get through to him for us?' She couldn't make much progress either, so eventually I lost the plot and said to Bex, 'Come on, love. We're off.'

I called the club, explained the situation and asked if we could see the club doctor. He agreed with the dates from Stoke, but we still couldn't convince the hospital. In the end, Bex was three weeks overdue when George was eventually born on 12 September. He weighed in at 10lb 2oz, but he had an infection and spent the first 10 days of his life in a special care unit. Bex needed 22 stitches, internal and external. She also picked up an infection and had to stay in hospital for 10 days. It was a shambles.

GHOSTBUSTER

It was also a poor way to start our new life. And things weren't made any easier by the reception I received from some of my new team-mates. There were problems both on and off the field and the team made a disastrous start. We lost 5 of our first 7 games and drew the other 2. I was coming in for a load of abuse from the fans and although I could handle that kind of thing during games, it soon developed a more sinister side away from Home Park.

When I signed I was given a club car, a red Cavalier with my name on the side, and it soon became a target for my growing band of enemies among the supporters. Twice, soon after George was born, Bex came home in tears and said she'd been almost forced off the road when a van cut across her. I'd had kids chucking stones at the car on my way to training and, a couple of times, I came out of the pub to find that my tyres had been slashed.

I wasn't taking any chances with the safety of Bex and George so I bought some red masking tape and covered over my name on the door panel. I don't suppose the sponsors were too pleased, but that wasn't my problem.

And things took a turn for the worse in early October when Zee, our Great Dane, died. She was a hell of a big dog, weighing in at around 13st. Or she should have. But soon after we arrived in Plymouth, she started losing weight big-style. I took her to the vet, who said she had become diabetic and that we would need to give her a daily insulin injection.

He injected her with 10 units of insulin and said we'd build up the doses until we got the balance right. I took her back the following day, a Friday, and learned how to give her the injection myself, 12 units this time. As Saturday was match day, Bex took her the third time and came back saying she'd had to give her 2 doses.

I rang the vet to find out why and he said, 'Bring her straight back, we've given her 140 units instead of 14.' I had to set off for the game against Wycombe Wanderers so Bex took her back. The vet said he'd leave her on a drip overnight. He assured us that everything would be OK. But I was a worried man as I set off for Home Park, Wycombe Wanderers, my unfriendly team-mates and around 6,000 abusive fans.

I was a bloody sight more worried an hour into the match when I collected a broken cheekbone. I'd gone up for a header, took a whack in the face and heard the bone crack. I could feel a hole in my face. Paul Sumner, the physio, came on and I told him what had happened. 'No,' he said. 'You're OK.'

I stuck my finger in the hole and said, 'What the fuck do you think this is, then?' He just started asking me silly questions to see if I was concussed. That was the least of my worries. I went back for 20 minutes before the referee stopped the game. He looked at my face and said, 'Are you all right?' By this time, I couldn't put my finger in the hole anymore because my face was so swollen. I told the ref I'd be OK, finished the game, came off the field and asked to see the club doctor. He took one look and sent me straight to hospital. My cheekbone was broken in three places and I needed an operation straightaway.

So there we were, in a strange town, George's birth had been a nightmare, we had a dog on a drip at the vet's and me in hospital waiting for an operation to repair a smashed cheekbone. Thank God Bex's mam and dad were on their way down to give us a helping hand.

I had the operation on the Sunday morning, about the same time as the in-laws were on their way to collect Zee from the vet. They got her home: she walked through the door, collapsed and dropped dead. I was still groggy after the op when they told me, but alert enough to say we'd have to ask for a post mortem. So she was sent to another vet, no doubt a pal of the first one, who said she'd had a weak heart. Believe that and you'll believe anything.

We'd only been there a few weeks and already I was having serious misgivings about Bex and George being around. I said,

'Come on, let's piss off back up north and I'll commute for training and matches.' But Bex wanted to stick it out for a while and stay together as a family. So I agreed. Little did we know our real nightmare was only just beginning.

It all seemed innocent enough to start with. One of us would wake up in the middle of the night and notice the lights were on downstairs. At first, I assumed we'd left them on by mistake and go down and turn them off. Sometimes we'd be woken by voices downstairs. I'd find the telly switched on, even though I was certain I'd turned it off last thing. So I started unplugging the telly before we went to bed.

That worked for a while, but then the voices started again and I'd go down to find the plug back in the socket and the telly switched on. Once we went for a night out, turned the lights off and drew the curtains closed when we went out. We came back to discover the lights on and the curtains wide open.

Sometimes we'd find an ornament had fallen off a shelf or a table and smashed. Or we'd be sitting watching the telly and hear footsteps upstairs. We even heard the sound of our dog running around. Once, when we were having a cup of tea in the lounge, Bex asked if I wanted a KitKat, Zee's favourite. The second she said the word KitKat, we heard the sound of a dog running down the stairs. We looked at each other and ran to the stairs to see what was going on. And there, on the landing window that she'd cleaned not so long before, was the print of a dog's nose; *our* dog's nose.

'I thought you'd cleaned the windows,' I said.

'I did.'

Then one morning I went down to make a cup of tea and discovered that the electric kettle had come on in the night and burnt itself out. We called in two electricians to check all the wiring right through the house and they both said everything was OK.

I'd never been into all that poltergeist stuff, but believe me, we were shit scared by what was going on. We couldn't work it out at all. The missus and I have never been as close in bed – holding on tight in case something supernatural happened!

It wasn't every day, perhaps just once or twice a week. Then one day, when I was chatting to Marie, our next-door neighbour, I mentioned what was going on. She said she had a friend who was into the supernatural and claimed to have exorcised a few evil spirits. So I asked if she could come round and explain what was happening.

As soon as the exorcist walked through the front door she started laughing. 'Oh yes, there's something here, I could feel it straightaway, but it won't harm you.'

'Won't harm us?' I replied. 'It's already broken half the ornaments, the telly comes on when we've turned it off, so do the lights, we've heard our dead dog running downstairs and we're scared shitless. Hasn't it done enough bloody harm already?' But she wouldn't perform an exorcism because she said the ghost was friendly.

In the end, we decided Bex and George would stick it out until Christmas and go back home before New Year. 'Look,' I said, 'there's too much going on down here; the players, the fans, drivers trying to ram us off the road, the dog and now this. We'll never be right here.' So they left, but the weird happenings didn't end there.

After they'd gone I used to divide my time between Plymouth and Stoke and spent all my weekends back home. Martin Hodge, our keeper who'd also signed in the summer, had been staying in a hotel. Once, when his partner was coming down from the north to visit, I said they could stay in the house for a couple of nights while I was away.

He picked her up at the station, drove to the house, unloaded their bags and they went out for a meal. They left all the lights and the telly switched on. When they got back, the place was in darkness, the telly turned off and the curtains shut. Hodge told his girlfriend the background and they didn't hang around.

GHOSTBUSTER

As Bex had taken most of our personal belongings back home, I put a camp bed in the front room and more or less lived downstairs. I didn't really fancy that bedroom on my own. One of the things they'd left behind was a little sponge ball that George used to play with at bath-time. One afternoon when I came in after training, I spotted the ball on the landing floor. I gave it a kick as I walked by and it hit a picture of Zee that we'd put on the wall after she died.

At that instant, there was a smash downstairs. I ran down to see what had happened – I reckoned some pillock had put the window through – and there on the floor in smithereens was our Royal Doulton figurine of a Great Dane. There were pieces all over the place. I scraped them all together, put them on a table and double-checked there were none left lying around. I rang the missus to tell her what had happened, said I'd see if it could be repaired and went out for the afternoon. When I got back, there were two pieces of the figurine, a leg and the tail, lying on the carpet. There was no way I could have missed them when I was clearing up.

That turned out to be the last weird experience because I didn't spend much time in that house after Bex and George left. We later learned that, a few years earlier, a young girl had died in the house, in George's bedroom. I wouldn't even begin to try and explain what had been going on. Perhaps the ghost or whatever was trying to tell us we weren't welcome in Plymouth because we heard later that the people who moved in after us hadn't experienced the same thing.

So I became a football commuter. It was 240 miles each way from Stoke to Plymouth and I did the journey three times a week. I drove home after the match on a Saturday; then set off back at 5.30am on the Monday morning. I stayed in Plymouth on Monday night, then went back home straight after training on Tuesday. We usually had Wednesday off, so it was back to the 5.30am start on Thursday morning, stay over Thursday and Friday nights and then home again on Saturday evening. Sometimes, just so I knew who was boss, I'd report to the training ground and one of the coaches would say, 'No training today, lads. We'll just take it easy and have a bath.' So I'd travelled nearly 250 miles for a soak.

The first time I did the trip was on 31 December. We had a game on New Year's Day, so I set off late the previous evening. There only seemed to be one other car on the road and for 60 or 70 miles, we kept passing one another. I thought to myself, 'What's that sad bastard doing on his own on the M5 on New Year's Eve?' And then I realised he must be thinking the same about me. Just after midnight, he pulled alongside, we slowed right down, wished one another a Happy New Year and then pissed off on our separate ways.

Commuting became a regular part of my life, but things started to go downhill for me on the days when I stayed in Plymouth on my own. I began going out on the piss straight after training. It just became a habit, a way to beat the boredom, I suppose. Once, when a televised snooker tournament was taking place at The Pavilions, Plymouth's major arts and entertainment venue, I got some tickets through Willie Thorne for the television hospitality unit. He was a top player in those days and knew Martin Hodge from his time at Leicester, where Willie lived. I had a few beers, took my seat on the front row ... and fell asleep.

The camera zoomed in and the commentators made a few jokes about me being riveted by the action on the green baize. My auntie Doreen was watching the telly back home in Leeds and rang on my mobile, which was on silent mode in my pocket. The vibration woke me up and I waited until the end of the frame before calling back. She wasn't impressed by my behaviour.

Neither was I. But so what? When I wasn't doing my commuter runs, there was nowt else to do but train in the morning and then go out boozing. I'd have two, sometimes three, bottles of wine, go home for a kip, then out to a casino or a nightclub. When I'd had enough, I'd get a taxi back and collapse on the camp bed. I'd train the next morning and, if I wasn't hitting the road to Stoke, I'd hit the bottle instead. On the day before a game, I wouldn't go out. I'd have a couple of bottles in the house ... and a romantic meal for one.

I tried never to drink and drive but once I did and nearly killed myself. I'd been in a bar and probably had the best part of two bottles of red wine when a fan came up and started giving me hassle. I wasn't having any of it, so I staggered into the car park and clambered into the car. I knew I shouldn't be anywhere near a steering wheel, but thought I'd just move the car round the corner and then get a taxi home.

The car park was overlooking the sea and I'd parked facing forward in the last space before the barrier wall became a chain fence. I selected first instead of reverse. The car jolted forward and crashed into the wall. If I'd parked in front of the fence instead of the wall, I'd have been over the top and history.

I even received a call from The Samaritans. I was in the club office collecting my abusive mail when one of the receptionists said there was a call for me. There was a woman on the other end of the line. She explained that she was a Samaritan and had been told I might need help. Did I want to talk? I assumed it was someone from up north who'd heard I was having a bad time and was trying to take the piss. I started laughing, but she was deadly serious. I politely declined the offer – I hadn't reached that stage yet.

In fact, two things kept me from hitting rock bottom: my trips home each week and an ex-paratrooper called Tom Brown. Tom and his wife Brenda lived across the road and they were just about the only neighbours who talked to us on a regular basis. He was a Plymouth fan and knew what most of the supporters thought about me, but he was prepared to give me the benefit of the doubt.

He was in his fifties and did a lot of charity work. He and Brenda had two kids, a daughter Tammy, who had left home, and a son, Alistair, who was about ten. Tom and I would go for a pint sometimes and he was just about the only person I could confide in. With the missus up north, I needed someone I could talk to who understood what I was going through. He was always prepared to listen.

He tried to do his best for me and used to defend me when Plymouth fans were having a go. In the end I was worried for his sake. I said, 'Look, Tom. I'll be here today, gone tomorrow. Don't lose friends because of me.' But he continued to fight my corner.

He and Brenda knew I was going home to an empty house, but they didn't realise the state I was in and that I was sleeping on a camp bed in an empty room. When Tom found out, he said, 'You can't carry on like this. Come and live with us.' And even though the club were still paying the rent on the house, I moved in with him. I knew I couldn't really handle things on my own any more. They both went out of their way to help. Brenda would cook my special pre-match meals and I moved into Tammy's old bedroom. That was my own space. Tom was a lovely bloke. He and his missus were just about the only people in the whole of Plymouth who'd made me feel welcome. I'm still in touch with them today.

It was a dreadful time. The move should have meant a new start with a new-baby. And who knows, if things had worked out, we might even have settled in the south-west. But instead it was one trial after another and the most difficult time of my life. Perhaps, if things had been working out at the football club, it might have been a different story. Maybe I would have been able to handle things better. But instead, down at Home Park, life was almost as bad.

14

I'M AN ALIEN

When I signed for Plymouth on 20 July 1994, Port Vale had just been promoted to the old Division One. Plymouth had missed out. They'd finished third, three points behind Vale, and then lost to Burnley in the play-off semi-finals.

In the game against Plymouth at Vale Park, I made a last-ditch goalmouth tackle to prevent a goal. Vale won 2-1. Just before I joined Plymouth, one of the local television stations showed a clip of my tackle. The presenter pointed out that if it hadn't been for Peter Swan, Plymouth rather than Port Vale could have been promoted.

That went down like a lead balloon with supporters. And when my name was announced in the line-up for Plymouth's first pre-season friendly, some fans started booing. As I was walking down the tunnel after the warm-up, a couple of kids spat at me. I couldn't work it out, until someone told me about the television clip of the Vale game.

To make matters worse, Peter Shilton took the captaincy off Steve Castle, a big favourite with the fans, and gave it to the new boy. And I soon discovered there was a strong clique in the dressing room, mainly southern players, who resented this big, brash northerner coming in as the club's record signing. Shilts had boosted me up by saying I would be the difference between missing out last season and winning promotion this time. That didn't go down well with some of my new team-mates. There was an atmosphere right from the start.

I decided to attack it head on and on the bus back from a pre-season game, I asked if anyone fancied going out for a beer when we got back to Plymouth. They all started to fidget and found something hugely interesting to gaze at through the window. Eventually, one of them said, 'No, we don't bother going for a drink, we just get off home.'

Fair enough. I managed to persuade Mark Edworthy, who was a young kid and not part of the clique, to stop for one instead. We found a pub near the ground, walked into the bar and there, standing in the corner, were ten or more of the Plymouth players, drinking and laughing. I clocked them all, had a beer with Mark and went home.

Not all the players were involved. Martin Hodge, who'd started his career in Plymouth before going off to play in goal for 9 clubs at all levels, joined at the same time as me. He kept himself to himself, but I got on well with him. He was a teetotaller, but even so, we'd pop out sometimes and put the world to rights. Steve McCall, the former Ipswich midfield player who became caretaker-manager later in the season, also got on with his own routine and wasn't part of any particular group.

At the start of the season, Darren Bradshaw came down on loan from Sheffield United. He stayed at our place and soon afterwards, Mick Quinn, who'd scored a shedful of goals for 6 clubs and earned legendary status on Tyneside, also arrived on loan from Newcastle. He stayed with us, too, although he was only around for a few games. I got on OK with Mark Patterson, another Yorkshireman, who could see what was going on, but my mates at the club were few and far between, and that pub incident confirmed what was going on.

I'M AN ALIEN

The message was reinforced during a practice match between the first team and the reserves. One of their lads came in for a challenge and, just before I made the tackle, I heard one of my team-mates shout, 'Break his fucking legs!' I thought it was Alan Nicholls, the goalkeeper, who was killed in a motorbike accident in 1995. I turned round and pinned him to one of the posts, but the rest of the players came in quickly and pulled me off. They said it wasn't Nicholls. Maybe not, but someone shouted and the incident left me in no doubt where I stood.

Even so, I assumed that once the season began for real, our differences would be left in the dressing room and not taken across the white line. I was wrong. Like any club, we worked hard on set plays in training and I was always involved, coming up for corners and free-kicks. During the first few games, however, it became obvious my team-mates had other ideas. By the time I'd arrived in the box, the set piece would have already been taken and I'd be getting stick from the crowd for being slow.

Mind you, I did strike lucky in the first game against Brentford. As I reached the box after a corner had been taken, a shot came in, hit me on the leg and flew into the net. I'd put £20 on myself to score the first goal as a publicity stunt for a new Ladbroke's shop in the ground, so I was 400 quid in pocket. Happy days! But it wasn't a good day for Plymouth Argyle: we were stuffed 5-1 at home.

Our fourth game was in the League Cup against Walsall at Home Park. We'd lost 4-0 in the first leg so there wasn't a lot to play for and I was getting my usual share of abuse from the fans. We won a free-kick, which as usual was taken quickly before I got into position, but this time the ball came out to me about 35 yards from goal. On the half-volley. I hit it perfectly first time on the half-volley and it flew into the net past Trevor Wood, their keeper, who'd been at Port Vale with me. Right into the top corner.

A couple of the lads came up and tried to jump on my back to celebrate. I shoved them off with my elbow and gave an 'up yours' salute to all four corners of the ground. I was saying, 'Fuck you lot, I'm here for me now. I don't want any help from anybody. The players don't talk to me, the fans hate me, that's it.' And I didn't really mix with most of the other players from then on.

On top of everything, we made a disastrous start. We let in 15 goals in our next 5 league games and only scored 4. Throw into the mix the first-round League Cup exit and it was very bad news indeed.

Before long, I went to see Shilts. I said, 'Look, this isn't going to work out. I was wrong to come here. Just let me go. I'll ask for a move.' He told me to hang on for a while. Clearly he was hoping things would settle down. He didn't want people to think he'd made a mistake with his record signing. As it happened, John Rudge had heard I was unsettled and offered £150,000 to take me back to Port Vale. There was no way Plymouth were going to lose half their money in such a short time, but if I'd known about Rudgie's offer, I might have been a bit more persistent in my efforts to get away.

It didn't take long before news leaked out that I wanted out. The story made banner headlines in the local press. When it broke, I was asked to do a television interview. One of the first questions was, 'If you're so desperate to leave, why did you come to Plymouth in the first place?'

'For the money.'

It was an honest answer and I knew it would upset people. I hoped it would give me an excuse to push harder for a move. Straightaway, the whole town seemed to be in uproar and I was public enemy number one.

After fracturing my cheekbone against Wycombe in October, I was out of action for 5 games. I couldn't train and, when I returned to action, the atmosphere in the dressing room was even worse. As Christmas approached, we were in deep trouble at the wrong end of the table. We lost our last 3 games before the Christmas programme – 1-0 at York, 3-0 at home to Brighton and 7-0 at Brentford – but that didn't stop the players having a Christmas bash.

Even though hardly any of them were speaking to me, I thought I'd better show my face. I asked Martin Hodge what he thought and he said, 'Don't bother.'

'But I'm captain. The least I can do is turn up and show them I'm trying, even if they want nowt to do with me.'

'Fair enough, but don't say I didn't warn you.'

It was a fancy dress do and they'd arranged to meet in a bar in town. I arrived with Hodgey and found the rest of the players gathered in a corner. We walked over to them, but no one acknowledged me. So I minded my own business until Kevin Nugent, one of the strikers, came walking past on his way to the gents. I decided it was time to try and build a bridge or two, so I grabbed him and was just starting to say 'Kev ... ' when a button popped off his shirt.

'What are you doing?' he asked. 'You've ripped my fucking shirt.'

'No, I haven't, it's just a button come off. The shirt probably only cost a quid, anyway.'

He was holding my arms and wouldn't let go. I could see the rest of the lads watching and I pushed him away, but he came straight back at me. I got the first one in by head-butting him under the chin. Next thing I knew they'd all jumped on me and soon we were outside, scrapping in the car park. I'd only been in the pub ten minutes to say Merry Christmas and I finished up with a fat lip.

Shilts left early in 1995. After missing out in the play-offs, Plymouth had been down among the dead men since day one and not many managers will survive that. But I liked Shilts a lot. He was a football legend, but he still came across as an ordinary bloke; he made me feel welcome and did everything he could for me. But I sensed straightaway that he wasn't at ease with the job. Tactically Shilts was pretty naïve. Obviously, he enjoyed working with the goalkeepers and, from where I stood, he looked pretty capable as a goalkeeping coach, but otherwise he didn't have a lot to offer.

In a way I felt sorry for him. He seemed lonely. A couple of times when I was out injured and the team were playing away, he asked me to go along, too, and stay overnight. He seemed to want someone to talk to, although he was never the best conversationalist, so our chats were always a bit stilted.

It was the same with people in the hotel reception area or the lounge. With a record 125 England caps and over 1,000 league games to his name, Shilts was instantly recognisable. People always wanted to go and shake his hand and perhaps have their picture taken with him. But he didn't appear to understand why and seemed ill at ease. He liked to have a familiar face near him as a diversion.

Shilts loved a bet and there were all sorts of stories doing the rounds about his betting, although how many of them were true was another matter. Mick Quinn, though, had his own take on it. Quinny was well known for his love of racing and ended up training racehorses himself. With his goalscoring record Quinn could have made a big difference at Plymouth, but he hardly played at all during his short stay.

'Shilts has only brought me here to give him a few tips!' he used to joke.

John McGovern was Shilts' assistant. They'd won European Cups together at Nottingham Forest and McGovern had managerial experience at Bolton and Rotherham. They'd done well the previous season, but it seemed to me they were on a different wavelength about how we should be playing. Shilts would say one thing, McGovern another and we'd be in the middle wondering what to make of it all.

And it didn't help that McGovern was a very dour character.

Ideally the manager and his coach should be different personalities, one to play the straight man, the other the joker. Shilts was the quiet one, but I can't really recall McGovern ever really having a laugh and a joke with the players. It just wasn't his style.

I even think that if he'd been a bubbly character, he might have helped me through the sticky time at the start. Having a laugh has always been my style, but there was never much fun and banter on the training ground at Plymouth.

Steve McCall, who'd already made over 100 appearances in midfield for Plymouth, took over as caretaker when Shilts left. He was a big man with the fans, even though he hadn't really featured that season. He was very professional and did everything right – eating, drinking, training. He was a father figure to the younger players – some of them even called him Dad.

He wasn't daft. Before his appointment, he'd seen what had been happening in the dressing room. However, he hadn't approved of the way I had been handling the situation and didn't really have anything to do with me. Before his first training session, he pulled me to one side.

'You might as well piss off. After what you've said about only coming for the money, you can't stay down here.'

'Cheers, that's all I wanted to know.'

After treatment, I got in the car and drove straight back home to Stone. As far as I was concerned, that was me finished with Plymouth, but I was told by the PFA that I would be breaking my contract if I stayed away without a proper reason.

As it happened, I was out with an Achilles tendon problem at the time, but McCall tried to fix me up with a move to Cardiff. Mark Aizlewood, an old Leeds team-mate, was the manager there. It looked as if I was finally going to be on my bike once I was fit again, but before the deal could go through, McCall had one or two new injury problems, so the move was called off and I was back in the side after missing 5 games.

Funnily enough, the fans came round to me a bit towards the end of the season. They weren't daft and, eventually, I think they spotted what the clique within the team was up to. They knew I was playing to get away, but at least I was trying, which was more than could be said for some of the others. They started chanting 'Swanny, Swanny, give us a wave!' And I thought, 'Fuck off! You've made my life a misery. No chance!'

With 8 games to go and relegation looking more and more likely, I broke a couple of ribs in a game against Bristol Rovers at Home Park. I was obviously going to be out for a while and missed the next 2 games. By that stage, McCall had been replaced by Russell Osman, the ex-Ipswich and England defender. He was given the title of managerial adviser, whatever that was supposed to mean, and he tried to build a few bridges.

'Swanny, I need you to come back and play for me. How do you feel about it?'

'Yeah, I'll give it a go. But not with these ribs, I can't even jog.'

'Come in and we'll stick a couple of injections in. You'll be OK.'

I'd no axe to grind with Osman and playing would give me a chance to show potential buyers what I could do. So I agreed. I had injections before training and then again before matches. I played in the next two games, a defeat in the return game against Bristol Rovers and a home win over Swansea that gave us an outside chance of staying up. He was pleased with me.

The next game was at home against Birmingham. They would eventually gain automatic promotion. Playing up front for them was 6ft 7in Kevin Francis, the man I'd been marking against Stockport in the Autoglass final less than 12 months earlier. It seemed like twelve years. Kevin was obviously a real handful and in the first-half his challenge left our keeper Alan Nicholls struggling with a knee injury. Early in the second half, I was booked for a foul on Francis and Birmingham scored from the free-kick.

Then, 24 minutes later, he broke away down the left and I went across to tackle. Some tackle! Two-footed, waist-high – and Kevin's waist took a bit of reaching. I didn't even look at the referee. Another yellow, followed by a red. And once again, the free-kick led to a goal on the way to the 3-1 defeat that just about sealed our fate.

I had to cross the pitch to reach the tunnel and, amazingly, the fans gave me a standing ovation. It occurred to me that they might be saying sorry for the treatment they'd handed out over the last 9 months, but I didn't respond. I walked straight down the tunnel, into the dressing room, picked up my clothes and shoes, ran to my car, climbed in, put it in gear and drove north. Still wearing my kit and boots.

I didn't care whether I ever saw Plymouth again at that stage, but after more injections in my ribcage, I was back in the squad and heading north for our game at Crewe, who, like Birmingham, were going for promotion. Plymouth's club doctor didn't travel with us. Instead, a doctor at Crewe gave me my pre-match injections just five minutes before kick-off. There was no way they were going to take effect for at least fifteen minutes, so I was in absolute agony from the start. Minutes into the game, Ade Adebole nudged me in the ribs and I went down in a heap. That was the end of my season.

Two weeks later, a home draw against Oxford, coupled with unfavourable results elsewhere, condemned Plymouth to the bottom tier of the Football League for the first time. Was I sorry? Was I fuck! My nine months at Home Park had been a nightmare both on and off the field and I would honestly have been hard pressed to say whether I was happier about Vale being promoted the previous season or Plymouth going down on 6 May 1995. I never wanted to see the place again.

On 30 May, Huddersfield Town beat Bristol Rovers in the Division Two play-off final at Wembley. Two days later, their manager Neil Warnock resigned. On 22 June, he took over at Plymouth.

I didn't know much about Warnock at the time. After Plymouth's game at Huddersfield he'd said some complimentary things about the club and some of the players. He claimed it would be 'criminal' if Argyle went down, adding among other things, 'I've always had quite a lot of time for Swanny.' I knew we needed to talk and managed to get hold of a phone number. I gave him a call: 'Neil, it's Peter Swan, one of your players at Plymouth. I don't want to be there, I have to get away.' I explained some of the background.

Warnock replied, 'It looks as if we won't be able to build bridges after all that. I'll try and sort you out, but come to pre-season and we'll take it from there.'

'Where are you now?'

'Huddersfield.'

'Can I come round and see you, thrash it out now?'

'Right.'

He gave me the address. Bex and I were in Yorkshire that weekend, so we got in the car and drove to Warnock's house. I was expecting to sit down, face to face, and sort out my future. Instead, he switched on the telly, stuck in a video of the play-off final and made us watch Huddersfield winning and him prancing around on the touchline. He told me this was what we could achieve at Plymouth the following season.

I stuck it out for a while and then told him we hadn't come to watch his stupid videos; that I didn't want to be at Plymouth and something needed to be sorted. I ended up stalking out of the house with nothing resolved.

So it was back to Plymouth for pre-season. When I arrived I

discovered that neither my wages over the summer nor the second part of my signing-on fee had been paid. I contacted the PFA straightaway and they slapped an embargo on Plymouth, preventing them from buying or selling anyone until my situation had been sorted out.

Warnock wasn't happy. I could see where he was coming from because it wasn't his fault in the first place. I said to him, 'Look, just get rid of me. All your problems will be solved at a stroke.' But still nothing happened.

So I thought, 'Bollocks to this.' I became totally disruptive, like a big kid. If we were doing hurdles for speed training, I'd run through them instead of jumping over them. I kicked people up in the air in practice matches, took shots at goal from inside my own half, anything to annoy Warnock. Finally, he pulled me to one side. 'Right, I've sorted out a deal with Burnley. Go and talk to them.'

Try stopping me! I met Jimmy Mullen, the Burnley manager, and agreed a 3-year deal and a signing-on fee. Warnock called that night to ask if everything was sorted.

'Yes.'

So he told me to sign the next day.

I said no.

'Why not?'

'Because Plymouth still owe me the second half of my signing-on fee.'

Warnock argued that Plymouth had fixed me up with a move, that I was getting a signing-on fee from Burnley and that I should just forget what I was owed, sign and start afresh.

'No chance. The only reason I came down here in the first place was for the money, so I'm not going to leave it behind. You give me my money and I'll fuck off.'

He insisted they wouldn't pay me anything.

'Fine. See you in the morning.'

He called back a few minutes later to say he had a few injury problems and I was in the party for a pre-season tour of south Devon, playing against one or two local clubs. The tour started the following day. I hopped on a train, arrived at Home Park as the bus was pulling in, slung my bags into the hold, jumped aboard and found myself a seat at the front. I didn't talk to anyone: players, manager or coaches.

When we arrived for the first game, we trooped into the dressing room and first off, Warnock said, 'Right, these are your overnight rooms for the weekend.' He read out all the pairings before turning to me. 'Swanny, you don't like any of these lads, do you? So I've put you in a room by yourself. OK?'

'Yeah, fine.'

Then he announced the team. I was No.14. I assumed he was taking the piss. He'd called me all the way back to Plymouth to go on tour because he was short of players and then stuck me on the bench. No way was I going to warm my arse alongside him and any of the players. So I went and sat in the stand with the fans. They thought it was a huge joke. I played along with them and at half-time, I said to a few of them, 'Right, come on, let's go and have a game.'

We trotted out on to the pitch and began kicking a ball around. Straightaway, the PA system boomed out: 'Would the fans clear the pitch. No playing on the pitch.' My new mates started to move, but I told them to stay put. I was a player warming up and they were helping. Eventually Dan Macauley, the Plymouth chairman, arrived, expecting to reason with the fans, but when he saw me, he turned and walked away.

We went back in the stand after a few minutes. I was having a natter with the punters as the players came out when Mark Edworthy came rushing over. 'Swanny, you're playing.' I counted ten players, chucked my tracksuit top to one of the fans, jumped over the fence and lined up in the back four.

But I was determined to wind up Warnock as much as I could, so I failed to intercept easy through balls, booted straightforward clearances miles into touch, missed tackles and played people onside. He was seething. So I turned the screw a bit more the next time I had a clearing header. Instead of meeting the ball full on, I ducked under it at the last minute, leaving the centre-forward through one on one with the keeper. He missed.

'What's going on?' yelled Warnock from the touchline.

I walked slowly over, very quiet and polite and winking at the fans in the stand. 'You expect me to head the ball when we're going to a beach party tonight? If I cut my eye going for a header, I'll miss the party.'

The punters were killing themselves laughing, which wound up Warnock even more. 'Just get off that pitch,' he ordered. 'Now!'

'You come and get me,' I replied and trotted out again. He tried to substitute me several times, but each time I just stayed on ... and carried on ducking out of headers.

I made it to the beach party. There was a disco, plenty of food and booze, and some Plymouth fans joining in the fun. When I spotted the chairman arriving with his wife, I seized my chance. I grabbed the microphone and boomed out, 'Let's hear it for the chairman! A big round of applause for the man who has come along in person to deliver a cheque for the money the club have owed me for three weeks. I've got a wife back home who's driving round in a car that isn't paid for, so he's bringing the cheque to get me out of bother.'

The fans started clapping and I put my arm round the chairman's wife and gave her a big smacker on the cheek. I put my arm round him, too, and, to be fair, he was OK. I think he would have been happy to get me away at any price and would have paid up, but there was still no big fat cheque waiting for me next day.

Instead we had another friendly. After the match, I decided to hang around in the bar when the rest of the players went to bed. Warnock and his staff were in there and, after a while, he told me I should go to bed, too. I replied, 'Nobody tells me when to go to bed, not even my dad. So don't you start telling me what to do.'

I wandered over to the bar. I'm sure Warnock was hoping I'd buy a pint so that he could clobber me. Instead, I ordered an orange juice, picked up a paper and sat down with them all. Nobody spoke for half an hour. As the club hadn't paid either my wages or my signing-on fee over the summer, there wasn't much point fining me. After a while, I stood up, put the paper down and strolled off to bed.

I carried on playing in the pre-season friendlies because Warnock had injury and illness problems to contend with. And I continued to cock everything up. He kept telling me this situation couldn't carry on – and I agreed. 'Just get rid of me then,' I said, knowing that Burnley were still keen. I'd told them I'd soon be on my bike, that Plymouth would crack first.

And finally, with just a few days to go before the start of the season, he sent for me. 'Let's get this sorted, shall we?'

'Right.'

'We'll give you £15,000.'

'Thirty.'

'The most we'll give you is £20,000.'

'Twenty-five.'

'OK.'

I signed for Burnley on 4 August 1995. It felt as though I had just got out of jail.

Of course, with hindsight, I could have played it a different way. At first, I didn't realise what a big club Plymouth is down in the South West. At the time, Torquay and Exeter were also in the Football League, but Plymouth were the big news in the area. I rubbed people up the wrong way, but no one really attempted to solve the problem. The southern clique dominated the dressing room and most of the other players just went along with them. That was never going to be my style.

Funnily enough, it might have been different if Warnock had been manager when I signed 12 months earlier. He would almost certainly have brought in more northerners and I suspect, deep down, that he liked me as a player and wanted me to stay. But by the time he took over, I was determined to make the break. Everything had gone too far, inside and outside the club, and it was clear that no one was going to climb down.

People have asked why I didn't just walk out, but I was never going to do that. They owed me a lot of money, after all. As things got worse, I just became more and more determined not to be ground into the dirt. One way or another, I was going to sort it out myself. And I suppose that, in some ways, Plymouth made a man out of me.

In the end, I started to enjoy being the odd man out. I was on my own with a battle to win and I relished the fight. I believed the world was against me. At the time, there was a song around by Sting, 'Englishman in New York'. Those lyrics about always feeling like an alien were spot on for me. And I used to sing it to myself all the time, replacing 'Englishman in New York' with 'Yorkshireman in Plymouth'. And when I won, I knew I was a stronger person because of what I'd been through.

I hadn't quite heard the last of Plymouth, though. Just before I left, I spoke to a reporter from the local paper down there about the awful time I'd had at the club. An article appeared the following day. A little while later, I received a letter from a member of my Argyle fan club. It was addressed to Peter Swan, c/o Burnley Football Club. It contained a copy of the article with the words, 'Never mind, darling' scrawled across the headline. And it made very different reading from the letter I'd received from the Port Vale supporter two years earlier.

Peter Swan,

You are another failure for Argyle. You can slag off our team and our town but we know you are poor. Last year, Argyle finished third in the league and Burnley sixth. But the usual fiddle in football saw Burnley promoted. And Peter Swan is there now.

Never mind! Eat your black pudding and swill your beer before you cry in it. Get a couple more dogs and some Northern Rock. And you'll still tell us how rubbish we are and how wonderful you are.

Farewell, Burnley Bollocks!

There was no signature ...

15

HOME SWEET HOME

I sat on a bench in the dressing room at Burnley's Gawthorpe Hall training ground, letting the gritty northern accents, the jokes and the banter wash over me. I leaned back, rested my head against the wall and smiled to myself. It seemed like a very long time since I'd smiled in a dressing room. I was home, back where I belonged in the north of England. I was back among friends.

Moving clubs is like starting a new school or a new job. You can never quite be sure about the players around you. They are all different personalities and have to be approached in a different manner, and just as a player assesses his new team-mates, they are assessing him. Twelve months earlier at Plymouth I'd sensed straightaway that something was wrong. But here I knew almost immediately that I was going to be welcome. I felt relaxed.

After a few minutes, a voice shouted, 'Come on, lads. Let's be having you!' I was fastening my boots at the time and there was a table between me and the man behind the voice, so I could only see him from the waist down. I noticed straightaway that one of his knees seemed to bend inwards. I raised my sights and saw a middle-aged guy wearing shorts and a club tracksuit top. It was Clive

Middlemass, the first-team coach. I was used to coaches being younger than the manager and not a lot older than some of the senior players, but Clive looked like something from another era and I couldn't imagine him sprinting around the training ground.

But what a lovely bloke! What a good coach! He made me feel involved straightaway in the first training session. And I soon realised that while Clive might not have been in the first flush of youth, what he didn't know about coaching probably wasn't worth knowing, and he knew how to put it across.

I seemed to slot into the dressing room from the word go, although I soon discovered that some of the pranks that had become my stock-in-trade at Port Vale were out of date. I'd spent a year more or less in isolation at Plymouth and you can't take the mickey out of yourself, can you? I didn't like them, they didn't like me, so there wasn't much to laugh about. So I was a bit ring rusty at first and discovered that cutting off the end of people's socks and moving cars in the car park were yesterday's jokes. Instead, I started to learn how it felt to find my underpants in the teapot or Swarfega in my shampoo bottle.

When I signed we were still living in Stone, but I decided that from then on, I was going to stay in the north. We soon started looking for a house back home in Yorkshire. Our first stop was a converted barn in a village called Barkisland in the hills above Halifax. Richard Jobson, my former team-mate at Hull, who played nearly 700 games for 10 clubs, lived opposite. He went to work for the PFA after retiring in 2003.

We took out a six-month lease but, after three months, found a place of our own in Holmfirth, the village where *Last of the Summer Wine* is filmed. Harry, our second son, was born while we were there and we're glad he and George have been able to grow up among their own kind. We sold the place in Holmfirth after I moved to Bury in the summer of 1997 and found a house near Wakefield. We've been in and around the area ever since.

I used to joke that I only crossed the Pennines to Burnley and Bury to take the Red Rose money, although I've always got on OK with Lankies. But living in Yorkshire meant we could see more of our parents and the rest of the family. It was good to be on the doorstep as they were growing older. And, after a gap of four years, Mam and Dad were able to come and watch me play on a more regular basis. It hadn't been easy for them when I was at Vale, never mind Plymouth.

Usually the three of us who were based in Yorkshire – Liam Robinson, Ian Helliwell and me – travelled over to Burnley in one car. The most direct route was over the top from Hebden Bridge, near Halifax. It wasn't far as the crow flies, but involved climbing up a narrow, winding road called Mytholm Steeps. It more than lived up to its name. Then there was a rollercoaster ride over the tops between places with weird and wonderful names, like Blackshawhead, Kebcote and Cliviger, before dropping down into Burnley, right by the ground at Turf Moor.

On the journey back, we had a competition every day to set a new record for freewheeling. We'd flog the car up to around 70mph at the top of the final rollercoaster hump, just past a pub out in the middle of nowhere called The Sportsman's Arms. Then we'd bung the gear lever into neutral and head off through Blackshawhead and down the Steeps. If we met anything coming up the Steeps, the record bid was knackered. And when we hit the main road in Hebden Bridge, we prayed for a gap in the traffic so we could sweep straight out without having to halt. The all-comers record eventually stood at 4.4 miles ... or, to the technically minded, the second lamp post heading towards Hebden Bridge!

It could be a tough trip in the winter and once I had a lucky escape. Liam was doing the driving, but I'd arranged to stay overnight in Burnley, so I didn't make the return trip. Soon after setting off, he clipped another vehicle on a bad bend and his car turned over. The whole of the nearside of the car was caved in on the passenger's seat – just where I would have been sitting.

I actually signed for the Clarets on loan to begin with and my first match was the final pre-season game against Manchester City. Bury's manager Jimmy Mullen had signed me as a central defender and I was desperate to impress to make sure the deal was made permanent. The other 21 players were treating the game as just another friendly, but not me. I was marking Niall Quinn and he must have thought he was playing in a World Cup final. I kicked lumps off him from the first minute until I was taken off midway through the second-half. I might easily have been sent off, had it been for real.

To be honest, it was a relief when my number went up. I'd hardly done any serious pre-season work at Plymouth and I was completely knackered, but the fans liked what they saw and gave me a massive ovation. Before long I was known as 'Godzilla' or 'The Incredible Hulk' in the local press, who seemed to be looking for a positive angle. It was a completely different world from my nightmare in Devon.

I signed a two-year contract before our first league game against Rotherham. As it happened, Jamie Hoyland, the club skipper, was suspended for the first two games and, the day before the Rotherham match, Jimmy Mullen called me into his office. He said I'd be wearing the captain's armband. I'd only been around five minutes, so it gave me a real lift. Twelve months earlier at Plymouth, I'd led out a team of strangers, feeling I was on my own. Here, I knew that I was among friends and that the other players were supporting me from behind, not stabbing me in the back.

After we'd won our first two games, I thought I might have a chance of keeping the armband. Then Jimmy called us both in. He said he'd promised Jamie the job for the season and would stand by that. He added that it had been a tough decision. I really fancied it, but shook hands with Jamie and said, 'Right, let's crack on with it.' We were good mates from then on.

I played in central defence alongside Mark Winstanley. Strong, quick and a good left peg. Right foot? Non-existent. Jamie and I sometimes used to wind him up by passing the ball at pace to his right foot. He used to get into all sorts of contortions trying to run round the ball so he could use his left instead. Jamie and I would be in stitches.

Afterwards Mark used to ask why we'd done it. 'Because it's funny,' I'd reply. And before games, he'd plead with us not to mess him about. We never did it when there was any danger, of course, but one day his lack of a right peg backfired badly. A cross came in from the left and the ball skidded past me and headed straight for Mark, who was covering behind. It was on his right foot and he just smashed it first time towards his own goal. The idea was to concede a corner but instead, the ball flew like a bullet into the top corner from 15 yards. Marlon Beresford, our keeper, never had a chance.

Warren Joyce played in midfield. We used to call him 'Weirdo' ... but don't get the wrong idea. He was a lovely lad and, like me, had spent a season at Plymouth before joining Burnley in 1993. He's done well since retiring and, in 2006, was appointed manager of Belgian club Royal Antwerp. At times Joycie seemed to live in a little world of his own. Sometimes one of the lads would report early and go to the gym to loosen up. The place would be in darkness but when the lights were switched on, Joycie would be in the corner doing his yoga. He didn't seem to notice that the lights had gone on and that someone was working out on the treadmill or the weights.

David Eyres was thirty-one at the time and little did any of us know he'd still be going strong 11 years later. By the time he quit league football at Oldham in 2006, he'd played over 700 games in an 18-year career. He possessed a great left foot, spent 7 seasons at Turf Moor and was a good man in the dressing room, always up with the banter.

Kurt Nogan scored 26 goals in my first season. Like Andy Payton and Bernie Slaven, two more of my former team-mates, he was a penalty-box predator and only interested in scoring goals. But even though he became a bit of a folk hero and won the Player of the Year award, he never settled at Burnley. He once went on local radio and said he wanted to get away and go back to Wales. This caused a bit of a stir, but after my experience at Plymouth, I knew where he was coming from. Even though he may have been doing well at Burnley, he couldn't settle and wanted to get back home. Instead, he ended up down the road at Preston.

Marlon Beresford, our keeper, was a great shot stopper, but we used to call him 'Dracula' because he hated crosses. His nickname was 'Gorgeous George' because all the women loved him. He lived in Sheffield and used to wheel his family over the Pennines for home games. There seemed to be hundreds of them. He ended up with a £500,000 move to Middlesbrough in 1998, although with Mark Schwarzer around, he didn't play much first-team football. He still picked up decent money playing in the reserves, money that would probably have set him up for life.

The physio was Andy Jones, another top man and a real favourite with the fans. He had a curious style of running, with his arms down by his sides, and if there were two players down from opposite sides, he hared on to the park, desperate to beat the other team's physio to his injured player. He was a little dumpy chap, so the crowd loved seeing him come out of the blocks like an Olympic sprinter and go dashing on to the pitch.

When he ran on to treat a player, he had this strange habit of sliding the last couple of yards on one knee. In one game, Gerry Harrison, one of our midfield players, was pole-axed and lay prone on the turf, dead to the world. Andy dashed on and slid in towards Gerry on one knee, but he'd overcooked the slide and his right knee went straight into Gerry's bollocks. I've never seen anyone come round so quickly.

Andy used to work one-to-one with injured players and sometimes he'd take us to a nearby sports club at the Dunkenhalgh Hotel. I went along with him one day and when we arrived there was a women's keep-fit class going on in the gym. Most of them were young, they were all wearing highly-coloured leotards and, all in all, they looked pretty fit. Andy was obviously keen to impress.

We were both working on the treadmill with our backs to the keep-fit girls, and after a while, I said, 'Hey up, Jonah, your lace is undone.' Even though the treadmill was going fairly quickly, he stopped and looked down to check. Mistake! The treadmill didn't stop and Andy went hurtling backwards into the group of women. He picked himself up, muttered a few sheepish apologies and headed straight for the changing room. We never used the Dunkenhalgh again.

We started well enough with 4 wins and a draw in our first 5 league and League Cup games, but we were a bit hit-and-miss after that and it wasn't long before Mullen started to come under pressure. He'd been in charge since October 1991, succeeding Frank Casper with the Clarets standing in eleventh in the old Fourth Division and apparently going nowhere. Six months later they were promoted as champions and, after a season of consolidation, went into what is now the Championship via the play-offs. They were relegated after one season. I arrived at the club after relegation for a change!

But after our patchy start, we were knocked out of the Cup in the first round – beaten 3-1 at home by Walsall – and although we had a decent December, the alarm bells were ringing for the gaffer. A run of 4 successive defeats between 20 January and 10 February signalled the end.

I hadn't been around for long, but I'd always got on well with Mullen. In my early days the lads used to tell me he could be a bit unpredictable. There were tales of how he'd fallen asleep in the toilet before one game and another time how he'd announced a 12-man team in the dressing room before kick-off!

Once, when we were playing Carlisle away, we stopped for a pre-match meal. The players ate their food, had a stroll round the hotel grounds and then climbed back on the bus to wait for the manager and directors. We waited and waited, and by the time the top brass returned to the bus, having obviously had a good lunch, we were behind schedule. When we arrived, we had to get changed in a rush while Jimmy gave his team talk – or tried to do so against stern opposition from the PA system, which was broadcast into the dressing room through a loudspeaker.

One day I took a rugby ball out for our warm-up before a practice match. It was a frosty day so we were working on the Astroturf pitch. We had a few minutes of touch-and-pass before Jimmy arrived. He put a ball in the centre circle and walked to watch from the touchline. While his back was turned, I swapped the football for my rugby ball and we kicked off.

You can imagine how a rugby ball behaves on Astroturf so we were obviously all over the place. Jimmy was ranting away on the touchline and eventually, he blew his whistle and shouted, 'Here, give me that ball!' We chucked the rugby ball across and he was just about to show us how it should be done when he spotted what was going on.

Not long before he left, we lost 3-0 at Shrewsbury, a third league defeat on the bounce. I'd been thrown up front to try and snatch a goal and get us back into the game, only to be substituted five minutes from time. I muttered something under my breath in Jimmy's direction as I stalked off down the tunnel. Afterwards, I was chatting to my dad in the players' lounge when one of the lads told me the gaffer wanted to see me.

I sensed another bollocking was on the way and went back to the dressing room. He wasn't there. So I went out on to the pitch and spotted Jimmy sitting in the dug-out. I walked over and saw he was in tears. I tried the humorous approach. 'Come on, gaffer, we weren't that bad!' He turned and told me he'd had enough, that he was going to see the chairman there and then and resign. He said the pressure was getting to him. I told him not to rush into anything, to think about it over the weekend, to have a chat with the missus first and make a decision in the cold light of day.

We went back in on the Monday morning and Jimmy was as right as rain. I walked past him in the corridor and he never said a dickie bird. He didn't resign and carried on as normal. I was sure he'd call me in to say he'd listened to what I'd said and thanks, but nothing. It was as if the conversation had never happened.

After he left, Clive Middlemass took over as caretaker while the board found a replacement. One of the first names in the frame was Adrian Heath. He'd made his name with Stoke, won a championship with Everton and established himself as a big favourite with the fans after joining Burnley in 1992. Two or three months before Mullen left, Heath had moved to Sheffield United as assistant manager to Howard Kendall, his mentor as a player at Stoke and his championship-winning manager at Everton. Heath was obviously going to be a popular choice with the fans if he came back, but he sounded like bad news for me. We'd never hit it off from the day I joined Burnley.

At the time we both lived in the Potteries and travelled north together. We shared the driving, but that was about all. He used to go droning on about all the big names he'd played with and against while he was at Everton, about how he was going to be a manager one day and how he'd do the job.

One day I said, 'Look, if you ever got a manager's job, I wouldn't want to play for you.' He asked why. 'Because I think you're a pillock.' After a while, I couldn't be arsed with him any more, so every morning, I used to buy half a dozen daily papers. If he was driving, I'd start reading as soon as we set off; if I was behind the wheel, I'd hand him the pile of papers.

So when he was appointed to succeed Mullen in February 1996, I feared the worst. There was an uneasy peace between us for the rest of the season as we hauled ourselves away from trouble and finished in seventeenth place. In the summer, Heath appointed John Ward, who subsequently managed Bristol City, Cheltenham and Carlisle, as his No.2. He brought a lot of new ideas to the training ground and when we set off for a pre-season trip to Northern Ireland I was feeling pretty optimistic.

But Northern Ireland was the setting for my first major run-in with Heath. As a player, he'd been known to the lads by his nickname, 'Inchy'. But after taking over, he made it clear that he wanted to be called 'Boss' or 'Gaffer'. Not by me, he wasn't. I carried on calling him 'Inchy'. One day in Ireland, he pulled me to one side and asked why. I said, 'Because I don't respect you. You know I don't, I've told you often enough.'

Surprise, surprise, I didn't really feature in the senior side in pre-season and, Sod's Law, I was suspended for the opening game against Luton. He had the perfect excuse not to involve me, and with Vince Overson, an experienced defender who'd started his career with the Clarets in 1979, back at the club, my prospects looked pretty bleak.

And so it proved. We won that first game and, even though Overson was injured, I didn't get a look-in during the opening weeks of the season. It wasn't long before I was knocking on the manager's door. He told me there was an opportunity for me to go out on loan to Hartlepool or Hereford, who were both in the bottom division. No chance! I asked for a move and went on the transfer list in mid-September.

However, before long, the side started to go through a dodgy spell and I knew the fans wanted to know why I wasn't playing. A piece in the *Lancashire Evening Telegraph*, the local paper, in which I asked Heath why he wasn't selecting his best centre-half, kept the pot on the boil. On 29 October, we drew 1-1 in a midweek game at Preston. Winstanley and Overson picked up knocks and, afterwards, Heath told me I'd be in the line-up at York the following weekend. It was a chance I wasn't going to miss.

We lost 1-0, but I played well. Heath admitted as much in the press and kept me in the side. We won our next 4 games and, after a 1-0 win over Bournemouth at Turf Moor, the *Evening Telegraph* carried the headline: HEATH HAILS PETER THE GREAT. He'd given me the armband at half-time after Nigel Gleghorn was injured, and in the article, he enthused, 'Peter is a tremendous leader and he's done brilliantly since he came back into the side. His performances have inspired the people around him. I can't praise him highly enough.' Pass me the smelling salts!

Our next game? Plymouth Argyle at Home Park. The papers in Burnley and Plymouth went to town. In the *Evening Telegraph*, The Incredible Hulk had turned Ghostbuster and was going back to bury the memory of his Home Park House of Horrors.

And the *Plymouth Evening Herald* gave Warnock a chance to air his views: 'Peter is his own worst enemy. He's one of the best defenders in this league or one of the worst, depending on his mood. But he's done ever so well for Burnley lately. I didn't have any problems with Swanny. It's just that when I came to the club, he'd already made up his mind that he wanted to go.'

I'd told the lads all about my time there and warned them what to expect. But even so, my reception surprised them. There were far more fans around than usual when we went out for the warm-up 40 minutes before the start. They'd come early just to have a go at me and the booing started as soon as I appeared. They were going mad. The rest of the boys couldn't believe it. When we got back into the dressing room, I joked, 'It was like that when they were on my side, never mind playing for the opposition!'

We agreed that if I scored, I'd run back to the centre circle and stand with both arms raised. The Burnley players would form a circle round me and go down on their hands and knees and pay homage. And it so nearly happened. There were chants of 'Greedy northern bastard!' throughout the match, but late on, I had a shot cleared off the line that would have given us a 1-0 win. If only!

The following day's Sunday *Independent* summed up the mood in the South West. 'For much of the second half, with the game remaining goalless, the script appeared written up in advance for Peter Swan to mark his Home Park return by seizing the decider from a Burnley set-piece. Such a miserable outcome didn't bear thinking about for the Argyle faithful who, judging by the boos that regularly accompanied every movement by Peter Shilton's record signing, still hadn't forgiven him for the derogatory comments he made about their club and city after bitterly regretting his West Country move. But even the most uncharitable had to admit that he commanded his territory with a masterly dominance that was singularly lacking when he wore an Argyle shirt.'

But even though Heath had gone public to say how well I was playing and I had said all the right things too, there was no real chance of us burying the hatchet behind the scenes. I was still on the transfer list and made no secret of my desire to get away. I also knew that Stan Ternent was keen to take me to Bury. They'd come up from Division Three as champions and were in the process of winning back-to-back promotions. After I'd collected the Man of the Match award in a televised win over Bury in January, I bumped into Stan in the corridor. I pretended to be talking about the good old days at Hull, but when we were out of earshot, I said, 'For fuck's sake, Stan, get me out of here!' He replied, 'I'm trying, Swanny, I'm trying.'

On one occasion, I almost made it easier for him. We were getting ready to board the bus after an away game and I'd stashed two bottles of wine and six cans of beer in my Adidas bag as sustenance for the boys on the way home. All the bags were lined up outside the players' entrance waiting to be loaded and I was just about to collect mine and take it on board as hand luggage when Heath beat me to it and picked up mine instead of his own. I can't think how he didn't spot how heavy it was and take a look inside. I dashed over, explained that he'd got the wrong bag and made the switch. We were barely speaking at the time and if he'd discovered what was in the bag, I could have been on my bike.

Soon after the end of the season, Burnley and Bury agreed a fee of £50,000. I went in to see Heath to check that Burnley would pay me the rest of my signing-on fee, something like 20 grand. He said he didn't think there'd be a problem. Compared with my previous moves, it all seemed a bit too straightforward and I wasn't entirely happy.

I gave Stan a call. He wasn't interested in lengthy negotiations. He told me what was on offer, adding, 'If you're not happy with that, don't bother coming.' Like I said before, Stan doesn't mince words. The money wasn't brilliant, but I wanted to play for Stan again and even though Bury was a smaller club, they were going to be in a higher division. So I said yes. When I got home, I switched on the text. Heath had left for Everton as No.2 to Kendall.

Next day my first port of call was with Frank Teasdale, the Burnley chairman. I said, 'You'll know I'm going to sign for Bury, but

I just want to make sure everything I agreed with Inchy is still OK.' He looked blank. He had no idea about the transfer or paying the rest of my signing-on fee. The deal was off.

Chris Waddle took over, his first, and to date, only job in management. He was a hell of a big name and his appointment was seen as a coup, but it didn't work out and he left after one season. I spoke to him as soon as I could and told him I'd fixed up a move to Bury. He said we'd talk again after a practice match between the first team and the reserves. I was half tempted to toss it off and not really bother, but instead I went out and had a blinder. I scored twice from centre-half. After that, I thought there was no way he'd let me go, but he called me in and said, 'Right, get yourself away.' I signed for Stan soon afterwards.

Thankfully, it was au revoir and not goodbye to one of the best clubs I played for and I'd be back at Turf Moor 12 months later.

16
SILENCE IN COURT!

Stan Ternent was the reason I joined Bury. Most people saw it as a nothing club and, from the outside, there wasn't a lot going for it. Except Stan. I had a lot of respect for him after our time at Hull City and he'd guided Bury to 2 successive promotions, so I reckoned it was worth a go.

Stan was a strong character who wanted strong players around him. A lot of managers don't like forceful personalities in their squad; they're afraid their own authority might be undermined, but not Stan. He actively sought out strong players. Even though they might cause one or two problems off the field, he knew that they'd always do the business once they crossed the white line.

And there were some very forceful personalities at Bury, men like Ronnie Jepson, Gordon Armstrong, Andy Gray, Paul Butler, Chris Lucketti, Dean Kiely, David Johnson and Lenny Jonrose. And me. But Stan trusted us, and while there may have been a few bust-ups, there was never any real bother.

His man-management was different class. I'd discovered that for the first time after I'd torn my cruciate ligament at Hull. Stan lived in Burnley and used to travel over to Humberside every day.

Obviously I couldn't drive because of my knee, so twice a week he picked me up in Wakefield and took me over to Hull.

I can't think of many managers who would do that. A lot of them prefer injured players to be out of sight, out of mind. But he knew I was desperate to stay involved with the boys, even though I couldn't train, and because he'd been prepared to go out of his way to help me, I was always ready to do the same for him. Maybe I would play with an injury when I should really have been sitting it out.

Stan didn't have a problem about his players having a drink the night before a game. He wanted the ones who enjoyed a pint to feel they could drink in front of him rather than go behind his back. On away trips at all three clubs I played for under Stan, he'd sometimes call us all together in the hotel foyer before dinner. If there was a pub nearby, we'd pop out for a pint; if not, we'd use the hotel bar.

Quite a few players didn't want alcohol and just had orange juice or a soft drink, but the important thing was that we went there together as a team. Then we'd go back for our evening meal and Stan would say that if anyone wanted another half, then or afterwards, there was no problem. He knew that if he played ball with us, we'd go out and give everything for him.

But woe betide any player who crossed him or failed to give him 100 per cent. His bollockings were legendary and if anyone didn't buy into his 'We're all pissing in the same pot' philosophy, they were out the door. Like any manager, he's made one or two enemies over the years, but he's the best gaffer I've worked for.

I always respected him and I still do. A lot of his former players feel the same. I once called in at his home on my way to Burnley, where I was working for Radio Humberside. While I was there, Glenn Little, who'd played for him at Turf Moor, popped in for a chat and there was a phone call from Ronnie Jepson, another of Stan's ex-players.

SILENCE IN COURT!

There was an incredible atmosphere in the dressing room at Bury and it was probably the best dressing room I've known. I was only there for 12 months and, in some ways, it felt as though I was just there for a good time. After 4 years playing in central defence, Stan wanted me to play up front and I always saw that as a chance to have a bit of fun. Being a defender was deadly serious; one mistake and you could lose a game. As a striker, though, there was a whiff of glory around and if a few chances went begging, so what? Nobody seemed to mind.

There was no training ground at the club. Instead, we trained on some council pitches called Goshen Fields. To get there we had to jump over a cemetery wall, walk between the headstones and scramble through a fence at the far side of the graveyard. There were piles of dog shit all over the place. And time after time we'd be halfway through a session or a practice match when some punter would walk his dog across the pitch and argue the toss if we tried to stop him. 'I've as much right to be on this fucking pitch as you have!'

Mind you, there was one occasion when our primitive training facilities worked in one of the lads' favour. Halfway through a session with Sam Ellis, Stan's No.2, the gaffer arrived and called all the players together. He told us the drug-testing team had turned up at the ground to carry out some random dope tests. He said that if anyone had been doing anything they shouldn't have been doing, they'd better piss off now. One of the young reserves was out of there like shit off a shovel and we didn't see him again for 24 hours. If we'd had a proper training ground there would have been no escape.

Every Friday morning, Stan held a court in the dressing room. He was the judge and stood up at the front of the courtroom. The players were the jury and we dealt with any petty offences that other players or staff might have committed during the week. We'd all troop into the dressing room and Stan would stand in judgement. He'd announce that the court was in session and from then on, no one was allowed to talk without the judge's permission. Anyone who did was fined.

He had a handful of papers, each containing an offence committed by one of the lads. The accused would be asked to plead guilty or not guilty and could appeal against the sentence. A failed appeal meant double the fine. We'd fine people three or four quid for things like wearing someone else's training kit, wearing flip flops in the car park, moving another player's car, bad haircuts, bad sense of fashion, and – an offence invented by Stan – for being a complete pillock. That covered any minor offence not on the official hit list.

One of the players wrote down all the fines and they had to be paid within a week – or be doubled. There'd be about £50 worth of fines each week and all the money went into a pool towards a day out at the races or a trip off somewhere else. I've never known it happen at any other club, although when Jeppo succeeded Stan as manager of Gillingham in 2005, he maintained the tradition down there. It was great for team spirit and Stan loved every minute.

Harry Wilson, known to the lads as 'Harry the Bastard', was one of the coaches and we used to wind him up something rotten. Every week, he'd have to defend himself against some trumped-up charge, usually an offence someone else had committed. We really used to get to him. He knew I was the main man, and one day, decided to get his own back. After we'd all gone training, he moved my car. Unfortunately one of the lads was a bit late, spotted him and told me when he arrived on the training pitch. After training, I made a big play of looking for my car and eventually spotted it in a side street. I drove it back to the ground and said to Stan, 'Somebody moved my car – and the 100 quid that was in the glove compartment.' I made that bit up.

SILENCE IN COURT!

Harry turned white: 'Hang on, Swanny. I moved your car, but I never touched any money.' Stan told him we'd sort it out in court on Friday. There was no way Harry could avoid a fine for moving the car, but he swore 'til he was blue in the face that he hadn't taken the brass. Peter Hampton, the physio, started laughing and Harry just lost the plot. He had a go at Peter and the two had to be separated. Fine doubled.

Another time, I'd been doing a bit of extra training out on the pitch and couldn't be arsed to go back into the dressing room for a pee, so I pissed in the away dugout instead. Straight afterwards, Harry came down the tunnel and walked on to the pitch. He was followed by Stan, a minute or so later. The piss was just starting to trickle out of the dugout so I grabbed Stan and said, 'Gaffer, you won't believe what I've just seen ...' I pointed to the tell-tale stream and added, 'That was Harry. I saw him.' I called Harry back and told him I'd spotted him. He was livid. Stan told him we'd sort it out at court and Harry ended up with another fine.

We had to sign a book when we reported every morning. And at quarter to ten, it was taken into Stan's office. Anyone who hadn't reported went before the court. There were some incredible appeals against conviction. Tony Ellis once claimed he'd locked himself out moving his wheelie bin. His £4 fine was doubled on the spot.

Stan also went to great lengths to nick his victims. He and Ellis shared an office and every day an apprentice left their clean boots outside the door. Once a week Lenny Johnrose would pinch Sam Ellis's boots and either hide them or take them outside and rub them in the mud. He got away with it for weeks, but in the end, Stan was too clever for him.

There was a CCTV camera at one end of the corridor, aimed at the players' entrance. Eventually Stan climbed up a ladder and directed the camera on to his office door. Lenny hid Sam's boots the following Tuesday morning and thought he'd got away with it as usual, but when we arrived in court on the Friday, Stan was ready: 'Stand up whoever nicked Sam's boots on Tuesday!' Nobody moved. 'I won't ask again.' No response. 'Right, take a look at this.' He switched on the video and there was Lenny running down the corridor, pinching Sam's boots and making off in the opposite direction. Caught red-handed.

But while I found myself among a great bunch of players, off the field, the club was in a state of shock. Hugh Eaves, the main benefactor during the promotion seasons, had pulled out in the summer. All assets were frozen, the club was up for sale and there was no money for Stan to strengthen the squad. Staying in the division would have been a miracle if he'd been able to fork out a bit of money for new players; without them we were pissing into the wind from day one.

And because of the financial situation, we were told there probably wouldn't be any money to stay overnight before away games. Talk about the poor relations! While clubs like Sunderland, Manchester City, Nottingham Forest and Middlesbrough were shelling out for five-star luxury, we were going to have to pay our own hotel bills. At the end of October, we played Norwich and Ipswich away on successive Saturdays. Travelling on the day was a non-starter, so, for the Norwich game, we stumped up the money from the players' pool and Stan paid the Ipswich bill out of his own pocket. Towards the end of the season we had a 20-hour round trip for a night match at Portsmouth. Somehow we managed to get a point.

And from the start of the season, the fans were distinctly turned off by our new status. In theory, we were 46 games away from the top flight, but only 5,000 people turned up for the first home match against Reading. There'd been a crowd of over 11,000 for the final game of the previous season, but the novelty had worn off. Our only capacity gate was for a Friday night game against Manchester City in September. There were 8,000 City fans in the ground. Sunderland brought the same number in November, but we couldn't even fill the place with our own supporters.

So there was a siege mentality from the start and, despite everything, we had a decent side. Dean Kiely was in goal. Stan had picked him up from York in the previous year and he was always going to go on to bigger and better things. Like playing for the Republic of Ireland and a £1m move to Charlton and the Premiership. Bury did the right thing by him. They knew he'd be moving on sooner rather than later, so they put him on decent money until the right offer came along. It meant that, when he finally moved, he'd get a good deal – and the club could ask for a big fee because Dean was on top whack financially. They did the same for Chris Lucketti, who played in central defence alongside Paul Butler. Two more players who made it into the top flight.

Andy Gray was the main man in midfield. He was thirty-three and had played over 300 games for Crystal Palace, Aston Villa, QPR, Spurs, Swindon, Marbella and Falkirk. Oh, and once for England. When he was in the mood, he could run the game on his own. He was as strong as an ox. Andy was a real character off the field. As a Londoner, he stuck out like a sore thumb in the Gigg Lane dressing room, but he was always one of the boys. He had loads of contacts in London, and if any of the lads wanted to go to a club or a show or whatever, Andy could fix them up with tickets. The last time I spoke to him he was selling diesel in the Middle East.

I was among a group of strikers that included old pros like Ronnie Jepson, Tony Ellis and Nigel Jemson. Between us we'd clocked up over 125 years and 1,500 league games. That's a fair bit of know-how. Jeppo is still a good mate. He broke into the professional game late and had been working down the pit before joining Port Vale in 1986 at the age of twenty-five. Before arriving at Bury in 1996, he played for Preston, Exeter and Huddersfield. He used to come in for training with a fag in his mouth and he'd light up again before getting into the car to drive home.

We'd had a real ding-dong when Burnley beat Bury 3-1 at Turf Moor the previous season, a game that the *Evening Telegraph*'s Tony Dewhurst clearly enjoyed. He wrote: 'I'll bet Bury's tough-man centre-forward Ronnie Jepson is rubbing ointment into a few bruises this morning after a rare old battle with Turf Moor's Godzilla. Swan and Jepson had a battle that made Mike Tyson v Evander Holyfield appear tame. And Swan won hands down.'

There was also a bit of banter flying around during the match, but we had a laugh about it over a pint after the game. It was good to link up with Jeppo at Gigg Lane and we were room-mates on our handful of away trips. After dinner we'd sit down with a beer, Ronnie would have a cigarette and sometimes I'd light up a cigar. Stan often joined us for a natter. Jeppo became close to Stan, and when the gaffer joined Burnley in 1998, Ronnie soon followed. Eventually he became his assistant at Turf Moor and followed him to Gillingham in December 2004. When Stan left six months later, Jeppo took over. It never quite happened for him as manager, but, at the end of the 2007–08 season, he linked up with Stan again at Huddersfield. It's a good chance for him and I'm sure he'll make the most of it; he's a good coach.

Tony Battersby and David Johnson were the younger generation. Johnson had come in on a free from Manchester United and attracted a lot of attention during the two promotion years. Before the first game of the season, his wife got involved in a bit of barney. She'd brought their newborn baby along and was expecting to do a bit of nappy-changing in one of the lounges. But they were being used for corporate guests. There were no changing facilities in the ladies' so she ended up getting pretty pissed off about it. The story made it into some of the national papers, but baby-changing facilities at Gigg Lane? She must have been joking! There were hardly any changing facilities for the players, never mind babies.

I got off to a bit of a flier with 6 goals in my first 12 games, although I didn't notch any more in the next 15! Johnson didn't like me scoring goals. He wanted to be the main man. He used to say, 'I hate playing up front with you, Swanny. You score all my goals.' And I think he meant it. He scored 5 goals in 17 games before moving to Ipswich for £800,000 in November. It turned out to be a good bit of business for both Stan and the club.

From the start, we set out to make life as difficult as possible for the opposition ... on and off the field. The dressing rooms were tiny, and before a game, we'd hose down the walls in the away dressing room and turn up the heating to full bore. It was like a bloody sauna when they arrived! Some players refused to change in there and used the corridor instead.

The opposition had to walk past our dressing room on their way to and from the warm-up and we'd always leave the door open and make sure they saw us laughing and joking. We'd usually train on the pitch a couple of times during the week and Stan would tell the groundsman to leave the surface as we'd left it, all cut up and bumpy. It looked like a herd of elephants had been running around and this was a club playing in the equivalent of what is now the Championship! It wasn't cheating, it was a case of using everything in our power to stay in the division. On paper, we didn't belong there.

There were some real big hitters around that year. In the end, Forest, Middlesbrough and Charlton were promoted. Manchester City, Stoke and Reading were relegated and in between there were teams like Sunderland, Wolves, Sheffield United, West Brom, Norwich, Ipswich and Portsmouth. So Bury, with an average gate of around 6,000, along with Crewe, Port Vale, Stockport and Oxford, were very much the poor relations. Yet we all stayed up.

At home matches against the smaller teams there was virtually no atmosphere. It was like a reserve game, but we started the season OK and, after beating Tranmere in early September, we climbed as high as seventh in the table. We levelled off after that, but even so, a 2-0 win over Forest at the start of November kept us in fifteenth position. Then the wheels started to come off and we went 13 games without a win.

Nobody rolled us over – in fact, we only conceded more than a single goal in 5 of those 13 games – but one-all draws and 1-0 defeats weren't enough. And the opposition was strong. Take Middlesbrough, for example. Their squad included big names like Paul Merson, Andy Townsend, Michel Beck, Craig Hignett, Gianluca Festa, Mark Schwarzer and Emerson, the Brazilian midfield player, not to mention good pros like Steve Vickers, Craig Fleming and Robbie Mustoe. But they only beat us 1-0.

Emerson didn't last the 90 minutes. I caught him early in the game. It was a great tackle. I won the ball fair and square, but my studs gashed his thigh as I went through with the tackle. He went off for treatment and I thought there was no way he'd be back. Instead, he returned a few minutes later with a massive bandage round his thigh. He could hardly move and I couldn't work out why he'd come back. But I soon found out. I went up for a header and I felt as if I'd been hit by an express train. It was Emerson getting his own back. I had stud marks down my back. He was booked for the challenge and substituted a few minutes later. As he was walking off, he asked me if I wanted him to autograph the scar afterwards.

The following week we lost 1-0 at Bradford City. In the last minute, I was sent off. I was playing centre-half, marking Edinho, their Brazilian striker. Near the end, I tackled him, hard but fair. He went down like a stretcher case. The ball went out of play and one of our subs knocked it back towards me. I sidefooted it as hard as I could, straight back at Edinho, who was still lying on the deck. The ball hit him on the back of the head. He leaped to his feet and came running towards me. So much for his injury. He tried to head-butt me, but I leaned back and his head hit my chest. That was the signal for a full-scale brawl involving just about every player. Paul Butler was wading in with both arms; Kiely came running up from his goal area to get involved. And even Stan and Paul Jewell, City's coach at the time, were wrestling near the dug-out.

I was more bothered about talking to the referee. I wanted him to know that I hadn't done anything except kick the ball towards Edinho. That may have started the whole thing, but it wasn't exactly a sending-off offence. And I hadn't really been involved in the brawl. But I was wasting my time. When things calmed down, he called me over and gave me a straight red card. I walked towards the dressing rooms in the corner of the stadium. Jeppo, who was on the bench, joined me in time to see Edinho collect a red card as well.

I dashed into the dressing room and swapped my boots for my trainers and then headed back into the tunnel to wait for Edinho. I didn't want to slip if there was any action, but he must have known what was going to happen because, all of a sudden, he did a right turn and ran up the steps into the stand. From there, he took a left and into a corridor that ran into the club offices and then down some steps into the dressing room via a back door. Edinho 1, Swanny and Jeppo 0!

By the beginning of February we were twenty-third in the table and everybody was writing us off, but we went to Manchester City and beat them 1-0. The result kick-started a revival. We won 3 of our next 4 home games by a single goal, sneaked an away win at Birmingham and lost just once in 9 games. With 7 games left we were seventeenth and a decent bet to stay up. However, we lost 4 of the next 6 games with just a single win, at home against our old pals from Bradford City.

As a result, we were right on the edge before the final game at

QPR. Both sides were on 49 points with Rangers having a substantially better goal difference. The three clubs immediately below, Stoke, Port Vale and Portsmouth, were all on 46 points. They all had a better goal difference than Bury. If they all won and we lost, we'd go down with the bottom two, Manchester City and Reading. QPR would only go down if we beat them by a cricket score and if Stoke scored a hatful against City. But once again the club decided that we'd travel down to London on the morning of the match. We weren't having that and had to stump up the money for a hotel out of the players' pool. It cut a bit of a hole in the fund for our end-of-season trip to Majorca, but it was a massive game and we didn't want to take any chances.

Some outsiders will look at a fixture like this and think the two teams will just go through the motions. Why spoil a week in Magaluf by picking up a knock in a tough tackle? Why risk relegation when a point apiece will guarantee safety for both sides? But it doesn't work like that. Professional pride kicks in ... and it certainly did on this occasion.

As we were leaving the pitch after the warm-up, I found myself walking alongside Vinnie Jones, who was playing for Rangers at the time. I joked that we should be settling for a nil-nil to make sure we were both safe. Vinnie laughed. So did I. We knew there was no chance of that happening. And almost straight from the kick-off Vinnie and I challenged for a 50-50 ball and he went straight through me. It was every man for himself from then on and the tackles were flying in all over the place.

We ran out 1-0 winners. Gordon Armstrong nicked a goal in the twenty-fourth minute and we hung on. We were safe. So were Rangers, thanks to their superior goal difference. Port Vale and Portsmouth won to join them on 49 points. Manchester City beat Stoke but they both went down with Reading.

Even though there was no money around, we'd been on a

reasonable bonus to stay up, but Gordon Armstrong and I had decided to make sure we wouldn't be out of pocket whatever happened. A couple of days before the game, we called the bookie. We asked for a price on Bury losing at QPR and then going down on goal difference because the three teams below them had all won. He offered us something like 25/1 so we each lobbed 100 quid on, just in case. It was one bet we were delighted to lose.

It was a miracle that we stayed up. The odds had been stacked against us from the start and having to sell David Johnson to keep the bank manager happy could have been a killer blow. But there was a strong team spirit running through the squad and we scrapped for every minute of every game. If it's true that you get what you deserve in football, then we deserved to stay up ... and we certainly deserved our break in Magaluf.

On the flight back, I sat next to Stan. He told me he'd had an approach from Burnley. What did I think? 'It's your hometown club,' I told him. 'Potentially it's a big club and you might never get another chance.'

'Yes, but if it goes wrong, I'll still have to live there, won't I?'

'You've got to give it a go, Stan. But if you do, make sure you take me with you!'

First off, though, Bex and I were going to the World Cup. France '98. I'd given David Batty, my old Leeds team-mate, a call a few months earlier and asked if there was a chance of any tickets. He came up with two for each of England's group games. Against Tunisia in Marseille, Romania in Toulouse and Colombia in Lens. So we found ourselves some hotels and set off.

First stop: Marseille. It was a baking hot day and, around lunchtime, we were milling about with the England fans in the old port area. The atmosphere was OK at first, but as the ale started to take effect, we could sense things were turning nasty. There were carloads of England fans driving by, waving flags, chanting 'En-ger-land, En-ger-land!' and taunting the French. I was worried for Bex and decided to make a move, get out of the area and set off to the ground.

We'd reached a street corner when we found ourselves stuck in a crowd of England fans. I was stood next to a big chap with a shaven head. He was topless and had a Union Jack tattooed on his belly. He was eating a sandwich. All of a sudden, he chucked the sandwich away, high into the air. It was obviously a pre-arranged signal for the bother to kick off. The place erupted. It was as though World War Three had started. Everything that could be moved seemed to be flying around. We turned and forced our way back through the crowd to the door of a nearby hotel. It was locked. We were in a really dodgy situation.

Just as we were trying to work out what to do next, the hotel door was unlocked. A voice shouted, 'Swanny, get yourselves in here.' It was Viv Anderson, No.2 to Bryan Robson at Middlesbrough at the time. He and Robbo were doing some corporate work at the hotel before commentating on the game for one of the satellite channels. They'd come to see what was happening outside and spotted us fighting our way through the mob. We stayed with them for about half an hour until things calmed down a bit. We then went to the stadium with them – escorted by their bouncers. The following day, the front page of the *Sun* carried a picture of the ringleader who'd thrown the sandwich. Fortunately I was out of frame by that time!

The drama didn't end there, however. We found our seats, among a load of other people who'd received tickets from the England players, and who should be sitting two rows in front? Terry Robinson, the Bury chairman, and Neville Neville, the commercial manager and Gary and Phil Neville's dad. They soon spotted me and Terry was laughing all over his face. He called out, 'I'll introduce you to your new manager when you get back home, Swanny!'

I couldn't work out what was so funny. Then it dawned on me. 'Just tell me it isn't Neil Warnock.'

'It is.'

'Then I won't be playing for you again.'

I kept my word.

Warnock had left Plymouth in 1997, a year after taking them to promotion through the play-offs in his first season. On his first day at Gigg Lane, he came into the dressing room to introduce himself to all the players. When he reached me, I kept my arms folded and just shook my head. He walked straight past and carried on shaking hands. When he left, some of the lads wanted to know why I'd ignored him. 'Don't ask,' I said. 'I just don't want to go there.'

Warnock called me in soon afterwards. He said he loved me as a person, but that he didn't want me anywhere near his first team. 'Right, get rid of me then,' I replied. He said he'd do his best. I didn't train with the first-team squad. Instead, Warnock told me to work with the reserves and the kids under Kevin Blackwell. He'd joined Warnock at Plymouth as reserve goalkeeper and one of the coaches, and followed him to Bury. They stayed together at several clubs before parting company at Sheffield United in 2003.

There was a rumour going round at the time that Blackwell used to cut the manager's lawn on his afternoons off while they were at Plymouth. I didn't know whether that was true or not, but when Warnock told me to train with Blackwell, I told him I wasn't going to work with his gardener. So I went off and trained with a young goalkeeper who was on trial from Ireland. His name? Paddy Kenny. He eventually followed Warnock to Sheffield United and into the premiership.

Even though I wasn't working with the first team, Warnock included me in the squad for a friendly against Aberdeen. I was No.17 or 18. A couple of the lads, Dean West and Dean Barrick, were injured and after treatment they decided to go out for a few pints before the game. I assumed I wouldn't be involved, so I went along. I got back to the ground in time to get changed. I joined the lads for the warm-up, but spent most of the session chatting to a few of the punters. When the game started, I resigned myself to sitting on the bench for 90 minutes.

I made sure I was sitting well away from Warnock so he wouldn't smell the ale. With about 20 minutes left, he turned round and said, 'Get yourself stripped off, Swanny. You're going on.' There was no way I was going to play with four or five pints on board. So I stood up, ran to the goalline at the far end of the pitch and then straight back past the dug-out. I carried on into the dressing room, got changed and pissed off. I'd travelled over from Yorkshire with West and Barrick so we linked up after the game. The next day Warnock called me in. He wanted to know what had happened.

'How do you mean?'

He asked why I'd disappeared after he'd told me I'd be going on.

'Going on? You said, "You won't be going on, so get yourself off." That's what I did.' He just shook his head and I didn't even collect a fine.

Warnock introduced a new regime from the start and among his rules was a ban on jeans on match days, when all the players also had to be clean-shaven. His first home game was against Huddersfield, the club he'd taken to promotion three years earlier. As I wasn't going to be playing, I decided to do a bit of training beforehand. I arrived around lunchtime, worked out for a while and I was having a shower when the players started to turn up.

I joined in a bit of banter as I was putting my jeans on. Then I checked in the mirror that the designer stubble was coming along nicely. I was still messing around when Warnock arrived to give his team talk. He turned round and walked out. He came back ten minutes later to find me still there, larking about. He left again. It was about ten past two when he returned for a third time and asked me to go. I pretended not to hear, but some of the lads decided enough was enough and told me it was time to leave. As I was walking away, Warnock called after me. He told me to go and watch Burnley instead, because that's where I'd be the following week. It was music to my ears!

In the end, another three weeks passed before Stan came calling for me and Gordon Armstrong. It was the only time in my career that I didn't stick out for my signing-on fee before I left. In fact, I agreed to take a cut just to make sure I could get away.

17

THE BEGINNING OF THE END

I returned to Turf Moor in time to play against Millwall on 1 September 1998. I felt as though I'd never been away. The fans gave me a standing ovation before the kick-off, we won 2-1 and I picked up the Man of the Match award. It was a false dawn ... for both Burnley and for me.

I'd been looking for a two-year deal, but Stan would only give me one. He liked to keep his players hungry. Not a bad idea on balance. A three- or four-year contract spells comfort zone to a lot of players, but the knowledge that you might be kicked out at the end of the season tends to focus the mind. It certainly did for me. I was only three weeks away from my thirty-second birthday.

After using me as a striker at Bury, Stan now wanted me to play at the back. I didn't have a problem with that, but the season went pear-shaped more or less straightaway. In all, I started only 11 games and made 6 substitute appearances, but it was an on-off business all season long. I was sent off in my third game at Reading and it took the best part of a month to complete the three-match ban. Sometimes it can be over in a week. Then I missed a couple of games with a chest infection and seemed to struggle with one niggling injury after another.

The team never got off the ground, either. Stan had brought three of us with him from Bury – me, Ronnie Jepson and Gordon Armstrong – but he wasn't happy with the squad he'd inherited from Chris Waddle. And there wasn't much money to strengthen. At one point, he sacked four players he believed were not pulling their weight and, by the time he turned on the town's Christmas lights, Burnley sat nineteenth in the table and Stan was public enemy No.1.

When we travelled down to face Wycombe Wanderers on 20 February, we'd won just 3 of our last 14 games. We were heading for the relegation zone. Wycombe might easily have been the beginning of the end for Stan. Instead, it was the beginning of the end for me. And it started with a little pop in my right knee. Just like I'd felt at Hull 9 years earlier.

I started the game on the bench. Stan sent me on up front early in the second-half. I went for a harmless 50-50 ball with a lad called Jason Cousins. His knee caught my knee. Pop! My knee buckled. I collapsed. Agony. Andy Jones ran on. 'What's up?'

'My knee. Just went pop.'

'Get off and we'll have a look in the treatment room.' Already I was fearing the worst.

The St John's Ambulance team ran on with the stretcher and started trying to lift me on board. Stan wasn't having that. 'Fuck off you lot! Leave my player alone.' He called everyone off the Burnley bench and they carried me into the dressing room on the stretcher. My knee was numb. Andy put a compression bandage around it and, after the game – which we lost 2-0 – I was lifted on to the bus for the journey back to Turf Moor.

I couldn't drive home so the club put me in a hotel in Burnley for the night. The knee was heavily bandaged and I was due to have a scan the following morning. When I got to my room, the pain had eased a lot so I took off the bandages and went for an exploratory trot along the corridor. The knee felt fine. I convinced myself that I might get away with it. The next morning's scan confirmed my worst fears. The cruciate had snapped.

It couldn't have happened at a worse time. There were three months of the season to go and it would be 9 months before I would be fit again. My contract was due to expire in the summer, I had a wife and two kids to support and I was knackered.

I went back to the ground with Andy. Stan sent for me. He asked if there was any particular surgeon that I wanted to do the op. A consultant called David Dandy, from Cambridge, had done the same operation on Paul Gascoigne 8 years earlier so I said I'd see him. The club made an appointment. I was also booked in at Lilleshall for some rehab work in the hope that an operation might not be necessary. After all, I'd got away with it at Hull in 1990, why not now?

I drove to Cambridge from Lilleshall on my own. The appointment didn't last long. I climbed on to the couch. Mr Dandy took hold of my heel and foot, lifted my leg, twisted and pushed at the same time. Pop! Operation. He was going to take a section of my right hamstring and staple it to my kneecap as a replacement ligament. I walked back to the car and rang Stan. As I started to speak, I began to cry. That doesn't happen often, believe me, but all of a sudden the reality had hit me. I believed that to all intents and purposes my career was over. I turned the phone off.

When I thought I was OK to talk, I switched it back on and rang again. Stan said he'd been trying to get back to me. He must have noticed there was a catch in my voice. 'Are you down there by yourself?'

'Yeah.'

'*What*! Right, leave that with me. Get yourself back up here and we'll talk as soon as you arrive.'

I suspect someone at Turf Moor was about to cop for a massive bollocking for letting me go to the appointment on my own. I saw Stan as soon as I arrived.

He said, 'Get yourself booked in and have the operation.' Then he shook my hand and looked me straight in the eye. 'And I'll look after you until you're fit again.'

'But my contract expires ... '

'Don't worry about that. I'll look after you.'

I had to wait for the swelling to go down before Mr Dandy could operate, so it wasn't until the last week of the season that I caught a train down to Cambridge. I was in for four days, on my own and with no visitors, but that didn't bother me. On the third day, I had a call from the lads. They'd just arrived at Northampton for the last game of the season and wished me all the best. To rub it in, I had another call later to say how much they'd miss me at the end-of-season piss-up that night. The following day, Bex drove down and took me home.

At least the boys had something to celebrate: survival. After the Wycombe defeat, Burnley lost their next 3 games, 5-0 against Gillingham, 6-0 against Manchester City and 1-0 to Preston. All at home. We were in the drop zone and a 1-1 draw at Wrexham hardly looked as though it was going to save Stan. If he'd gone then, there would be no one around to 'look after' me, but the board held their nerve and Stan stayed. We beat Macclesfield 4-3 next up and didn't lose again all season, finishing fifteenth.

We all knew there were going to be big changes in the summer. Barry Kilby, who'd taken over as chairman midway through the previous season, was prepared to put a bit of money in and I sensed there was a feeling among some board members that I wasn't going to be much use to the new-look Burnley. Swanny was coming up to thirty-three, was out of action and out of contract. In their minds, it was time to move him out, but Stan stood by me and fought my corner. There was no way he could give me a one-year deal, but he set me up on a month-to-month basis until I had a chance to prove my fitness.

I spent hours working on my own. On the track and in the gym that was part of a new leisure complex behind the Longside stand at Turf Moor. It was a long, boring grind. When I'd finished I used to nip into the café and have a coffee with anyone who happened to be around. I became pals with a chap called Jim Fallon. He was blind. He and a mate used to come and play indoor bowls and worked out in the gym as well. And with Jim around, I was never short of a laugh.

I was always trying to wind him up, but he obviously had a sixth sense that I was around. If he was on the treadmill, I'd sneak up behind him. I'd be about to move it up a gear when he'd call out, 'Swanny, I know you're there.' Or if he was doing weights, I'd try and move the pegs up so he was lifting a heavier weight, but I never got away with it. We had some real laughs. Because he was blind, I suppose people were afraid to take the piss out of him. Not me. What's more, he used to have a go back.

I finally came out on top when he was playing in a bowls match against a pair of women. Jim and his mate were bottom of the league and I used to rib them about it. One day, Jim told me his pal wouldn't be around for the game the following week, so did I fancy taking his place? I turned up for the big match and asked him what I was supposed to do when he was bowling. 'You line me up right and tell me how far the jack is from the opposite end of the mat.'

'OK.' I guided Jim to his starting position, told me where the jack was and then lined him up ... facing the wrong way. He was 3ft away from a concrete wall instead of 45ft away from the jack. When he let go of the ball, it hit the wall with a crack and then rebounded into Jim, sending him flying backwards on to the mat. Our opponents didn't see the funny side of it, but Jim was killing himself and it took five minutes before we settled him down and he was ready to start again for real.

Three months after the op, I had to go back to Cambridge to make sure everything was OK. It was. I could step up my schedule, but pre-season had come and gone without me. Jeppo and the rest of the lads did their best to involve me in the banter, but until I could train properly, I was just an outsider looking in. I had to see the physio every Monday morning. First Andy and then Paul Lake, who took over when he left, to check how things were going. They wanted to see if my movement had improved, if the knee was stronger, if there was any unexpected swelling. And each week I was able to step up my workload a little bit. It meant less time in the gym and more on the training ground.

But every week I was told that if I had any pain, I had to stop and take it easy for a while. That was vital. If it hurts, stop. They told me time and time again, but I'd never worried about pain before: I'd always reckoned that it was a temporary thing, something to put up with, so I took no notice. Even though my body was yelling at me to slow down and take it easy, I ignored the warning signs and insisted I wasn't in pain. So, every Monday, I told a load of half-truths and was given the go-ahead to move up another gear.

And there was another reason for trying to rush back ahead of schedule. I'd felt all along that I had to repay Stan. He could easily have let me go when my contract expired, but he hadn't. He'd kept his word, and in November, after 7 months of what should been my 9-month rehab, I said I was OK to give it a go in the reserves against Oldham. It was madness. Jeppo was also playing and he kept chivvying me along. 'Are you OK, Swanny? How's it going? You're doing great!' I played for 45 minutes then called it a day.

To be honest, I could have come off after 10 minutes because I knew straightaway that I wasn't ready. I spoke to the local reporter afterwards and told him it had gone really well, but I'd decided enough was enough at half-time. That was the signal for a summons from Stan the next day. He told me in no uncertain terms that he made the decisions at Turf Moor, not his players. Then he asked how it had gone. 'Fine,' I lied. 'Yeah, it went really well.'

But the knee wasn't fine and the more I pushed myself, the more it complained. I was living with pain twenty-four hours a day and firing down the painkillers every three or four hours. It was the only way I could get through training.

In the end, my stomach rebelled against the constant bombardment from painkillers. I started passing blood. I'd be standing at a bar, sitting in the car or walking round town when I'd feel the tell-tale signs in the seat of my underpants. Did I heed the warning? Did I fuck! All I was interested in was a new contract or a move; and another year's football.

So instead of the tablets, I used suppositories. Four a day. Just to train. Obviously I couldn't get them from the club doctor because he would have reported back to Stan, so I went to my own GP and managed to convince him everything was above board. Incredibly, no one found out. I used to flush the empty suppository tubes down the bog, but sometimes I needed two or three attempts before they went away. Once one of the lads followed me in and spotted the empty tube. 'Who's sticking these things up their arse?' Nobody answered and I never said a word. If anyone had told Stan, I'd have been flushed out, as it were.

It was hopeless. Because I was coming back from such a long-term injury, other parts of my body started to play up: ankle, Achilles, calf. I used to go to the sauna or have a Jacuzzi to try and loosen up the joints. I'd stay in for hours at a time. I got up early to do extra gym work before training, just so I'd be reasonably loose.

It was around then that I had my first real bust-up with Stan. I'd put a bit of weight on while I was out of action and I couldn't lose it because I wasn't training properly. I cut down on how much I ate; I even cut down on the booze, but no joy. After I'd played a couple of reserve games, Stan called me in. 'Look Swanny, you've got to lose some weight. If you don't, I'll have to get rid of you.' I thought he was just looking for an excuse.

'Right, fucking well get rid of me then!' And I stormed out of his office.

I came off the bench in a couple of first-team games in January, but I knew it wasn't right. I'd done everything and it hadn't worked.

One day at the beginning of March, just over a year since the injury, I was late for training. Stan saw me arrive, which would normally have meant an automatic fine. Instead, he just said, 'Morning Swanny, all right?'

'Yeah, fine, gaffer. You?'

'Yeah.' I sensed something was wrong. After training, he said, 'Can I have a word?' I knew what was coming. We went into his office. 'I'm going to have to let you go,' he said.

I stood up, shook hands. 'OK. Thanks for keeping your word and standing by me. That's meant a lot. I'm fit again. I've got a chance.'

'I'll make a few phone calls; try and sort something out for you.'

'Thanks, I appreciate that.' We shook hands again. I walked away from Burnley for the last time. It was a lonely drive home and my knee was killing me all the way. For me, the Turf Moor party was over.

But for Burnley, it had only just begun. And the man who lit the spark was a football legend: Ian Wright, who'd arrived not long before I left. The boys had been up with the front runners all season without attracting much attention, but when news leaked out that Wright, Arsenal's all-time record goalscorer with 33 England caps to his name, might be on his way to Turf Moor, the football world sat up and took notice.

THE BEGINNING OF THE END

He'd joined Celtic from West Ham in October 1999, but it hadn't worked out. Stan heard on the grapevine that he might be available, but it looked a long shot. Wright was 36, a London legend, and the word was that if he was going anywhere he'd be on his way back to the Smoke. But Stan didn't give up, and on Valentine's Day 2000, a month before I left the club, he pulled his rabbit out of the hat. Wright joined the Clarets. Lights, camera, action!

Wrighty had an incredible impact at the club and in the town. He had an aura about him, and at a stroke, Stan convinced people inside and outside Burnley that we meant business. The media came calling and over 20,000 fans rolled up for his first game against Wigan, an increase of 7,000 on our previous match against Bristol Rovers. It was a goalless draw.

Wrighty started only four games, made eleven substitute appearances and scored four goals. But his presence set the dressing room alight and sparked a successful promotion challenge. After losing their next 2 games, Burnley won 9 of their last 13 matches and clinched promotion with a 2-1 win at Scunthorpe on the final day of the season.

I was long gone by then, of course, but I'd still had time to write my name into Wright's legend. I'd always admired him. He was a fantastic player, a natural goalscorer and a great personality. And I wanted a slice of the action. Needless to say, the YTS lads were queuing up to be his boot boy, but they reckoned without me and Jeppo. On his first day, we strode into the boot room. 'Who's doing Wrighty's boots?' One of the kids put his hand up. 'Right, fuck off!'

Jeppo took the right foot, I took the left. We cleaned his boots, trainers, rubbers, the lot. We were like two big kids. I can still see Jeppo, fag in the corner of his mouth, giving Wrighty's right boot an extra shine, talking about his impact on the training ground and how good his sessions with the strikers had been.

I'm sure Ian had no idea who his boot boys really were. He

certainly didn't offer us any tips! But to this day, Jeppo and I can sit back over a pint and tell anyone who's prepared to listen that we were once Ian Wright's boot boys.

Burnley was a great place to be. Even though I was playing at the third level of English football, I always felt the club belonged much higher up the ladder. The facilities were good and you could almost smell the tradition behind a club that had been a founder member of the Football League way back in 1888. It always felt like a big club waiting to happen.

And the fans were something else. The ground is surrounded by terraced streets, where everyone seems to be a Clarets supporter. I used to do some coaching in local schools and all the kids would be wearing the claret and blue of Burnley, not Premier League strips belonging to clubs based somewhere over the horizon. These were Burnley kids, they supported their home town team and they were proud of it.

I was chuffed to bits when news came through that Burnley were back in what is now the Championship. They've been there ever since. Will they ever go back to where they belong in the top flight? It won't be easy, but I for one would love to see them do it.

18
THE FINAL CURTAIN

Five days after I left Burnley, the phone rang. It was Terry Dolan, my manager at Hull eight years earlier. He was in charge at York, in the old Fourth Division. 'Will you come and train with us for a few days and play for the reserves at Scarborough on Wednesday? We'll see how you are. If it goes OK, we'll give you a contract to the end of the season.' It was a lifeline.

I'd always worked on the basis that if I was OK with people on the way up, they'd be all right with me on the way down. With one or two notable exceptions, that was how I'd played it with the managers I'd worked for. I could be a pain in the arse sometimes but, by and large, they got value for money. Dolan and I had always been straight with one another at Hull and now it was payback time.

I reported on the Monday morning, stuffed a suppository up my arse and trained well. The pain was manageable. By Tuesday morning, everything had stiffened up. I could hardly move, never mind train. I rang Terry and told him I'd been asked to go for talks at another club. 'I'll have to see what they're offering but I want to play for your reserves tomorrow.' I sat in the jacuzzi most of

Tuesday and, the next day, headed off to Scarborough's McCain Stadium. The pitch was frozen, it was blowing half a gale, the young kids in the York side weren't on my wavelength and I had an absolute stinker.

I drove home, had a couple of brandies to kill the pain and went to bed. Bex woke me at seven o'clock next morning. 'We've won the lottery! We've won the lottery!' She was sprinting upstairs. I sat bolt upright, leaped out of bed, and we ran downstairs to check our ticket. I never felt a thing from my knee.

She was holding the slip and we went through the numbers. We had five out of six. No jackpot, but we reckoned a hundred grand-plus. Bex rang up. It took ages to get through. When she put the phone down she said we'd won around 1,500 quid, but she'd have to go to the local outlet to find out exactly how much. She came back in tears.

'What's up?'

'We've only won £500. They said 1,500 people had won £500, not the other way round.'

Some you win, some you lose. We've never done the lottery since.

I arrived at Bootham Crescent on Thursday fearing the worst. Dolan looked pretty downbeat, but having said that, he usually did. He said, 'OK, we've seen enough.' I tried not to let my disappointment show but instead, he went on, 'Train with us next week and we'll sort something out.' I couldn't believe it.

I trained on the Monday, made my excuses again on the Tuesday, played another reserve game on the Wednesday. On Thursday, Terry called me in. 'We'd like to give you a contract until the end of the season. How much are you on?'

I'd been on around a thousand a week at Burnley and I would have settled for less, but the money was OK and I was in the starting line-up for the game at Shrewsbury on the Saturday.

THE FINAL CURTAIN

Neither the suppository in the morning nor the one before the game were enough. My knee was killing me after only 20 minutes and I'd already collected a yellow card. I knew I wouldn't last 90 minutes. Just before half-time, I made another clumsy challenge, received another yellow card and was sent off, but the lads hung on for only their second win in 18 games and a one-match ban gave me some breathing space. I played 8 more games to the end of the season and we only lost once. A potential relegation battle became mid-table respectability.

People said I'd made the difference. It was flattering, but I didn't see it that way. OK, I'd done well, tightened things up at the back and lifted the atmosphere in the dressing room, but from where I stood, I was just part of a side that suddenly clicked. It happens. A team can be struggling, then they get a couple of little breaks and they're away. A similar thing happened at Burnley the season before. They'd looked doomed with ten matches left but found an extra gear and a 'Get Out Of Jail Free' card. We'd done the same.

Dolan wanted to offer me a new 12-month contract and fixed up a meeting with Douglas Craig, the chairman. I hadn't seen much of him up to then, but he seemed a decent bloke. We sat round a table. My knee was throbbing. Terry told me what was on offer, but Craig interrupted. He wasn't happy about my knee. He said it could go at any time and he wanted a clause in the contract saying that if I had to quit because of my knee, the club wouldn't have to pay me.

Dolan came straight back. 'I'm not having that in one of my players' contracts.' They were arguing between themselves and getting nowhere. So I joined in. I was just desperate for a contract, *any* contract. 'I'm happy with my knee. If you want to put that clause into the contract, fine.' But Dolan stood firm, and in the end, Craig accepted Terry's argument. I honestly hadn't felt as strongly about it. I genuinely believed that one way or another, I'd get through the season.

Terry made me captain, the first time I'd been given the job full-time since my year at Plymouth, but I'd also skippered Port Vale and Burnley a few times and always really enjoyed the job. As a kid, the captain tends to be the best player in the side, but it doesn't work that way in the professional game.

The captain needs to be a leader, an organiser and a man the other players respect. He has to be able to keep his players going even if he's having a tough time himself. They must be able to turn to him in confidence if they have a problem or an issue they don't want to take to the manager. So to be given the armband is seen as a big honour for any player at any level. I was chuffed to bits.

I went away for the summer to celebrate a new contract, the captaincy ... and my recently acquired status as a television celebrity. It began during my spell in rehab at Lilleshall earlier that year. Rob Ullathorne, who played for Norwich, was there at the same time and soon afterwards he appeared on Helen Chamberlain's *Soccer AM* show on Sky. Rob was the man in the firing line on their question-and-answer session and one of the questions was: 'Who is your best mate in football?' Just for a laugh, Rob said, 'Peter Swan.'

The following week, they featured John Beresford. He was asked the same question: 'Who is your best mate in football?'

'Peter Swan.'

Helen did a bit of a double take although, unlike Ullathorne, Bez was speaking the truth, the whole truth and nothing but the truth. But Helen and the rest of the team spotted a storyline and, for the next few weeks, persuaded the featured player to pretend his best mate was Peter Swan. All sorts of people I'd never met in my life joined in the fun and I even turned out to be big mates with Steve McManaman, who was with Real Madrid at the time.

They filmed Steve in Spain and he bought into the idea big-time. 'Your best mate in football?'

'Peter Swan. He was here a couple of weeks ago. Usual nightmare with Swanny. He always says he's just here for a day or two and ends up staying for a week. I couldn't get rid of him.'

Macca did well for me there, but Dean Windass stitched me up big-style. He was with Bradford City at the time and the previous week had played in a testimonial at Hull. I went along, too, and we were both in a club afterwards. Dean introduced me to his missus while we were standing at the bar. I just said hello and moved on. The following week he appeared on *Soccer AM*. 'Who's your best mate in football?'

'Peter Swan,' he replied to order. 'And I've got a story about Swanny.'

'Go on then, tell us.'

'We were out in a club a few nights ago and Swanny came over and told me he'd just pulled a bird at the bar. It was my wife.'

I was watching the show in a hotel room in Burnley at the time and the mobile went straightaway. It was Bex. I told her Windass was only messing about, and that I was hardly going to chat up his wife five minutes after he'd introduced us.

In the end, I was invited on to the show, just to prove to the viewers that Peter Swan really did exist! It was an all-expenses paid trip: first-class rail travel on Friday, overnight in a London hotel and chauffeur-driven transport. The car called for me early on the Saturday morning and when I arrived at the studios, I was shown into the Green Room. There was a contract for me to sign, a cup of coffee and then out on to the sofa with Helen and Tim Lovejoy. They showed a clip of me in action, we talked about my career, how I knew Robbie Williams and what I was doing now. I had a chance to chip in on the other issues that were discussed throughout the show and, in the end, we all had a good laugh.

Afterwards, I thanked Helen and said that if I could ever help her in the future, she only had to give me a shout. The mobile rang not long afterwards. She's a big Torquay fan and was helping to organise a testimonial for one of the players. Because of my

Plymouth connections, she thought it would be a good laugh if I played in the game. Did I fancy it? No problem. When I asked about a hotel, she said I could stay with her and her partner at her place, a smashing flat overlooking Torbay. It was a great night and we've been pals ever since.

In July, I reported back for what turned out to be my last season as a professional footballer. Terry told me that I knew my own body better than anyone and to pace myself through pre-season and to make sure I was ready to go when the action got serious. I got through pre-season without too many problems and plenty of suppositories and played in all the friendlies. It was probably a mistake. I should have picked my matches a bit better.

It was a boiling hot day for the first friendly. I drank about six cans of Red Bull to lift the energy levels, stuck in the suppository and I was all set. Then I spotted the shorts hanging on my peg. I always wore size Double XL, these were struggling to make large. I tried them for size. No chance! They looked like lycras. The lads were absolutely pissing themselves. I called the kit man over. 'These shorts, they're far too small. I take Double XL.'

'They're all we've got!'

'What do you mean, they're all you've fucking got? I can't play in them! They'll split if I bend down.'

'I'll see what I can do.' I put on a different coloured pair for the warm-up and wore a long kagoule over the top. Nobody noticed anything, but I knew there was no way I could wear the shorts that were waiting for me back in the dressing room. Then I spotted Yorkie the Lion, the club mascot, arsing around in front of a handful of fans.

Over the top of his lion outfit, he was wearing a York City shirt and ... the biggest pair of shorts you've ever seen. I broke off my stretches, jogged over to Yorkie and started to stretch again. 'Yorkie!' I called. No answer.

I moved nearer. 'Yorkie!' Still no response. Was he deaf or something? I took a few more steps in his direction and yelled, 'Yorkie!' This time he looked round. For the benefit of the punters, I put my arm round his shoulder and pretended to be sharing a laugh.

But this was serious stuff. 'Look, can you do me a favour? Go into the dressing room, take your shorts off and hang them on my peg.' I could hear him laughing inside his lion's head. 'I'm not joking. Go and put those shorts on my peg.'

'You're serious, aren't you?'

'Too right I am.'

'OK, no problem.'

Yorkie waved to the fans and jogged off in the direction of the tunnel – and then I noticed the long, brown tail attached to the back of his shorts. 'Oi, Yorkie!'

'What?'

'And cut that fucking tail off while you're at it!'

By the time I reached the dressing room, I'd psyched myself up to wear Yorkie the Lion's shorts, complete with his name on the front and a chopped-off brown tuft at the back. But waiting on my peg was a brand new pair of Double XLs fresh out of the club shop. So Yorkie kept his shorts ... and his tail.

The last friendly was against Manchester United. Jonathan Greening, one of the kids at York, had joined United and part of the deal was a pre-season game at Bootham Crescent. I desperately needed a break before the first league match, but I wasn't going to miss United. I was playing at the back. I looked at the United line-up: Beckham, Keane, Scholes and Giggs were in midfield and Yorke and Greening were up front. I didn't bother about the make-up of their back four.

Because it was Man United, I wanted to give the extra ten per cent. That extra ten per cent fucked me up, but I lived the moment. Midway through the first-half, I decided that as a former

Leeds player, I ought to give Beckham something to remember me by. I went charging into a tackle, he saw me coming, stepped aside, let me have the ball, gave me a smile and prepared to take the free-kick.

As we were lining up, Paul Scholes decided to have a word. Apparently he doesn't normally say much during a game, but this was an exception to the rule. He said, 'Watch this. Beckham's going to smash the ball in to me, I'll lay it off, he'll flick it over to the far post, Giggsy will come in for the volley.' I thought, 'No way'. Beckham seemed to be setting up to float the free-kick to the far post, but at the last minute, he belted it low and hard to Scholes. He played it back to Beckham as promised and when the flighted cross came in, Giggs volleyed inches over the bar at the far post. Scholes didn't even look at me as he ran back to the halfway line.

I also learned to my cost about the quality of Beckham's crosses. I'd always reckoned I could handle more or less anything in the air, but as I went for Beckham's first cross, I suddenly realised I was way out of position. I mistimed my jump and the ball flew over my head. I couldn't work it out.

The same diagonal ball next time ... and the same result. At the third or fourth time of asking, I worked out what he was doing. It was like hitting a golf shot with topspin. The spin carried the ball beyond its obvious flight path. Mark Sertori, who was also playing in central defence, tried his luck soon afterwards. 'You're not going to get it!' I shouted. He didn't. His diving header missed the ball by about four yards. I cracked out laughing.

Bex had come to the game with George, who was five at the time. As we were leaving, I spotted Beckham standing near a turnstile, signing autographs. 'Sorry about that challenge.'

He smiled and said, 'No problem.' He ruffled George's hair and gave him the remains of his Gatorade. Then he bent down and pulled a pair of boots out of his holdall. 'There you are, son.'

'I don't want them,' said George.

'Go on, they're a present.'

'No chance. I'm a Leeds fan.'

Typical!

The first league match was at Chesterfield. We went in front through Peter Duffield after 43 seconds, the season's quickest goal. I didn't have much to smile about after that. I'd been OK through the week, but I knew almost straightaway that my knee wasn't right. I couldn't turn. I said to Sertori, 'Look, if anything comes over the top, it's yours.'

'Leave it to me.'

I knew I shouldn't have been out there. I was frustrated, angry and disappointed that things had gone wrong so quickly. We were still in front at half-time, but they hit us with 3 quick goals after the interval. With 15 minutes left, we won a free-kick inside their half. I went into the box. Steve Blatherwick, a team-mate at Burnley, was marking me, jostling, tugging my shirt. Normally I would have shrugged it off as part and parcel of the game. Not this time. I said, 'Do that again, Blathers, and I'll fucking whack you!' He did it again. I boiled over and went to butt him. He saw it coming, pulled away and I failed to make contact, but the ref was three yards away. Red card.

Dolan pulled me afterwards. 'Did you butt him?'

'No.'

As it happened I had Blathers' number in my phone, so before we got on the bus, I gave him a call. 'Do us a favour, Blathers.'

'What?'

'If I ring you in five minutes, will you tell the gaffer nothing happened?'

'OK.'

Dolan called me over as I was getting on the bus. 'Look, did you do it?'

'No.'

'We'll be having a look at the video and if you did, we'll fine you two weeks' wages.'

'I've got Blathers' number here. Do you want me to ring him?' I dialled the number, handed Terry the phone. He asked what had happened. Blathers told him he'd been tugging my shirt and I'd swung round, but there had been no contact, so I escaped a fine, but not the three-match ban. That would start the following week, after our first home game of the season against Cheltenham. I staggered through training that week and led the side out for the first and only time at Bootham Crescent. We lost 2-0, but somehow I lasted the full 90 minutes.

On the Monday morning, I went in to see Terry. 'Look, I'm banned for two weeks. Can I go in for some keyhole surgery, just to clean up the knee? I should be right for the season then.' The club booked me into a hospital in York. Deep down, I knew the knee was knackered, but I thought this might give me a few more months.

The day after the op, I saw the specialist. He was shaking his head. 'How have you managed to play with that knee? The mess in there is unbelievable. First, the good news: the cruciate is fine. Your operation was a success and that's not going to be a problem, but a knee should be shiny and round; yours is dull and concave. There's no cartilage, there are bits floating round everywhere and it's riddled with arthritis. If I was in charge, I wouldn't even let you out for one more training session, never mind a match.' He added that if I did any more damage, I could end up in a wheelchair.

I'd been playing through the pain barrier for two years, first, with the help of tablets, then suppositories. I shouldn't have been playing at all. I knew he was right, but I walked away refusing to believe the injury was so bad. I wanted to give it one more go.

Terry had the specialist's report in front of him when I walked into his office the next day. I sat down on the other side of the desk. 'This isn't good, is it?'

'No, but I want to play on.'

'Bring your missus in tomorrow. We'll have a chat.'

Bex and I went back the following day. Dolan said, 'You've got your life to live, Swanny. You've got your wife, your kids. You want a proper life with them. This is just a game of football. I've seen the report. You could be in a wheelchair before long if you're not careful. There's no way you should train again, there's no way you should even think about playing again. It's in your hands, but don't think you owe me anything. You did brilliantly for me last season, you kept us up. The club will pay you what you're owed, there'll be a pension payment from the PFA and that will give you time to get yourself sorted out. Above all, remember that you haven't let me down.'

I still wasn't going to go quietly. I said, 'Look, Terry. I'm not going to make a decision here and now. I want to go back to Lilleshall and see what they say, then we'll look at it again in a month's time.'

I tried Lilleshall, I tried to train again at York. It was hopeless, like living with toothache. Nothing worked. If I rested, the knee stiffened up, if I worked, the pain was even worse. After 4 weeks, I accepted defeat. I was thirty-four and washed up. Sixteen years, 7 clubs and 503 senior games after signing professional forms for Leeds United, my career was over.

19

WILL SWANNY BE THERE?

Every cloud has a silver lining. Even a career-threatening injury. And at least the bad news from the specialist in York gave me the chance of a farewell trip to Lilleshall. I'd already had five spells there on rehab while I was at Leeds, Hull, Port Vale and Burnley. Now I was going back for a last desperate throw of the dice.

It was a fantastic set-up: a country house set in acres of grounds with a two-mile drive leading to the front door. The facilities and treatment were top drawer. The centre was run by Pauline and Phil Newton, a husband-and-wife team. Phil was the director in overall charge and Pauline worked alongside him. They were both highly-qualified physios and around them they had a team of specialists in all areas of sports injury treatment and rehab.

They were great people who became good mates. But they ran a tight ship and this was a tough regime. Instead of just spending a morning working with the club physio, it was 9 to 5 with only a short break for lunch. Five days a week, usually for four weeks, sometimes longer. It was as hard as anything I've ever done. During the first couple of days, I'd be in bed having a lie-down after an 8-hour stint. Sometimes it was all I could do to manage a couple of pints after the evening meal, but made up for that as the weeks went by.

My first visit to the centre was in 1986, the year it opened. Come to think of it, I must have been one of their first patients. I was with Leeds at the time. I'd had an operation to clear some scar tissue away from my right knee and the physio suggested a four-week course at Lilleshall.

I jumped at the chance. Over the years, I've met a lot of players who thought a visit to Lilleshall was some sort of punishment, but not me. I used to hate being an injured player hanging around the club. I felt like an outsider. But down at Lilleshall there'd be anything up to a dozen players going through rehab and we were all in it together.

I wasn't just the solitary player with a bad injury, working on his own to get back: I was part of a group. And there was always someone more seriously injured than me, someone to talk to about how they were coping, someone to encourage, someone who would encourage me in return. I saw people from all sorts of different sports with horrific injuries, all of whom were determined to work their way back. Seeing everyone making progress gave us all a lift.

There was always a target to aim for and I needed that. I'd arrive on the first Monday of a four-week programme and see players who were far fitter than me. They'd be starting their last week. So I knew that, if I worked hard, I'd be up there, too, at the end of my programme. We were all working towards the same goal: being fit to return to our clubs and just about ready to join in full training again.

The courses were designed to make sure that when we did go back, we wouldn't pick up the little niggles that so often follow a long spell out with a big injury. For example, in the summer of 1993, while I was at Port Vale, I went to Lilleshall for rehab after my hernia op. After two weeks, I felt fine and said I was ready to go back. Instead, they kept me down for another fortnight to build up my groin and abductor muscles and I slipped back into training without any problems.

The programmes were competitive, but they were also fun. Sometimes, if we'd all worked well, there'd be croquet or sit-down cricket on the lawn as a bit of light relief. As the years went by, however, health and safety started to kick in. At first, for example, we'd be told to jump on a bike at the end of an afternoon and ride to the end of the drive and back. The last one home had to do it again.

We'd just leap on the nearest bike and set off at top speed. All sorts of bumping and boring went on before we made it back to HQ. By the time I went down there for that last time, we had to wear helmets and fluorescent jackets and each bike had to be tested before we climbed on. I could see where they were coming from. The last thing a club wanted was a million-pound player going back with a broken arm after falling off a bike, but some of the fun had gone out of it.

On my first visit, I ganged up with Jan Molby, who was with Liverpool at the time, and Bob Beardmore, who played rugby league for Castleford. I went through hell for a couple of days and behaved myself at night, but by Wednesday, I was ready for a bit of action. So were Jan and Bob. We headed off to a pub in Newport, a little market town nearby. It was full of bikers. We'd had a couple of pints when Jan called one of them over. A real bloody man mountain. 'This lad wants to arm wrestle with you,' said Molby, pointing at me.

I thought, 'Hang on, Jan! I don't do arm wrestling with anybody, let alone a hairy-arsed biker with forearms like billiard table legs and tattoos all over the place.' And the biker obviously fancied his chances. 'How much for?' he asked.

'Fifty quid,' said my second.

'Right!'

I'd never arm wrestled in my life, but I grabbed hold of his hand, we grappled, grappled and grappled again. After a while, it was obvious we were going nowhere fast and the bout ended in a draw. Honours even. Fifty quid intact. Over to you, Jan.

Molby and another biker linked hands and the second bout began. There were about 15 bikers cheering their mate on, with just Bob and me in Jan's corner. It was a one-sided affair. Jan obviously knew what he was doing and he soon had the biker down on his knees, banging his arm on the floor. He was deadly serious and, for a split second, it looked as if he would break his arm. His mates were crowding round us, they were distinctly hostile and I thought we were going to be done over. But, at the last minute, Jan let go, shook hands, collected his money, walked over to the bar, ordered a full round and shouted, 'Right, let's have three of you for a scrum down!'

With Molby and Swan propping and Beardmore pretending he'd never done anything like this before, we packed down. Best of three with an ashtray as the ball. The landlord rushed over, thinking there was a brawl. But he soon realised what was going on and stayed to watch as our 'novice' hooker shovelled out the ashtray twice to give us an unassailable 2-0 lead. Another fifty notes in the kitty.

Eventually we all piled out of the pub and said a noisy farewell. The bikers put their helmets on, revved up and roared off into the night ... just as a police patrol car rolled into view. A neighbour had decided enough was enough. I tried to explain to one of the coppers that we were working at Lilleshall and had just popped out for a quiet pint. He was OK about it and told us to get off home.

And we would have done if Molby hadn't chosen that moment to have a pee behind the patrol car, waving at a woman who was peering out of her bedroom window. I managed to keep the coppers talking until he'd finished.

WILL SWANNY BE THERE?

The law obviously reported us to the Lilleshall staff, though, because when we went back the following Monday, there was a book at reception laying down the rules about what we could and could not do. As well as signing the register, we were all supposed to sign a form to prove we'd read the rules. Anyone who fell by the wayside would be sent home. 'You don't expect me to sign this, do you?' I asked.

Jan and Bob were just two of the professional sportsmen I linked up with over the years. There were footballers like Mark Dennis, John Fashanu, Geoff Thomas, Julian Dicks, David Howells, Rob Ullathorne and Garth Crooks. Richard Guest, the National Hunt jockey, was there for a few weeks and so too were England cricketer Phil de Freitas and Mick Hill, the Olympic javelin thrower.

And then there was John Beresford, the former Manchester City, Barnsley, Portsmouth, Newcastle and Southampton defender, who is now front man for a shop-fitting company, a Newcastle match-day host and a TV pundit; not to mention my best mate.

We'd played against one another at schoolboy level in Yorkshire and the first time I went to Lilleshall, Bez arrived, too, recovering from an ankle injury. We developed a bond straightaway. We go on holiday together now and we've enjoyed our fair share of nights out. It's a pity we never played in the same side, although I can't think of many managers who'd have agreed with that!

Every time I went to Lilleshall, I'd give Bez a call. 'I'm off to Lilleshall on Monday.'

'Right, see you there!'

We weren't trying it on with anyone at our clubs, but it was amazing how often our spells out of the game coincided. And we both had the same approach: work like hell during the day, play hard at night and if there's any chance of a practical joke, go for it! After a while, stories about our pranks down there were buzzing round the grapevine and other injured players wanted a piece of the action.

The third time I went, when I was recovering from my hernia op, Phil greeted me like a long-lost friend and told me how people booking themselves in for treatment would sometimes ask, 'Will Swanny be there? What about Bez?' If word got round that Bez and I would be there at the same time, the place would be booked up in no time. It reached the stage where, when we all got together on our first night, we'd be asked what we'd got planned for the week ahead. We were the social secretaries.

Phil and Pauline usually turned a blind eye to the two of us. They knew we'd give everything during the day and that we could still hack it the next morning after a night out. Anyone who came out with us who couldn't stand the pace the following morning got a bollocking from Phil and Pauline ... and from me and Bez!

But Lilleshall wasn't just for professional sportsmen and women. Amateurs used to go there, too. Sometimes people with no sporting ability. People like Andy. He had an office job in London and had paid for treatment to a knee problem out of his own pocket. He was totally uncoordinated, had no athletic ability at all and stood out like a sore thumb among all the pros. Bez and I took him under our wing. Well, sort of.

He seemed to like being around professional footballers and enjoyed the banter, but he was the easiest person to wind up that I've ever known. If Bez and I needed to let off a bit of steam and have a laugh, Andy was the perfect candidate for a few practical jokes. In fact, as soon as I spotted him, I said to Bez, 'We've got a corker this week.' And we started to make plans straightaway.

It just so happened that another of the patients during Andy's first week was a professional masseuse, who'd injured her ankle in a parachute jump. She was a real looker. She had her own clinic in

Birmingham and used to commute to Lilleshall every day. Over lunch one day, she was telling us about the value of deep massage. She suggested that Bez and I should try it some time; she said it would help take out some of the stiffness after all the hard work during the day. We arranged to go over that night.

'And can we bring Andy along, too?' I asked. 'He isn't a pro and he feels a bit out of it. This might help him to bed in a bit.' We set off straight after tea, telling Andy that this girl ran a massage parlour and he'd be all right for a bit of the other. He didn't believe us at first, but a few lurid stories got him going and by the time we arrived in Birmingham he was well fired up.

We parked outside the clinic and I said to Andy, 'Right, I'll go first, Bez second and you third, but before you go in, take your underpants off so you're ready for action as soon as you get rid of your trousers.' He nodded.

I went in, had a massage and 20 minutes later staggered out the door, trying to look completely knackered. 'Fucking hell, Bez. You've never had 'owt like that!' Bez dashed straight in. I waited outside with Andy, who was desperate to find out what had gone on. I told him to wait and see for himself, but finally admitted to a candlelit orgy of delight. Another twenty minutes went by before Bez emerged, doing his impression of another satisfied customer. We exchanged high fives. Andy leaped to his feet. 'Hang on', I said. 'You remembered to take your pants off, didn't you?'

'Yes.'

'Right, get in there, rip your trousers off, lie on the couch and the job's a good 'un. Leave the rest to her.' He dashed in. Bez and I rushed to the door to listen in. Seconds later a female voice boomed out, 'And what the hell do you think you're playing at?' We opened the door to see a shamefaced Andy yanking up his trousers and heading out of the room as fast as he could.

I tried to apologise on his behalf. 'He just wouldn't listen', I told her. 'We said it wasn't that sort of place, but he kept saying there were always a few "extras" on offer when you had a massage.'

Understandably, Andy was a bit subdued on the way back. He accused us of stitching him up. We acted the innocents. We claimed we thought he knew we were only joking and offered to stop for a pint to cheer him up. While we were playing pool, he went over to the bandit and, before long, he'd racked up £25 in winnings. I tried to convince him it might be an idea to cash in while he was in front, but he insisted on carrying on. Bad move.

I'd spotted the plug behind the bandit earlier so while Bez was at the table, I sidled over and nudged the switch with my cue. The screen on the bandit went blank. Andy couldn't believe it. He rushed over to the bar. 'I've just won 25 quid and the machine's fused.' The barman gave him an old-fashioned look, and while Andy was trying to convince him, I clicked the switch back on. The screen lit up again, but Andy's winnings had been wiped. Meanwhile he'd finally persuaded the barman to have a look, only to find the bandit in perfect working order with no record of his winnings.

'You want to watch him,' I told the barman. 'He's nowt but bother. He's already tried messing about with a masseuse in Birmingham.'

He was always immaculate when he started work in the morning. White T-shirt, white shorts, white socks. The pros made do with a couple of changes a week, usually from one battered old strip to another, but Andy's kit was always perfect. We couldn't work it out. So one day, after we'd finished, Bez and I decided to follow him. He went back to his room, showered and then, with us tiptoeing in pursuit, set off for the on-site launderette. While we watched from outside, he put his white gear in and switched on to cool wash. We had him!

We hid behind a tree as he was leaving and then nipped into the launderette. We switched off his washing, chucked in a pair of red socks Bez was wearing and switched the washer back on ... at maximum temperature. Next day, Andy reported for duty dressed from head to toe in a fetching shade of pink.

That morning, we decided to try out the old prank of moving Andy's car. We nicked his keys, hid the motor out of sight round the side of the building and went back to work. At lunchtime, we asked Andy for a lift into Newport, around four miles away. We went outside. 'My car, where's my car? Somebody's nicked my bloody car.'

'Well, you'd best ring the police.'

He got straight on to the blower and the cops said they'd be round as soon as they could, probably mid-afternoon. Garth Crooks was with us that week and knew what had happened. When he heard the plod were on their way, he suggested it was time to call off the hounds. No bloody chance! Instead, as soon as Andy was safely back in the gym, we returned the car to its original parking place. When the copper finally arrived, he sent for Andy, who was still dressed head to toe in pink.

The officer looked him up and down, asked what had happened and Andy led him round to where his car had been. It was still there. We looked on as Andy frantically tried to explain that he wasn't messing about, but it was obvious the copper wasn't impressed by excuses from a man dressed in pink. Andy came back in. 'I can't believe it. When I looked earlier my car had gone. You saw it had gone, didn't you?'

'Nay,' I said. 'Don't ask me. I never saw where you were parked in the first place. I just believed what you told me. You'd obviously forgotten where you'd left it.'

'It's being in this place with you bloody lot,' he replied. 'I must be going mad. And now they're threatening to do me for wasting police time.'

We decided to make it up to Andy that night and took him for a drink. Bez was teetotal in those days, so he drove my car back from the boozer. By prior arrangement, as we were going up the two-mile drive, he started 'chugging' the engine as if he was running out of petrol. Andy piped up from the back straightaway: 'Do what Formula One drivers do! When they're running out of petrol, they swerve the car around to use up the last dregs of fuel. Try it, Bez!' So Bez started weaving around in the drive, at the same time easing the car forward again. 'Told you!' said Andy.

But soon afterwards, Bez started chugging again and this time he let the car grind to a halt. 'That's it, we'll have to push,' I told Andy, and we clambered out. After 20 yards or so, Bez kicked the car into life again. I leaped into the front seat but, as Andy was trying to climb into the back, Bez slammed on the brakes as if he'd run out of petrol again. Andy clattered full force into the open door and fell on to the drive, clutching his bad knee. Next morning he was suffering from a monumental hangover and his knee had swollen up like a balloon 'What shall I do?' he asked.

'You've probably caught a cold in the joint,' I told him. 'It happens to players all the time. We rub some Vicks in it to loosen it up.'

'You're kidding.'

'No. Just tell Phil your knee's caught a cold and you need some Vicks.' We watched as Andy explained the situation to Phil, whose expression said it all. But he saw us watching, smelled the alcohol on Andy's breath and decided to go along with us.

'Right,' he said. 'Here's your Vicks, rub some in your knee and then go and lie upside down on the back-stretcher to get rid of the fluid. It might get rid of your hangover as well.' It didn't. After 20 minutes lying upside down, his face was a dull green colour. I was on the next piece of equipment.

'Swanny, I think I'm going to be sick.'

He was still struggling by the time we went for our late afternoon swim. Whoever finished last in the previous programme had to cycle to the swimming pool in Newport while the rest travelled in a minibus. So Andy was on his bike. The swimming exercises were really tough: we had to tread water in the deep end and throw a ball to one another. Anyone who dropped the ball had to swim a couple of lengths as a forfeit. Sure enough, Andy kept dropping the ball. After about six extra lengths, he leaped out of the pool and puked up.

As it was the end of the day, Phil usually let us have ten minutes in the sauna before setting off back in the bus. And while Andy and the rest of the lads were relaxing, I slipped outside with a spanner I'd hidden in my bag. I unscrewed Andy's saddle and stashed it in my bag with the spanner. After our sauna, we all piled on to the bus, leaving our answer to Lance Armstrong to pedal back up to the main house four miles away ... without a saddle.

The bikes were perfect for a joke or six. As well as removing the saddle, we'd flick off the chain, let the tyres down, turn the handlebars round. You name it. And then, once a week, there was the long bike ride along the country lanes round Lilleshall. We went out in threes and Andy drew the short straw. He was the third member of a team already featuring me and Bez. We set off at a fairly gentle pace, encouraging him all the time. 'Come on, you're doing well, Andy lad! Try and keep up a bit more!' Gradually the gap between the pacemakers and the weakest link increased.

The circuit was mainly on fairly straight roads and led back to Lilleshall, using three or four left turns. But there was also a right turn about a quarter of the way round. That was definitely off limits because it led on to a winding road that disappeared into the middle distance. We left just enough distance between us for Andy to spot us turning right when we should have kept straight on. And then we switched on the power for a few hundred yards, jumped off the bikes and hid behind a bush.

We could hear Andy puffing up behind. 'Swanny, Bez, where are you?' He cycled past. We waited until he was safely out of sight, came out of hiding, retraced our steps and headed back to base on the correct route. Everybody had to be back for lunch at 12 o'clock and it was only when 1 o'clock passed, and there was no sign of Andy, that we began to wonder if he'd fallen off. But he came staggering in at half past after a 7-mile detour. 'What happened?' he asked. 'Where did you get to?'

'Back here. We did our best to help you keep up, Andy, but we're professional sportsmen, we're here to get fit. We had to put our foot down after turning right down that lane. Didn't you see the left turn 100 yards further on?'

'What left turn?'

On our last night of the week, Bez and I were having a laugh in our room before going for a farewell pint. We were recalling all the tricks we'd played on Andy. We couldn't work out how he hadn't cottoned on to us. Then I heard a scratching noise outside the door. I flung the door open and there was Andy. He'd been listening in.

'You bastards!' he said. 'You've been stitching me up all along. You bastards! And I thought you were trying to help me.'

I wasn't having that. 'Hang on a minute, Andy. If you come here wanting to hang around with professional footballers, you play to our rules. We took you in because we thought you'd be lonely and wanted to be one of the lads. It's not our fault if you couldn't work out what was going on, so you might as well fuck off.'

He did. But when we got back after a session in the boozer, a note had been pushed under our door. It was from Andy, apologising for eavesdropping and saying what great people we were after all.

The following day we all went our separate ways and I assumed we'd seen the last of Andy, but when Bez and I reported back on the Monday morning, I was first to sign the register. I looked at the names of the people who'd already checked in. 'Bez, you're not going to believe this ...'

We went easy on him for most of the week, but the sight of a couple of campers pitching a tent on one of the lawns alongside the main drive was too good an opportunity to miss. When we got back from the boozer, the three of us crept up to the tent. The couple were either fast asleep or hard at it in a little world of their own because they can't have heard a thing. We loosened all the guy ropes and then gave Andy a nudge. He staggered into the tent, which collapsed in a heap.

Bez and I headed off behind some bushes and watched the action as Andy tried to extricate himself from the collapsed tent. He was racing against the clock to clear off before the couple climbed out. He lost the race. We sneaked off while the couple were threatening blue murder. Andy finally returned about an hour later. He'd managed to persuade them not to tell the staff there was a Peeping Tom on the premises.

We never saw Andy again after his second week, but our fellow pros always provided us with plenty of opportunities for a laugh. When David Howells, who was playing for Spurs at the time, rolled up in a yellow Aston Martin, I told him I'd always dreamed of driving a car like that. The next day, I went for a pint straight after work with a lad called Spenner from Shrewsbury, a Scouser. I was halfway down my second when Howells drove up, threw the keys on the table and said, 'Right, Swanny, all yours.'

Spenner jumped in the passenger seat and we set off down a nearby dual carriageway. It was fantastic. The only fly in the ointment was Spenner, who kept banging on about letting him have a go. In the end, I gave in ... but only for a quick spin. I pulled into a lay-by and pressed what I thought was the automatic parking button that immobilised the car. But while we were both out of the car, it started rolling down the slope towards the main carriageway. Injured or not, I covered the 20 yards to that Aston Martin like Linford Christie coming out of the blocks. I leaped into the car, slammed on the brakes and waited for Spenner. 'Get in!'

'But Swanny, you said I could have a go.'

'No chance. Just fucking get in!' All the way back, the thought of an £80,000 Aston Martin taking itself for a spin down the A518 brought me out in a cold sweat.

'How was it?' asked Howells after I'd parked the motor in the pub car park.

'Fantastic!'

'Great. I meant to tell you, Spenner could have a go as well ...'

Geoff Thomas, who was playing for Wolves at the time, was there on rehab after repair to both his anterior and posterior cruciates. He didn't drink so he was behind the wheel when we went for a pint. One of our watering holes was a pub called The Mermaid, about twenty minutes away. On a Thursday night, they held a kipper tie competition. If you didn't have a tie, you hired one.

Thursday night was also Singles Night and there were always loads of birds on their own. They knew that injured footballers from Lilleshall often went there on their last night and moved in like a wolf pack. They'd crowd round us, flashing all sorts in our direction. It wasn't a pretty sight.

There was also a club called Cascades, about seven miles away. We renamed it CatchAids. There were some right slappers in there. The older lads knew what was best for them and steered clear, but sometimes one of the young kids, who'd been missing the girlfriend, would be tempted. They'd tell us they were just popping outside for ten minutes and ask us to hang on. We'd wait for thirty seconds, jump into our cars and set off back. One or two of them failed to appear for breakfast the next morning.

Thursday was also yellow shirt day. At most clubs it's a Friday and the player who's performed the worst in training during the week has to wear a yellow T-shirt, usually unwashed. On away trips he has to wear it for dinner. At Lilleshall, I was judge and jury to decide who'd wear the shirt and, as a matter of principle, it always went to one of the top performers, preferably someone who fancied himself as a sharp dresser. And once sentence had been passed, there was no going back. So instead of going for a night out in his best gear, the winner would be stuck with a tatty old yellow shirt with 'I'm a wanker' written on the back.

I was re-living the memories as I drove down to Lilleshall for the last time in August 2000. Phil and Pauline were waiting in reception. She gave me a smile and a hug and said, 'Good to see you again, Swanny. What is it this time?'

'To be honest, love, I don't think I'm going to make it. I don't think I'll ever play again.' I told them what the specialist had said, how Terry Dolan had told me I should finish and how York had agreed to let me have one last shot with them.

Phil shook his head and laughed. 'So you're here for a farewell piss-up, then?'

'If you say so.'

I worked as hard as ever, but for the first time in 14 years, I knew deep down that it wasn't going to be enough. Each time I really pushed myself, the knee said no. All of a sudden, going through the pain barrier didn't seem such a good idea after all. And the surgeon's words were there in the back of my mind all the time.

Towards the end of the second week, I went in to see Phil and Pauline. I didn't mess about: 'This isn't going to work. I'm wasting your time and mine. I've been coming here since I was twenty, I've had some great times and you've kept my career going. But you won't be seeing me again.'

I packed my bags, climbed into the car, motored down the drive and set off out of the gates for the last time. Ahead of me was a 125-mile drive home. And I'd absolutely no idea what the future might hold.

20

IS THERE LIFE AFTER FOOTBALL?

Throughout my pro career I always had a hankering to play real grassroots football. I even had a go while I was at Leeds, just after my bust-up with Howard Wilkinson in 1988. I knew Wilkinson wasn't going to play me in the first team so, just for a laugh, I had a game with a local side, Rothwell Town. They were based between Wakefield and Leeds.

Some mates played for them, and on a free Saturday afternoon, I went along to watch. The regular centre-forward didn't turn up, my boots were in the car and so they threw me on instead. There were only a dozen or so people watching and I knew I'd be OK so long as I didn't do anything stupid, like playing an absolute blinder or getting sent off. Mind you, I'd have been in massive bother with Sgt. Wilko had word leaked out. It was a possible sacking offence.

I was playing up front and did just enough to help us win 3-1 without attracting too much attention. I made sure I didn't get whacked. The opposition soon worked out I could do a bit, so I played everything one-touch without lingering on the ball. If I had, someone would have clobbered me. We were awarded a penalty late on, but I didn't take it. Two weeks later, I was playing at Nottingham Forest in the third round of the FA Cup!

When I left York in the autumn of 2000, I was convinced I'd never play another game of football at any level. Shane Embleton, captain of New Wheel FC, a pub team from my old home village of Wrenthorpe, near Wakefield, had other ideas, though. First, he asked if I fancied coaching the lads one night a week. They'd pay me in pints. Then, when they were a man short one Sunday, Shane cajoled me into turning out.

We knew I wouldn't be able to do much running, but we reckoned I could sit in central midfield and knock it around from there. As I'd been expecting to watch from the touchline, I only had a pair of rubbers on my feet and it wasn't the best of surfaces. Grass roots? Mud roots, more like! I was up to my ankles. On top of that, the knee was throbbing and I could hardly move. Shane was playing on the right so, after about twenty minutes, I called him over. 'Look, I can't play in here. I'll go out wide where there's a bit of grass. Just keep knocking it out to me there.' We swapped places.

Seconds later, our keeper cleared the ball upfield, Shane went up for a header, missed, and when he landed, he was caught with a two-footed tackle that broke his leg in three places. That could have been me if I'd stayed in the middle. It was a freezing day. Someone called an ambulance and I made sure no one tried to move him. I lay alongside him, to try and keep him warm, but he was shivering in shock.

As a pro, I'd been used to the best medical attention being available immediately. This time it seemed like an age before the ambulance appeared and Shane was carried off on a stretcher. I went to hospital with him and hung around until I was sure he was OK. During the next week I got John Beresford and John Sheridan to go and see him, taking a signed shirt along.

I didn't play again for a while after that. Shane re-appeared with his leg in plaster, and whenever he asked me to turn out, I told him my missus had thrown my boots away. But he wouldn't take no for an answer and late in the season he pulled me to one side again.

'Swanny, we've got a Cup quarter-final on Saturday. Help me out.'

'I can't, Shane, I'm knackered. I'm never going to play another game.'

We won 3-2 in extra-time and I scored a hat-trick. I was in agony, but going back to the pub to celebrate made up for it. All the lads were absolutely over the moon and I felt great knowing that I'd achieved something for them. But there was no way I was going to be fit to play in the semi-final.

Instead, I promised to go and watch. On the Saturday night, I'd been to a party with John Beresford and had still been boozing at dawn. The match kicked off at 11am and I got a lift to the ground, a local miners' welfare club. It cost a quid to get in. I breezed into the dressing room. 'All the best, lads!'

'Never mind all the best, Swanny, you're playing!' They'd got hold of some boots and a pair of shin pads. How could I say no? After 20 minutes, I went in for a header. The keeper came out to punch clear and hit my nose instead. It was the first broken nose I had suffered during my career. It was pointing sideways ... and there was blood everywhere.

At half-time, I asked if one of the lads would put it back in for me. There were no volunteers. So I went to the bog, cupped my hands around my nose, gave it a crunch and pushed it back where it belonged. One of the boys was in there having a pee. He took one look at my face and puked up. I felt like doing the same.

What the hell was I playing at? Standing in the gents at a miners' welfare, blood pouring out of my nose, feeling sick, hungover and in line for a major bollocking for playing at all when I got home? Somehow, I made it through the second-half. We got beat and apart from the odd charity game, I have never played again.

But I stayed in touch with New Wheel and joined them on a few trips. I never bothered with luggage. Just the clothes I stood up in, a toothbrush and a couple of pairs of kippers. First there was a stag do in Amsterdam. Then a Christmas bash in Blackpool, where I went dressed as a cowboy. And finally another stag do for Mark Bird, one of the players, in Magaluf. The boys were there for a week but I just went along for the weekend. And the kippers really came into their own in that heat!

On the first day, I wedged one pair of kippers into the U bend under the wash basin in Mark's bathroom. After a few hours, they started to stink the place out. It took the hotel staff two days to find them. Mark's holiday improved significantly from that point ... until he discovered the other pair of kippers in the lining of his suitcase as he started to pack for the flight home.

But coaching and playing for New Wheel was just a bit of fun with the lads. The hard part began the day I walked away from York as a man with a past but with no idea about his future. At first, my main emotion was relief. I knew I wasn't going to wake up in the morning and face a battle against pain just so I could do the day job. But relief soon turned into panic. Fear, almost. How was I going to support my family? This wasn't just about me; it was about Bex, George and Harry, and where we were going over the next 25 years or so.

As a player, you kid yourself that it's never going to end; that when you retire, there'll always be something on the coaching side. So you take a few coaching courses and, every now and then, you pretend you're making serious plans for the future by enrolling for some kind of training scheme. While I was at Port Vale, I did a pub-management course, although keeping a pub would have been madness. I'd have drunk all the profits. At Bury, I started to train as a driving instructor. That seemed to be a good idea at the time because I enjoyed the practical side of the course, but the paperwork! So when the axe fell, I was no further forward.

IS THERE LIFE AFTER FOOTBALL?

When I finished I ended up with about £40,000. I'd been on £750 a week at York and they paid me six months' money under the terms of the contract Terry Dolan had insisted on. There was also a pension payment from the PFA. But the total of £40,000 was never going to set us up for life and I considered it merely a nest egg to back up whatever I earned from a full-time job. I assumed that job would be in football, where I'd been for the last 16 years.

I was naïve enough to believe that I'd made a lot of friends in the game. I expected the phone would ring before long and that I would find someone from the past on the other end of the line saying, 'Come on, Swanny, I've got a job for you.' So I didn't push myself. One or two people said there might be something once I'd got my A-licence in coaching, which would qualify me to coach professional players. So I attended an intensive course in Wales and gained the licence.

The phone didn't ring until Peter Wilkinson, the chairman of Ossett Town, gave me a call. Would I be interested in helping Gary Brook, the manager, with some coaching? £150 a week for two training sessions and matches. I met Gary and he seemed keen to have me on board. I even managed to persuade John Beresford to join us. He'd packed in at the same time as me, but hadn't got fixed up anywhere else. So he said he'd come along. Gary put him on the bench for two games; Bez pissed off.

And I soon discovered Gary had other ideas about my involvement. He took all the first-team sessions and gave the team talk on match days. I just had to fit in around him. Halfway through the season, Mick Pollitt, the reserve-team coach, died. He was out training with the lads when he had a heart attack. It was a terrible shock for everyone. Obviously his death left a gap in the coaching set-up and I told Wilkinson I'd take over and coach the kids as well. He agreed. For the first time, I was really hands on. I got a good spirit going and the reserves had some great results.

Gary left at the end of the season. I knew he thought I was after his job, but I wasn't. I'd gone to Ossett to gain some coaching experience in the hope that I might find a better job higher up the ladder. Managing the club never really entered my head, but I knew that if I applied for his job, people would put two and two together and make five. A week or so after Gary left, Wilkinson rang.

'You haven't sent in your CV yet.'

'I'm not sending it.'

'Why not? You've got a real chance.'

'I've been here all season, you know exactly what I can do. If you want me to do the job, I'll consider it.'

'OK, but send a CV first.'

'I've already told you: no CV.'

'Right, if I put a CV in for you, will you come for an interview?'

'Yeah, if that's how you want it.'

I went for two interviews, with Wilkinson and two more directors. I thought they'd gone well, but an hour after the second meeting, he rang and told me I hadn't got the job. I blew up. 'You bastard! You tell me to apply, you write my CV, you put my name forward. And then you give the job to someone else.'

That was me finished at Ossett Town. It was time for Plan B.

Since packing in, I'd been in contact with John Beresford two or three times a week. He was in the same boat and in the end, we decided that if football was no longer going to give us a living, we'd have to get off our arses and go out into the big wide world.

John had a mate called Bertie, who did a bit o' this and a bit o' that. He knew the project manager for a firm who were laying down wooden floors in Revolution bars all over the country. He reckoned wooden floors were going to be the next big thing.

So Bez and I were into wooden floors. We set up our own company, based at North Anston, a village just off the M1 near Worksop, and we slung about six grand apiece at it.

IS THERE LIFE AFTER FOOTBALL?

The company was called Major Oak, but it never took off; not least because we spent a lot of our time messing about. It was almost as if we were back at Lilleshall or still involved with a club. Instead of calling potential business contacts, we'd be ringing old mates and chewing the fat about the good old days. Or just talking football. After six months, Major Oak hadn't even got past the acorn stage. We'd lost our office and our six grand and moved out. It was time for Plan C.

Enter BallMax. Bez's idea. Put simply, it was a piece of equipment involving a soft football, attached to a stick by a piece of string. The idea was to teach young kids how to head the ball. Most youngsters are afraid of heading because they think it will hurt, but this was a soft ball and a coach would hold the stick above their heads and show them how to position themselves, how to time their jump and so on. There was a more advanced version with a harder ball aimed at young professionals.

We tried to market the advanced BallMax around league clubs and actually went to Manchester United and saw Sir Alex Ferguson. He said he'd give it a go with the academy kids. We sold some at Sunderland and Newcastle and a few clubs lower down the ladder also bought a few. We made our own DVD and sent it round all the clubs.

We even went in a camper van to a trade fair in Munich to try and attract some interest in Europe. Toys R Us also showed a bit of interest. With proper business minds at the helm, it might have taken off, but as usual, we never really took it seriously and in the end it went belly up. I'd bunged another five grand plus expenses into the project and Bez had spent more. It was time for Plan D.

Next up was some agency work. Billy Jennings, the former West Ham striker, was a pal of Bez and had set up as an agent. He was looking for ex-pros who'd just left the game, people who still had contacts in football. I met Jennings and agreed to give it a go. His company was called Premier Management, based in London.

They had one or two decent players on the books, but were also looking to sign younger pros at smaller clubs who might be in line for a decent move. There was a company car and a reasonable wage and it meant I was back in football, so it looked like a good move.

I was on the road just about every day, talking to young lads, convincing them we were their best bet, but it was a cut-throat business. No sooner had I fixed up a young player than one of the big-hitting agencies came in over my head and whisked him away. When we complained, the big boys would laugh and tell us to take them to court. There was no way we could afford to do that, so we lost out. I got a few players some reasonable moves, but time after time, we thought we'd got a deal worked out when a big hitter came in and wiped us out. So, after around 12 months, it was time for Plan E.

While working for Jennings, I'd bumped into Martin Wilkinson at a game at Scunthorpe. He'd been Allan Clarke's No.2 when I first started at Leeds and we'd always got on well. By this time, he was manager of Northampton Town. While we were chatting, I dropped in a mention of my A-licence and told him I fancied getting back in on the coaching side. He said he'd see what he could do.

They were struggling in the old Second Division at the time and ended up being relegated, but he offered me a chance to work with the youth team and then, hopefully, move me up to the senior players later. He gave me a three-month contract and said we'd have a look at a longer deal when I'd got settled in. I had to live in a hotel in Northampton and only saw the family at weekends. I never really had much of a chance to put on any sessions. The staff who were already in place saw me as a threat because I was better qualified, but I was confident Martin would eventually give me a bigger role. Two months later, however, he moved out and Colin Calderwood took over.

I was acutely aware that time was running out on my short-term contract, but Calderwood seemed to be OK about having me on board. So after a week or so, I went in to see him. While I'd been on my A-licence course, I'd been invited to also take the pro-licence course, which would qualify me to manage at the highest level. It would cost £5,000, but I reckoned that if Northampton were going to keep me on, that qualification would be a good investment for them as well as me.

I asked Calderwood if he thought the club would back me. He said he didn't think they'd pay for me to do the course, but said that if I wanted to do it off my own bat, fine. I told him I'd have a think, but that I would almost certainly go ahead on that basis. Half an hour later, I was driving home for the weekend when my phone rang. It was Calderwood. He said that as my contract expired in a fortnight, there wasn't much point me going back in on the Monday. In other words, I was out of a job. Why hadn't he told me to my face a few minutes earlier?

I didn't go ahead with the pro-licence; I just wasn't bothered about a career in football anymore. I'd had enough of people who said one thing and did another; people who weren't prepared to look me in the eye and be straight with me. From that moment on, I was going to be my own man. But I was still looking for a Plan F.

21

THE ROAD TO THE
WHITE HOUSE

Some of my best ideas have come to me over a pint of ale. OK, I've clean forgotten most of them the following morning, but not on this occasion. It was the summer of 2003 and finances were not good. I'd already made a big hole in the £40,000 I'd picked up three years earlier and it was time to pull in the purse strings.

Since 1999, we'd been living in Walton, a village on the outskirts of Wakefield. It was a nice house on a nice estate, but money problems dictated it was time to move on. We decided to down-size and moved down the road to a cheaper place in a village called Altofts, just off the M62. The house was smaller, but we had plenty of land where Sky, our new Great Dane, could have a runaround.

One evening, soon after we moved in, I was sitting in the garden with a beer, trying to work out what we could do with all the spare land. After a while, it dawned on me that there might be enough room to build another house. I reckoned there would be just about enough land for each house to have a reasonable garden.

The next morning, I called Shane Embleton, the skipper of the New Wheel football team who'd broken his leg when I had been playing for them a couple of years earlier. Shane was an architect.

He came round and did a few measurements. He said it would be a tight squeeze, but worth a try. I had a word with Andy, our next-door neighbour, who said he wouldn't have a problem. Shane drew up some plans, we put in for planning permission and were given the OK.

To raise the money, I sold Mam and Dad's house. Way back when I signed for Plymouth, I'd used some of my signing-on fee to buy the council house they were living in at the time. It cost me £12,000. When I decided to go ahead with building my own place, Dad had just come out of hospital after a quadruple heart by-pass. They needed to go into some sheltered accommodation, a council bungalow where people could keep an eye on them. So I sold their house for £90,000 and ploughed the money into our new place. The cash we'd made on the sale of our house in Walton kept us ticking over.

I appointed myself project manager. I went to a couple of exhibitions in Birmingham and collected all the info about how to build your own home. It seemed straightforward enough, but I knew that a few thousand people had said the same thing and fallen flat on their faces.

First, I made a month-to-month plan. One, find a builder: the Sennett brothers, Mark and Paul. They brought in Glenn Brown, the ground worker, who put all the basics in place underground. About a quarter of the costs of any house are out of sight: foundations, pipework, drains, soil stacks, water waste, damp course and so on. Once Glenn had finished, we were left with a concrete slab equal to the size of the ground floor. That slab cost me £18,000, but underneath were the vital body parts of our home. Then it was a case of pulling together all the different strands: from walls to roof, to floor, to windows and outer doors, to plumbing, to wiring, to plastering. Then along came toilets, bathrooms and kitchen. And finally, decorating, carpeting and furnishing.

It sounds simple, doesn't it? And it was. I never had any doubt that we'd get there. I didn't fear failure and I made sure I had the right kind of people around me. People who wouldn't let me down; not like some of my so-called contacts in football. I hadn't received too many favours from the football world since I'd been forced to quit. In the building trade, though, they seemed to be queuing up to help.

The work was physical, something I needed. But I had to use a bit of brain power as well, organising who I needed and when. I've always been a decent judge of character and I knew more or less straightaway whether I could trust the people who wanted to work for me. On their first day, I gave it to them straight: 'Look, I want you to come here and enjoy working with me. I don't want you getting out of bed at six o'clock in the morning, not wanting to turn up. In exchange, I'll play it right by you.'

There were one or two who failed to turn up without letting me know and I soon learned all about the old saying: if you're prepared to hire them, be prepared to fire them. My first plasterers bumped twice so I rang up and said, 'Come and collect your gear and then fuck off!'

'What do you mean?'

'You've let me down twice. I've found someone else.'

One of the electricians was the same. Perhaps I expected too much, but I was giving people work, looking after them, so the least they could do was pick up the phone and tell me they had a problem.

Most of the people who helped with that first project came back for my second one four years later. They knew I'd looked after them first time round and were keen to give it another go. It's down to man-management. If you don't treat people right, they come back and bite you on the arse. That's always been my philosophy and I like to think I could have used some of those skills in football, but that's history now.

Building our new home took 8 months and there were some hairy moments along the way, but I can honestly say I loved every minute. After scratching around for 3 years trying to find a life after football, I'd discovered something that gave me the same buzz. Maybe an even bigger one.

When it was ready, we sold our first house on the plot, moved into the new one and waved goodbye to the mortgage. Ask any journeyman pro to name his target as he nears the end of his career and he'll tell you it's to leave the game without a mortgage. If you can do that, everything else more or less fits into place. Well, I'd finally done it, 4 years late. We thought about throwing a party, bringing everyone back who'd worked on it and cracking open a few bottles of bubbly. In the end, though, we kept it low-key.

The house was proof that I could survive without a career in football, but I didn't want to turn my back on the game altogether and a chance encounter at Scunthorpe steered me towards another career swerve. This time into the media.

I was watching a game at Glanford Park when a bloke I'd never seen before came up to me. He was a bit overweight and starting to go bald. That's the polite version. These days I call him a fat, bald-headed old bastard. He introduced himself as David Burns from BBC Radio Humberside. Did I fancy doing a bit of summarising at Hull City matches? He said it wouldn't be every week at first, but if things went well, there might be a chance of some regular work. 'Yeah, I'll give it a go,' I told him.

I'd never really worn headphones before and the ISDN box in front of me looked like the controls of the space shuttle at first, but I soon got used to the technical side and it didn't take me long to develop my own style behind the mic.

I always try to be straight and honest and to say what the listeners want to hear, not the professionals. It's no good trying to protect players, to say they've done OK when they've been crap. They know when they've had a bad game and so do the fans. If a player has done well, then I'll say so. If he's struggled, I'll try to make a constructive criticism. And I like to introduce a bit of humour, too, which often involves taking the piss out of Burnsy.

I've upset a few managers and players, but that doesn't bother me. In fact, I knew I was on the right lines when, at a dinner, the wife of Andy Dawson, one of the Hull players, came up to me. She told me Andy didn't always agree with what I said, but that he believed I was expressing a genuine, honest opinion. And all his mates listened to Humberside when Hull were playing away because they knew we'd tell it as it was. That meant a lot.

Burnsy has been different class from the start and fantastic to work with. He helped me through the early days and we've become good mates, although I just wish he could stand the pace a bit better on overnight away trips. And one of the great things about the job is that there's usually a familiar face or two at games, ex-pros like myself who are doing a bit of media work. We can have a laugh and a natter about the old days. By and large, the journalists have accepted me for what I am. I don't pretend to be anything more than an ex-player with a few opinions to offer and there's always a fair bit of banter in the pressroom before a match.

Since the start of the 2004–05 season, I've covered just about all Hull's games, home and away. It can mean sitting in a car on the M1 instead of a Saturday night out on the piss, but I'll settle for that. And I hadn't been doing the job long when I was approached by the *Hull Daily Mail*, the local evening paper. They'd wanted Peter Taylor, Hull's manager at the time, to write a weekly column every Monday. That hadn't worked out and they needed someone else. Would I do it? I'd have to analyse the game from the professional's point of view and not pull any punches. I was working for the paper, not the football club.

My column is part of a two-page spread every Monday. At first, I used to email the copy direct, but now Phil Buckingham, their Hull City writer, or Mark Fewings from the sports desk gives me a call on the Sunday. I talk about why Hull have won, lost or drawn. I select the crunch moment, best player, worst player, the referee's most important decision and so on. And I give my overall view of Hull's performances.

About 12 months after that started, the paper asked if I'd be interested in another column, this time on a Thursday. Again it's part of a double-page spread, but about general talking points, not necessarily Hull City. Sometimes the desk give me some bullets to fire, but it's down to me whether I fire them or not. I try to make it pretty hard-hitting and we get plenty of readers' letters, about 50-50 agreeing and disagreeing.

The work has given me a new insight into what's involved for the media, both radio and newspapers, and I've learned what a demanding job it can be. I never realised how tight deadlines can be for the writers, and outside the Premier League, some of the press boxes and commentary positions can be pretty cramped, cold and inhospitable. The view isn't always brilliant, but that's of no interest to listeners. They just want to know what's going on, not how cold or uncomfortable we are.

As a player, I was reasonably media friendly. I've kept a few scrapbooks and they show I was usually up for a photo-shoot or a feature story during the week. But I was never totally at ease with reporters on match days. It was easy when the team won or I'd had a good game, but with hindsight, I should have handled it differently on bad days when, like most players, I went out of my way to avoid the media. Now I realise how good a time that is to front up and be honest, to admit you've been crap or to explain why the team has lost. It provides a good link with the fans. They don't want players who only want to talk on a good day; they want players who will stand up and be counted when things have gone wrong.

Working for Radio Humberside and the *Hull Daily Mail* has opened a few more doors, including some work for BBC Look North, the local television station. One or two people have suggested I should widen my scope a bit and maybe have my own radio chat show, but that's not down to me.

And 2003 also saw me pulling on the tracksuit again and doing a bit of coaching. It started with a call from Dennis Metcalfe, student liaison officer at the Leeds College of Building, the only specialist further education construction college in the UK. He told me that the students had a side who played in a league involving other local colleges and that he wanted me to do a bit of coaching. So every Wednesday during term times, I abandon the building site at lunchtime and head over to Leeds for a four-hour session with the students. I suppose it's a case of a footballer who became a builder teaching builders who'd dreamed of being footballers. The wheel has come full circle.

And now I'm on the road to the White House. Not long after we'd moved into our new house, we were chatting to Andy, the next-door neighbour. He has loads of land in the area and told us about a couple of houses he was planning to renovate in a place called Newlands. We took Sky and the kids for a walk to have a look. As we came over the brow of a hill, all we could see for miles and miles were fields. And what looked like a little bungalow in the distance. Painted white.

As we got closer, the bungalow grew into a detached house. Closer still, and it became a mansion with a drive that looked a mile long. The place was way down on its luck, but what potential! We fell in love with it straightaway. The next day I went to see Andy. 'I'll buy the White House. How much do you want?'

'Not for sale, Swanny. That house is my dream.'

He explained that he'd bought the White House and a couple of derelict properties as part of a deal for 250 acres of land. One day, he and his partner Kerry were going to live in the White House.

'Fair enough,' I said. 'But if you ever decide to sell ... ' I pestered him more or less non-stop for a couple of years, but there was no way he was going to budge.

Then one day, when I was sitting in the garden, Andy popped his head over the fence. 'Are you still interested in the White House?'

''Course I am.'

'Right, it's all yours.'

'You're joking!'

'No. Kerry and I have split up; we won't be getting back together. That was our dream, now it's yours. It's not really for sale, but you can have it.'

We sat down there and then and knocked out a deal. £180,000. We signed a contract that said I'd pay him when I sold my own house. He agreed that we could stay in Altofts until the White House was more or less up and running. I re-mortgaged our house to finance the renovation, which we estimated would cost around £130,000.

The White House is built on three floors and we went for three en suite double bedrooms and a family bathroom on the first floor. Plus three more double bedrooms on the top floor. The ground floor comprises a kitchen, lounge, dining room, utility room, cloakroom, office and a conservatory. And, eventually, we'll have a granny flat with a lounge, bedroom, kitchen and toilet. Work started in the autumn of 2007 and we reckoned it would take the best part of a year before we'd be able to move in and even longer before the house would be finished.

Soon after the renovation began, I bought a clapped-out old caravan. Even though the White House is in the middle of nowhere, there's an estate not far away that makes the Bronx look like Belgravia. We often had a load of valuable stuff on site so sometimes I used to stay overnight, with the dog as company, just in case any of the local tearaways fancied some fencing or whatever.

A few months later, we had to find a caravan big enough to accommodate the whole family. We'd arranged to let the house in Altofts to help pay the bills until the White House was ready. Bex and I moved in first while the kids stayed with her mam. Our move coincided with the coldest snap of the winter. Temperatures plummeted to minus seven at one stage, and when it warmed up, it started pissing down with rain every day. Then came the spring gales. Once or twice I thought the whole bloody lot would be blown away with us inside. It was a bit eerie at night. Sometimes we could hear voices and Sky would start barking. That kept potential intruders at bay, no problem, but sometimes, in the wee small hours, I found myself lying awake, asking myself, 'What the fuck am I doing here?'

However, when I opened the door in the morning all the negatives blew away and I couldn't wait to get started. I could look out over the site and think, 'Right, I'm going to get that sorted today and nobody can stop me.' If I'd been working for a company with a boss to answer to, I wouldn't have enjoyed it, but this way, I was my own man with my own business. And now I can honestly say that if I was given the choice of being the manager of a Championship club or running my own building development, I'd head straight to the building site.

The journey from Hunslet to the White House has taken 42 years and it's been a hell of a ride. A real roller coaster. On the way, I lost count of the times Mam and Dad told me I could have been a millionaire if I'd looked after myself and my money. I don't care – I've just had a fantastic life. And it's still going on.

After all, it doesn't get much better than sitting with the headphones on at Wembley, watching Hull City win promotion to the Premier League. What a day! Before the kick-off, I even managed to 'entertain' Radio Humberside fans with a brief solo version of 'Can't Help Falling In Love With You' when the touchline mic was switched off. I'm still waiting to hear from the record companies.

I've always enjoyed myself: I've laughed and I've wanted people to laugh with me. I like to think I put a smile on their faces – I love that. I'd rather give than take and I've always enjoyed helping other people. And after the way things have turned out for me in the last few years, maybe someone up there likes the way I live my life after all.

Usually, when I walk into a room, people start smiling. Sometimes, I feel like saying, 'What are you lot fucking laughing at?' But I like to think it's because they know the next few minutes will be fun. And while I've calmed down a lot over the last few years, I still have my moments.

Like at the 2008 Cheltenham Festival. It coincided with Hull City's game at Cardiff, so a few of us arranged to stop off at Cheltenham on the way home. Wednesday had been a heavy night and I was pretty knackered by the time we reached the course on the Thursday morning. A few pints temporarily solved that problem and I decided I'd have twenty quid on No. 5 in all 10 races of the extended programme.

There was no joy in any of the early races and, after seeing my fifth No. 5 finish nowhere, I decided I needed a crap. It was as hot as hell in the bog, my head was spinning and, before I knew what was happening, I'd fallen asleep. I woke with a start, looked at my watch and saw I'd slept through the sixth race and not placed my bet. You can guess the rest.

When I rejoined the lads to rousing cheers, they shouted, 'Where's the champagne, Swanny?'

'What champagne?'

'Number five. It just won. At 66/1!'

I got a load of stick about that when I reported at the KC Stadium for Hull's match against Southampton two days later.

The benders tend to be a bit rarer these days, though. Must be getting old, I suppose. But I still love the jokes, the laughs, the banter.

I want George and Harry to be the same. They're as different as chalk and cheese. George is the footballer. Even when he was playing for his kids' side, the Durkar Devils, he stood out. He's a big lad and started to play for the Under-14s at the Leeds Academy when he was still eligible for the Under-13s. They even made him captain. Soon afterwards they asked him if he fancied the Under-15s and he handled everything, no problem. He just takes it all with a pinch of salt. He's a decent rugby player, too.

Harry has tried his hand at a bit of everything: football, rugby, boxing, dancing, music. You name it. He does something for a while and then moves on. He says he'll make his money by robbing a bank. He has to live in George's shadow a bit, but that's often the way with football. Everybody seems to want to know how George is getting on, so Harry will have to learn to accept that's the way it's going to be if George goes on and makes it. But we've always told them the important thing is to look after one another. We don't want them worrying about me and Bex, we'll be all right. But they're in it for the long haul together. There will be people out there who'll want to shit on them, but if they stick together they'll be OK.

And Bex? Just about everybody who knows us asks her the same question: 'How the bloody hell have you put up with him for 20 years?' Sometimes I wonder the same thing myself. I haven't been an angel, after all. Maybe it's because just about every day of our lives I manage to put a smile on her face. I hope so, anyway.

Something I do or something I say. Even when she's low, we can usually find something to laugh about together.

She was never really involved in my football. During my career, my life had two compartments: football and family. Bex probably only saw around fifty of my 500-plus games and I tried not to take my work home. Sometimes if I scored a goal on a Saturday, she didn't find out until a pal told her the following Tuesday. She'd ask me why I hadn't mentioned it. I'd say, 'Why should I? It was just part of the job.' Mind you, she'd find out soon enough if I'd been sent off, because my next wage packet was smaller!

She always let me do my own thing, whether it was a night out with the lads or an end-of-season trip. I never felt tied to her or thought she was trying to hold me back. Far from it. Bex was determined to be independent. She was never going to be a footballer's wife who lived off her husband. She's always had a job and brought in her own money, most recently as a teaching assistant at the Cathedral High School in Wakefield.

I know I've been selfish. I love Bex and the kids to death, but I tend to want everything to be done on my terms. Bex will almost always be the one to bend and compromise. In some ways, she's too nice and sometimes the rest of us take advantage. We enjoy the ride, but every now and again she'll have a blow-up and then it's down to us to climb off the ride for a while and concentrate on her.

Of course, we've had our ups and downs. I've been a big drinker, but I've never turned to the booze when there's been a problem with Bex. Instead, I'll try to make sure we don't go to sleep on an argument. I may come across as hard-nosed, but deep down I'm soft and she knows that. She's given me the support I've always needed. Quite simply, getting married to her was the best thing I ever did.

The White House is going to be our dream home. When George was 13 we worked out that he'd lived in 13 different houses. Harry has now lived in 9. Those moves were always because of my football, but now we're in a position to put down some roots and I'd like to think we'll be there to stay. However, I suspect that, before long, I'll develop itchy feet and start looking for another project. When I'm ready and in my own time.

That's the big thing. In football you are always at someone else's beck and call, be it as a player, a manager or a coach. I've never been happy with other people running my life; I've kicked against it. But now I'm in control of my own destiny and that's where I want to be. I'll do it my way and, if things go wrong, I'm to blame. My way, not necessarily the right way. But that's been the story of my life. And you know what? I wouldn't have changed a minute.